G000141113

INTELLIGENCE CHIEF
EXTRAORDINARY

INTELLIGENCE CHIEF EXTRAORDINARY

The Life of
the Ninth Duke of Portland

Patrick Howarth

THE BODLEY HEAD
LONDON

To Bill
with affection, admiration and gratitude

British Library Cataloguing
in Publication Data

Howarth, Patrick
Intelligence chief extraordinary: the life of
the ninth Duke of Portland.
1. Portland, William Cavendish-Bentinck, *Duke of*
2. Intelligence officers—Great Britain—
Biography
I. Title
327.1'2'0924   UB271.G72P/

ISBN 0-370-30572-8

© 1986 by Patrick Howarth
Printed in Great Britain for
The Bodley Head Ltd
30 Bedford Square, London WC1B 3RP
by The Bath Press, Avon
Photoset by Rowland Phototypesetting Ltd
Bury St Edmunds, Suffolk

CONTENTS

Four pages of photographs follow page 112

FOREWORD

I am deeply indebted to the Duke of Portland for the many hours he spent in talking to me and for the care with which he read my typescript and suggested amendments or corrections. The book is not an official biography. It was begun on my initiative, and I am wholly responsible for its contents. Nevertheless without the Duke of Portland's words, in conversation and reports, which I have quoted verbatim, the book would have been a pale shadow of what I hope it is.

I also owe a considerable debt to Mr C. D. Chalmers, Head of the Search Department of the Public Record Office in Kew. In April 1982 I was officially informed that 'the records of the Joint Intelligence Committee have been retained in the Cabinet Office under Section 3 (4) of the Public Records Act, 1958'. The writer added: 'The chances of any access to them being granted to you are extremely remote.' Nearly eighteen months later I was given, by courtesy of the Cabinet Office, a list showing a limited number of JIC (Joint Intelligence Committee) reports which had been made available to the Public Record Office. I took this with me to Kew and was told that these reports were not collected together and there was no known means of tracking them down. At this point a lady, whose name I never discovered and who had overheard part of my conversation, said to me: 'Your only hope is to talk to Mr Chalmers.' This I did, and with minimal delay he called my attention to ninety-two volumes of the minutes of the meetings of the Chiefs of Staff during World War II and ninety-six volumes of memoranda. These contained all the JIC wartime reports apart from one or two which are still withheld. Transcripts of Crown-copyright records in the Public Record Office appear by permission of the Controller of H.M. Stationery Office.

I am indebted too to many other people who talked to me, wrote to me or helped me in other ways, in particular Mario Agliati, Lord Annan, Joan Bright Astley, Alan Banks, Phebe Bevir, John Blair, Lord Bullock, Lord Caccia, Robert Cecil, Lord Chelwood, Sir John Colville, Sir Michael Cresswell, Captain Charles Drake RN, Sir Charles Fletcher-Cooke, Dr Józef Garliński, Lord Gladwyn, Lord Hankey, Professor F. H. Hinsley, A. Horncastle, Lord Inchyra, Lieutenant-General Sir Ian Jacob, Lord Keith, Sir Laurence Kirwan, Vice-Admiral Sir Louis Le Bailly, the late Ronald Lewin, Piero Marazza, Lewis Massey, Lord Mayhew, Desmond Morris, Sheila Owen, Chapman Pincher, Terence Price, Sir Frank Roberts, the late Sir John Russell, Lady Russell, Lord Sherfield, M. Stephany, Andrew Tait, Lord Taylor, Dr Heather Tomlinson, John Webb, Sir Peter Wilkinson and Roy Wright.

CHAPTER I

Childhood. School.
First Assignment
(1897–1919)

Victor Frederick William Cavendish-Bentinck was born on 18
June 1897. In his forties he held the highest post in British
military and political intelligence. This he filled with exceptional distinction and with a record of success that is still little
appreciated.

Before his appointment as Chairman of Britain's Joint
Intelligence Committee, a post he held virtually throughout
the second world war, Cavendish-Bentick had been repeatedly present at great events. He was in Poland in 1920 when
the military engagement which Lord D'Abernon described as
the eighteenth decisive battle of the world took place at the
gates of Warsaw. A little more than two years later he was
serving under Curzon in the negotiation of the treaty of
Lausanne. In 1925 he was a member of the British delegation
to the conference in Locarno which the leading statesmen of
Europe believed had brought peace to the world and inaugurated a new era of hope for mankind.

After leaving his wartime intelligence post Cavendish-
Bentinck carried out another demanding assignment with
evident distinction. He was thereupon cast aside by the
Government he had been serving with a ruthlessness which
deprived him even of his pension rights.

His response was to begin a new career in industry at the age
of fifty. In this too his achievements were outstanding and
varied. In his late eighties, a few years after he had succeeded to
the title of ninth Duke of Portland, he was still chairman of a
company with an annual turnover of some £300 million.

His services to his nation, extending as they did over most of
the twentieth century, remain strangely unrecognized.

The Cavendish-Bentinck family has enjoyed an enviable

tradition of wealth and power. Horace Walpole wrote in a letter that 'no wise King of England would think it for his credit that he considered himself, or was considered by others, as personally at variance with a Duke of Portland'.

The wealth which supported the power, and made its exercise possible, was derived in the first instance from services to a monarch. It was later augmented by judicious marriages.

The founder of the English branch of the Bentinck family was a Dutchman, Hans Bentinck, who was a devoted adviser and friend of King William III of Orange. Among the services he rendered was to nurse his young master through smallpox. He came to England as an emissary to arrange the marriage in 1677 of his master to Mary, daughter of the future King James II, which served to bring William to the English throne. He was also wounded at the battle of the Boyne.

Although he spoke English poorly and seems to have been held in little affection by the English people, Bentinck was rewarded by King William with the post of Ambassador to France, and he was created Earl of Portland. His son became the first Duke of Portland.

The first Duke lost heavily by speculating in the South Sea Bubble, but his son, the second Duke, wisely married an heiress, who bore the names Margaret Cavendish-Holles-Harley. Through her mother's will she inherited Welbeck in Nottinghamshire, which became the Portland family home.

The Cavendishes, who had their roots in Suffolk, first became prominent in the sixteenth century. The third Duke of Portland strengthened the connections between the Bentinck and Cavendish families by marrying Lady Dorothy Cavendish, daughter of the fourth Duke of Devonshire. He also complied with the terms of the will of his grandmother, Lady Oxford, by changing the family name to Cavendish-Bentinck.

Estates in Scotland as well as England were acquired through these alliances, one of the most valuable possessions being the borough of Marylebone in London. The family connections with this remain evident in such names as Oxford Street, Harley Street, New Cavendish Street, Welbeck Street and Portland Place.

The member of the family who filled the highest political offices was the third Duke, who had the unusual distinction of heading both a Whig and a Tory administration. He was accepted as Prime Minister for his soundness of judgement and social standing rather than for brilliant political gifts. During his second administration he did not make a single speech in the House of Lords, and estimates of his ability varied from the Duke of Newcastle's description of him as 'that great and prudent man' to Lord Rosebery's reference to 'a dull, dumb Duke'. He was certainly a man of fortitude. When undergoing an operation for stone he spent seven minutes under the knife without an anaesthetic and without uttering a groan.

That the presence of a Duke of Portland was considered an asset to any British government in the early nineteenth century was shown by a letter which Canning wrote to the fourth Duke, when offering him the post of Lord Privy Seal. The office, Canning explained, had 'nothing in the way of business belonging to it'. He added: 'You need not remain an hour longer in Town for holding it, nor need you (if you do not feel disposed for it) even attend the Cabinet Councils when you are in Town.' The Duke, understandably, accepted the offer and continued to pursue his interests outside Westminister. He was largely responsible for the construction of the first railway in Scotland and the building of the harbour at Troon. The fourth Duke had a characteristic which was to become increasingly common in the Cavendish-Bentick family, that of longevity, for he lived to the age of eighty-six.

His son, the fifth Duke, who succeeded to the title in 1854, was the only one of the Dukes of Portland who could certainly be classified as an eccentric. He went to extraordinary lengths to avoid being recognized, or even seen, in public, and he dissipated much of his energies and fortune in the construction of enormously long underground tunnels. The two obsessions probably had a common origin. One of the tunnels at Welbeck was reputed to be the second longest in the world and linked the house to an underground riding school. Large numbers of workmen, mostly Irish, were continuously employed in the various works. Unlike Belloc's Lord Finchley, the Duke seems to have taken to heart the dictum that it was 'the business of the wealthy man to give employment to the artisan'. The Duke's tenants and clergy were not expected to greet him if they chanced to encounter him in the grounds of Welbeck, and as a form of partial concealment he habitually wore three pairs of socks and two overcoats.

As none of the sons of the fourth Duke married, the title passed to a descendant of a younger son of the third Duke. Both the sixth and seventh dukes died in their mid-eighties. Both fulfilled their public duties conscientiously but without great distinction. The seventh Duke, while known as Lord Titchfield, was a Member of Parliament for more than twenty years. It was his misfortune to come most prominently into the public eye when he advocated a tax on lipstick and face powder.

Some of the younger sons in the Bentinck family were men of exceptional distinction. Lord William Bentinck, son of the third Duke, may well be considered the greatest of the governors general of India before the title of the post was raised to that of viceroy. During his period of office, which lasted from 1827 to 1835, thuggery was suppressed, suttee was abolished, and the English language was instituted as a vehicle for education in Indian schools.

Lord George Bentinck, whose political biography was written by Disraeli, was a son of the fourth Duke. He was only forty-six when he died, yet he had already established himself as the leader of the protectionist wing of the Conservative Party after Peel had declared his conversion to the doctrine of free trade. He was also largely responsible for measures which extended greater tolerance to Jews and Roman Catholics.

It was largely at Lord George's instigation that the Bentinck family decided to adopt Disraeli as their protégé. Disraeli, they felt, lacked the solid advantage of a country estate, and to put this right they advanced him the money for the purchase of Hughenden. Unfortunately for Disraeli the eccentric fifth Duke later asked for the money back, thereby driving Disraeli to dependence on professional moneylenders. Not unreasonably Disraeli pointed out to the Duke that he had asked neither for the loan nor for the property and that in the meantime the property had cost him some £10,000.

Victor Frederick William Cavendish-Bentinck, known to his family and friends as Bill, was directly descended from the third (the Prime Minister) Duke through his youngest son Frederick. On his father's side his ancestry was the orthodox one which might be expected of a Cavendish-Bentinck. On his mother's side it was more irregular and, it might be thought, more colourful. There was even an infusion of gipsy blood.

This was a consequence of a chance meeting in Hyde Park between a son of the Duke of Somerset, who bore the courtesy title of Earl St Maur, and a pretty seventeen-year-old kitchenmaid, who was in a state of distress. Her name was Rosina Swan. Her father has been variously described as a bricklayer, a carpenter and a labourer. Her mother was gipsy.

Earl St Maur took the girl back to his bachelor establishment in Dover Street. Later they went to Tangier, where an illegitimate daughter was born. She was named Ruth and was to become the mother of Bill Cavendish-Bentinck.

Both Ruth St Maur's parents died of tuberculosis, and she was brought up in the home of her slightly eccentric grandmother, the Duchess of Somerset. She had little formal education but was allowed to read freely and was frequently taken to the theatre. It soon became apparent that she had a strong will and an independent mind.

Although precluded by her illegitimacy from being presented at Court, she attended the same parties and balls as other girls of aristocratic families. In between these functions she took to visiting Salvation Army hostels and the east end of London. What she saw led her to embrace a socialism which she would continue through the years to express vigorously and even spectacularly. She became an associate of Beatrice Webb in drawing up plans for the reform of the Poor Law. She enjoyed the friendship over half a century of George Bernard Shaw. She wrote a Fabian tract, and she was an active suffragette, on one occasion marching from Edinburgh to London to support the cause.

The husband to whom she was married in the Henry VII chapel in Westminster Abbey on 8 August 1887, Frederick Cavendish-Bentinck, was quite unlike her in temperament and philosophy. Sir John Colville, who wrote an admirable account of the life of Ruth St Maur in his book *Strange Inheritance*, called him 'the worldly and cynically tolerant Freddy'.

Bill Bentinck, who like other members of his family informally dispensed with the name 'Cavendish', later said of his father: *He was a younger son and became a barrister. In those Victorian days, the church, the army, the navy and the bar were respected professions. To go into the City was left to what they used to call City folk, more's the pity. He didn't go on with the bar, because he had throat trouble, which interfered with his oratory. He thought he would be well off, but unfortunately my grandfather invested money not very wisely—also in the theatre and women—and if the family had not paid off his debts, would have died a bankrupt. That was all very unfortunate.*

There were, however, other resources. Ruth St Maur had inherited £80,000 under the will of the Duke of Somerset. There was also a member of the Cavendish-Bentinck family, Lucy, who had married Lord Howard de Walden and who had inherited from the fifth Duke of Portland the Marylebone estate.

Old Lady Howard de Walden, Bill Bentinck recalled, *could remember as a girl hearing the news of the Duke of Wellington's victory in Belgium. She was well over ninety when she died. I cannot really remember her, but I do have a recollection of Queen Victoria's funeral procession, which I was taken to see from a stand in my Uncle George's house, 5 Richmond Terrace.*

Lady Howard de Walden invited Frederick Cavendish-Bentinck to manage the Marylebone estate, which he did until she died. She also provided the London house at 16 Mansfield Street, where Bill Bentinck was born.

Bill Bentinck was the third of four children. His elder brother Ferdinand, known as Ferdy, was born more than eight years before he was. He had two sisters, Joan and Barbara. Of his elder brother Bill Bentinck said: *He was intelligent, able, but a curious character, Ferdy. He did not hit it off with my father from a very early age.* Their mother even went so far as to describe him in an emotional outburst in a letter as 'a grief to us all our lives'.

There were grounds for parental disapproval. The chief of these was Ferdy's capacity for accumulating debts, which he did on a massive scale even while still at Eton. He later married a woman nine years older than himself against the wishes and advice of his parents, and the marriage ended in failure. His chosen profession was soldiering. After Sandhurst he joined the 60th Rifles and fought with distinction in France, but his career after the war was disjointed and he had the misfortune to contract tuberculosis. He recovered from this and, comparatively late in life, found an environment which seemed to suit him perfectly. This was in East Africa. He went out to Uganda as secretary to the Governor and later moved to Kenya. There he made a career in farming and colonial politics, eventually becoming Speaker of the Kenya Legislative Council and being knighted for his services.

At the age of eighty-nine he found himself Duke of Portland, the seventh Duke having died without a son. Two years later, in 1979, he died childless, and the title passed to his younger brother Bill.

The elder of the daughters, *very pretty when she was a young girl*, according to Bill, also contracted tuberculosis and spent some time in sanatoria in Scotland and in Switzerland. In Switzerland she was cured, and soon after the end of the first world war she visited her younger brother at his post in Warsaw. There she met her future husband, a diplomat named Reginald (Rex) Hoare, who later became British Minister in Bucharest. During a visit to the British Legation there in April 1938 Harold Nicolson recorded: 'I was met by Rex Hoare. A shaggy man and quite pleasant. His wife is a sister of Bill Bentinck and has that discontented look that settles upon the faces of English society women who marry English diplomatists.' It was an unflattering comment; Nicolson was far from being an unprejudiced judge of British diplomatic wives.

The youngest member of the family, Barbara, did not share her sister's good looks. She was shy and in later life suffered badly from sclerosis. She never married, and spent much of her life in Paris, where she died in 1980.

From the house in Mansfield Street the family moved to 78 Harley Street, which was taken on a lease and which was Bill Bentinck's London home until the end of the first world war. His father also took a lease on a house in the village of Corfe

Castle in Dorset, where there were good opportunities for riding and shooting.

At that time, Bill Bentinck said, Harley Street was only fifty per cent doctors and dentists. We lived in what would nowadays be considered considerable comfort. There was a nurse for myself, a governess for my elder sister and brother when he was on holiday, a butler and two footmen, a cook, a kitchenmaid, a scullerymaid, my mother's maid, a housekeeper, two housemaids and a coachman.

Every year at Christmas we used to stay with my uncle, Arthur James, and my aunt, Venetia, at Coton House, Rugby. These Christmas parties consisted of our family and about a dozen others. When I was very small my Uncle Arthur, who was both rich and generous, gave me a gold half sovereign. My aunt saw this and said: 'That's too much for the child. Give him a larger coin. He won't know the difference.' She took my gold half sovereign away, replacing it with a five-shilling piece. Though small I did know the difference, but refrained from saying so.

I can remember staying there some time after Christmas with my French governess when a general election was in progress. While I was in the drawing-room with the other guests somebody came in and announced: 'Arthur Balfour has not got in for Manchester.' I can still remember the frozen horror with which this news was greeted. Far greater than at the news of the defeat at Mons in 1914 or any other disasters in the first or second world wars. They all clearly realized at this news that the Liberals had won and that with Lloyd George as Chancellor of the Exchequer life in England would change for ever.

Freddy Cavendish-Bentinck did not share his wife's political views but followed a rather different tradition of public service. Among the honorary duties he performed was to give forty years of voluntary work to the Middlesex Hospital, of which he became Chairman. *My mother, Bill Bentinck said later, maintained she was an atheist. My father went to church regularly. He didn't take communion. He liked the music and the atmosphere and thought it was a good thing to do, a good example. I asked him, is it a particularly good example if they see you sound asleep?*

As he grew up the young Bentinck accepted in most respects his father's attitudes and beliefs rather than his mother's. In him they found expression in a general tendency to conform, combined with an amused scepticism and an exceptional sense of duty and conscientiousness in its performance. These were characteristics which were to endure throughout his life.

Although most of the early Fabians, referred to disparagingly as 'your mother's friends', regularly visited their home, the impact they made on Bentinck himself was slight. *Shaw was a nice old boy. Cunningham Grahame too. Sidney Webb a not very impressive little man with a beard.*

The interests which Bentinck developed as a boy were also for the most part those which he maintained later. *I read a good deal. I was interested in history. I was interested in animals. At one time I was rather keen on collecting coins, but I never got far with that.*

The first school which Bentinck attended was a preparatory school named Evelyn's, of which all he had to say in later life was: *It now lies under a Heathrow runway.* He stayed there from 1907 to 1910, by which time the choice of a public school had to be made. Eton, it was decided, must be excluded because of the opportunities it had afforded the elder son for piling up debts, and Wellington was selected instead. It was not a very happy choice.

Wellington College was founded as a memorial to the Duke of Wellington to provide for 'the gratuitous, or nearly gratuitous, Education of Orphan Children of Indigent and Meritorious Officers of the Army'. The site chosen was not far from that of the Royal Military College at Sandhurst. The first president of the board of governors was the Prince Consort.

In time, because of financial pressures, more and more fee-paying pupils were accepted, and Wellington acquired most of the characteristics of other English public schools in the nineteenth century, although there was always a strong emphasis on preparation for an army career. Among those who did much to shape the character of the school was a headmaster named E. W. Benson, a former classics master at Rugby, who came from a Birmingham evangelical background. Among his recorded dicta was a complaint against 'irresponsible enjoyment as tending to relax the moral fibre'.

The headmaster appointed in the year in which Bentinck entered Wellington was a Welshman named W. W. Vaughan, who was considered by many a surprising choice as he was not in holy orders. To a small boy he was an awesomely formidable figure, but he enjoyed an exceptional reputation within his profession, particularly for choosing good teachers.

Bentinck left Wellington blessedly free from the inhibitions and inclinations which the public school regime of his time encouraged, but he did not much enjoy his years there. Nor did he leave any impact on the school in the form of recorded achievements. *I was bad at games and therefore didn't like it. However I read a good deal, and at the age of sixteen and a half I got to the top of the form and so on, but owing to lack of prowess at games I was not doing much good there.* So with his parents' agreement he left.

Among Bentinck's contemporaries at Wellington was Ralph Stevenson, who was to be his immediate predecessor as Chairman of the Joint Intelligence Committee. Another, although a little younger, who was also to become a close wartime colleague, was Ian Jacob, later Director-General of the BBC. A slightly older Wellingtonian was Harold Nicolson, who had as little liking for the school as Bentinck, but who did not share Bentinck's attitude of detached tolerance towards it. After visiting Wellington in 1932 in the company of Raymond Mortimer, Nicolson wrote in his diary: 'I have no affection for the school whatsoever and no pride in it. I feel a grievance against it for having retarded my development.'

The next stage in Bentinck's education was one which he found much more congenial and also more memorable. His father had already formed the opinion that he ought to enter the diplomatic service. *In those days one did what one's parents wished. So in 1914 in the early spring I went to Germany to the family of Herr Geheimrat Professor von Öttingen, who was the keeper of the Goethe house in Weimar in the principality of Saxe-Weimar. In those days Germany was very agreeable.*

In addition to learning German he continued his study of Greek and Latin, was instructed by a Catholic priest and a Protestant pastor, and went with the professor's family when they went to Reichenberg. He had a companion, Charlie Law, who was the son of Andrew Bonar Law, the future Prime Minister. He was to be killed not long afterwards in Mesopotamia.

Bentinck's father was convinced that the Germans would

soon attack France, but he believed that the Kaiser would hold his hand until the death of the Emperor Franz Josef. *My instructions were, if he should die, I was to come home. Well, he didn't die, but his nephew was potted like a rabbit standing up in a car in Sarajevo.* By the time Bentinck left the country Germany was already at war with Russia. *I remember people singing war songs. There was not a sign of anything like that in England. I remember arriving at Harwich, where everything was very peaceful.*

Bentinck was still only seventeen when war was declared. He completed the business of matriculation and responsions as part of the normal procedure for a future Oxford undergraduate, but at the age of eighteen he applied to join the army. Although a fairly tall, good-looking young man, he was still inordinately thin, with a weak physique and rather poor eyesight. He was declared unfit for military service.

He tried to become a wireless operator in an aircraft, but at that time the consent of parents was required before the very young were given such an assignment, presumably in the belief that it was much more dangerous than trench warfare. In Bentinck's case the permission was not forthcoming. His father would have been content to see him serving in the Brigade of Guards, but, failing that, felt the best course would be for him to have an appointment as an honorary attaché at some British embassy or legation.

In an age in which it was assumed that the diplomatic service must be staffed by men who were able and willing to subsidize, in effect, the British government by drawing on their private resources, the appointment of honorary attachés was a logical arrangement for training young men at minimal cost to the Exchequer. Influence was of course required for such appointments to be obtained, but this presented no great difficulty, and on 28 June 1915 Bentick was appointed to the British Legation in the capital of Norway, which was then known as Christiania.

The British Minister in Christiania bore the name of Mansfeldt de Cardonnel Findlay. His diplomatic assignments had been to somewhat minor powers. He had served at the courts of Saxony and Saxe-Coburg and of Waldeck and Pyrmont. Before coming to Norway in 1911 he had been in

Bulgaria. Christiania was to be his last post, for he retired in 1923.

Findlay was a very nice man, Bentinck said, *but he was tremendously under the influence of a Naval Attaché called Consett, who liked to put a telescope to a blind eye and pay no attention to instructions. Consett wrote a book after the war called* The Triumph of Unarmed Forces, *all about the blockade. The blockade greatly weakened Germany's ability to continue the war. There's no doubt about that.*

The consequences of the naval blockade of Germany probably occupied more of the time of the staff of the British Legation than any other subject. Relations with the Norwegian Government were sometimes strained as a result. There were Norwegian protests against the censorship of mail carried by Norwegian ships and against excessive delays while ships, which had put in voluntarily to Kirkwall with perishable cargoes such as salmon, were examined.

The Norwegian representations had little effect. On 13 October 1916 Findlay received instructions from the Foreign Office that 'concessions by Norway to Germany as regards contraband and merchant shipping would endanger the whole success of our blockade measures and might seriously interfere with our overseas shipping'.

British policy on the subject of Norway's neutrality was also clearly defined. In a paper which General W. R. Robertson, Chief of the Imperial General Staff, signed in November 1916, it was stated that 'both naval and military interests would best be served by Norway remaining neutral and it would be detrimental to those interests if she became an Ally'.

Neutrality was certainly a popular policy in Norway, and there was little inclination among the people to side with Germany. In Sweden the problems were more complex. The British Minister there, Esme Howard, who later became Ambassador in Washington, was a friend of Findlay of long standing and seems to have influenced him considerably. Howard wrote a number of trenchant despatches in the first two years of the war with copies sent to Findlay, calling attention to the possibility that Sweden might enter the war on the German side. There was much pro-German feeling in Sweden. There was a fear of Russian aggression, and there were groups associated with the Court who were in favour of military intervention.

Howard did not go so far as to forecast that Sweden would in fact enter the war, but it could be deduced from his despatches that skilful diplomacy was required in promoting British interests in Sweden and, indeed, in Norway. 'If the situation is properly handled at the outset,' Howard wrote on 1 April 1915, 'Norwegian neutrality should be secured.'

Findlay's reactions to these possible dangers was to propose a secret agreement under which the Norwegian Government would inform Britain if and when a Swedish attack on Narvik, Trondheim or some other port was 'impending' and Britain, in return, would render 'all possible assistance in repelling such an attack'. Two months later he discussed the idea with the King of Norway who, as Findlay reported, urged that 'great care should be taken not to frighten the Norwegian Government by any appearance of desire to force them into a position which might endanger their neutrality'.

In October 1916 Findlay went rather further. Calling attention to the importance, both to Britain and France, of Norwegian factories which were producing nitrate ammonia for explosives and ammunition, he suggested a secret arrangement for providing Norway with anti-aircraft guns. He failed to explain how such an arrangement could be kept secret for long. His instructions from the Foreign Office were to 'do nothing to promote a breach between Germany and Norway'.

Findlay's intentions were of the best, but his judgement was sometimes questionable and occasionally expressed rather petulantly. 'I distrust the Minister for Foreign Affairs,' he wrote in February 1916. 'He is cunning but not courageous.' Eight months later, when Germany was demanding passage for her submarines through Norwegian territorial waters, he reported: 'I have no confidence in the power of resistance of the Norwegian Government. They are devoid of capacity, courage and sense of national honour.' To this the Foreign Office replied: 'We cannot believe that Norway will yield to Germany.' The Foreign Office was right.

Nevertheless Findlay must have been a likeable man, so likeable indeed that after nearly seventy years Bentinck remained not only loyal to his memory but more than discreet about his exercise of judgement.

To Bentinck himself Norway was a valuable training ground. An embassy or a legation in a neutral country in wartime provides variety and opportunities for using initiative which may not be found in the same country in time of peace. Shortage of staff meant that duties had to be shared out among a small number of people, and the hours of work were long. In June 1918 Findlay called the Foreign Office's attention to the problems of his clerical staff, who had to 'type continuously from 10 a.m. to 7 or 8 p.m. with a short luncheon interval'.

Bentinck also became aware of the activities of German diplomats of different kinds. *The German Minister in 1915*, he said, *was a very nice career man called Oberndorff. He was one of the people made to sign the armistice because other people wouldn't do it.* His successor was *rather an Abwehr type*. This was Admiral von Hintze, who came to Norway in 1917 from Peking, where he was thought to have organized attempts to sabotage the Trans-Siberian railway and the port of Vladivostok. Von Hintze's arrival in Norway was preceded by an incident in which a German was caught by the Norwegian police trying to smuggle in explosives disguised as lumps of coal, cigarettes and fountain pens.

Bentinck had continued his attempts to enlist in the army, and in 1918, when the standard of medical fitness required had been somewhat lowered, he was accepted. His period of military service began in August in the Household Brigade officers' training battalion in Bushey, where he learnt bayonet drill under the instruction of war-wounded NCOs.

The war came to an end before he could see active service, and he was demobilized in December and appointed a temporary clerk in the Foreign Office. He resigned from this position in order to continue his interrupted education. He did this in a manner which he came to regret later, for he decided not to go up to Oxford.

The greatest mistake was not going up to Magdalen, as I could have done, for two years, like Anthony Eden did. I would have developed much better. After I left Wellington I was never really with people of my own age group. I'd have been far better at mixing with people. I'd have been better equipped for writing and a bit more cultured. On top of that I think I'd have had a good time.

To those who knew him in later life Bentinck's ability to mix with people seemed effortless. Those who read his despatches appreciated how well expressed they were. That the lack of a university education made such skills difficult to acquire may therefore occasion surprise.

Instead of going up to Oxford Bentinck went to France to improve his knowledge of French. *My father didn't want me to go to Paris*, un lieu de perdition. *So I found a home in Neuilly-sur-Seine run by a professor and his wife. Very elderly. I came into the room and found them talking about l'Espagnole, who turned out to be the Empress Eugénie. The professor had been an artilleryman at the siege of Paris in 1870. I had a good time there. Dances and all sorts of things.*

Later in the year 1919 he took the examination for entry into the newly constituted Foreign Service. Until 1918 the Foreign Office and the Diplomatic Service had been separately staffed, but in July of that year the two were fused. At the same time the property qualification, which had been required of diplomats, was abolished, and rates of pay and allowances were raised to make it possible for a diplomat to subsist without other means of support.

It was a very easy exam. You were interviewed and passed on your personality and what you'd been doing and what you'd done during the war. The manner in which Bentinck had carried out his duties in Norway had of course been noted. He passed the examination, spent a brief period in the Foreign Office, and on 12 September 1919 was appointed Third Secretary to the newly formed British Legation in Warsaw.

CHAPTER 2
The Eighteenth Decisive
Battle of the World
(1919–22)

When Bentinck set off by train for Warsaw in September 1919, travelling via Paris, Switzerland and Vienna, he was heading for a country which faced prodigious difficulties.

The creation of an independent Poland in accordance with Woodrow Wilson's thirteenth point was, in one sense, the restoration of an ancient sovereign state. It was at the same time a fusion of three large areas detached from the Romanov, Habsburg and Hohenzollern empires without even a railway system in common and with differences in their economic and cultural levels which were immediately apparent.

Physically the consequences to the Poles of the first world war were appalling. Their territory probably suffered greater devastation than that of any other country. Many of the peasants, who provided the main element of continuity, had had their cattle slaughtered and their farms burnt. Typhus and grave food shortages occurred in a number of districts.

The Polish Government in the immediate post-war years clearly needed the support of the victorious Allied powers. The confidence of Western governments and banks was required if the currency was to be based on anything other than faith. The frontiers of Poland remained unsettled and were subject to bargaining, and the Poles were more aware than anyone else of the threat from communist Russia.

The extent to which support should be given to the new Government and to the nation was to be the principal concern of British diplomacy in Poland. The exercise of this diplomacy was complicated from the outset by the fact that the Poles in exile, with whom the Allied powers had negotiated during the war, were not those who were in a position to seize power when the restored Polish state came into being.

Towering above all the other Poles in exile during the war

was the figure of Ignace Paderewski, the great pianist. Saint-Saëns once said that Paderewski was a genius who happened to play the piano. Paderewski had a huge following in the United States, where he gave more than fifteen hundred concerts from the time of his arrival in New York in 1891. His handsome face and great mane of hair complemented his playing to make him a romantic symbol of the nation he represented. During the war he used his position, at first to obtain relief funds for the people of Poland, and later to campaign for Polish independence. His personal friendship with Colonel Edward M. House, the adviser whom President Wilson called his 'second personality', was of major importance in securing United States backing for the Polish cause. Clemenceau considered all this activity demeaning for such a man.

Paderewski was wholly committed to the Allied side. So was Roman Dmowski, the leader of the Polish National Committee in Paris. Józef Piłsudski, on the other hand, who had been brought up in the Russian Empire, where he had edited a socialist underground newspaper, attacked Russian trains in the Russo-Japanese war, and spent two years in prison before escaping, looked rather to Germany and her allies for the liberation of Poland. He even began to form a Polish legion, which the Germans foolishly expected to take an oath of allegiance to the Kaiser. Piłsudski thereupon disbanded the legion and was imprisoned in the Magdeburg fortress. He was released in October 1918 and made his way to Poland. There he received the support of the Polish irregular forces which had driven the German troops out of Poznania. When the war between the Western Allies and Germany came to an end Piłsudski was unquestionably the effective leader of the Polish nation.

Paderewski returned to Poland with the strong encouragement of the Western Allies. He landed at Danzig from a British cruiser and reached Warsaw on New Year's Day, 1919. Piłsudski accepted him as Prime Minister of a coalition government, he himself remaining Head of State and Commander-in-Chief of the army.

The struggle between Piłsudski and Paderewski which followed, and which members of the British Legation staff were able to witness at close quarters, was, because of the stature of the two protagonists, one of the great dramas of Polish political life.

Bentinck arrived in Warsaw in the company of one of those men to whom the Foreign Service owes much, but who do not reach the highest ranks, largely because their expertise keeps them rooted in one country. This was Frank Savery, who was going out as Consul. He was still Consul General in Warsaw when war broke out again in 1939. By then he enjoyed an extraordinary reputation among Poles as an authority on their national life.

Savery was a man of varied interests and discerning judgement. Among his closest friends had been James Elroy Flecker, who shortly before he died had discussed his latest poem *Burial* with him line by line.

On his outward journey to Warsaw Bentinck picked up Savery in Switzerland. Savery (*I called him The Prawn because he had rather big, bulging eyes and a red face*) had been serving in the British Legation in Berne. There his knowledge of Polish had been useful in negotiations with Polish émigré groups and also with Polish-speaking emissaries of the Austrian Government when it was putting out peace feelers. One of these emissaries, Count Aleksander Skrzyński, Bentinck was to encounter in other capacities later.

The British mission in Warsaw was headed for a time by Sir Percy Wyndham. He was something of a caretaker, for he retired from the Foreign Service in 1920. *An elderly man whose brain didn't function very nimbly. He was a nice man.* His successor as Minister was Sir Horace Rumbold.

Rumbold was a man bred to diplomacy. His father, who was also Sir Horace Rumbold Bart, and who was known in the service as Sir Horrid Grumbles, had been British Ambassador in Vienna, and the son had served under him as a Second Secretary in the same Embassy.

The younger Rumbold was a man of deceptive appearance. To Martin Gilbert, who wrote an admirable biography of Rumbold, Bentinck commented: 'He had the most important attributes for a Chief of Mission, viz: calmness—he was never flustered—shrewdness in observation, clarity in reporting and a capacity for inspiring trust and confidence. His appearance tended to disguise his ability. He would listen, then drop his eyeglass into his hand, shoot out his cuffs, and make a couple of observations that swiftly dispelled any doubts about his mental capacity.'

These doubts may have been occasioned by his heavy build and high colouring, attributable probably to high blood pressure. Be that as it may, the doubts were held by a number of people who had a limited acquaintance with him. Lord Derby, when he was Secretary of State for War, commented after one meeting with him: 'I have never come across a more stupid man in my life, both in appearance and conversation.' James Joyce, who felt slighted by Rumbold, wrote scurrilous verses about him. Harold Nicolson, on first meeting him in Berlin, wrote in his diary: 'He is a nice old bumble bee.' Of Rumbold, when seen in company with his wife, he wrote: 'They are really so appallingly English that it is almost funny, as English as bacon and eggs.' Yet he later dedicated his book *Diplomacy* to Rumbold and in it described him as 'the ideal diplomat'.

Rumbold was to prove an excellent choice as Minister in Warsaw. This was not only because of the qualities of calmness and shrewdness, to which Bentinck called attention, but also because he seems, in spite of periodic complaints, to have relished challenges and drama. He had been acting as Chargé d'Affaires in Berlin, because his Ambassador was on leave, when the Archduke Franz Ferdinand was assassinated at Sarajevo. Shortly afterwards he wrote to his wife: 'I am having the time of my life. Europe is in the midst of the most dangerous crisis in modern times.' After leaving Berlin he had been appointed Minister in Berne, where Savery had served under him and where, as Rumbold put it, 'day after day all sorts of fat spies walk into my parlour with really good information'.

The man who was Rumbold's deputy, with the rank of First Secretary, was Sir Percy Loraine, also a baronet. He took up his duties about a month after Bentinck arrived. He was later replaced by Bentinck's future brother-in-law, Rex Hoare. *I was devoted to Percy. We shared a flat in Warsaw. He was a good-looking baronet with money*. Although not having anything approaching Loraine's wealth, Bentinck was also comfortably off and, like Loraine, was able to enjoy his bachelor status. His starting salary was just £300 a year, and the annual increment only £20, but he had an allowance of £400 a year from his father which left him free of any immediate concern.

Another important member of the Legation staff was the Commercial Secretary, Richard Kimens. *He had been Consul in Warsaw before 1914. He was a mousy little man and was called Mousy. Mousy was half-Polish. His father became a sort of trading consul there. Mousy was very good. Quite easy to tease, but he was a dear fellow.* Kimens's reports, like Savery's, showed an impressive depth of knowledge.

The scene when Rumbold, accompanied by members of his staff, presented his credentials to Piłsudski as Head of State, made a lasting impression on Bentinck. 'I can still see him in my mind's eye,' he said of Piłsudski more than sixty years later, when addressing an Anglo-Polish gathering in London, 'an impressive figure in his grey uniform of the Polish Legion with no orders or decorations, standing with his hands on his cavalry sword. Behind him two ADCs, Major Beck, later Foreign Minister at the outbreak of World War II, and Captain George Potocki.' 'Piłsudski,' Rumbold wrote in a despatch in November 1919, 'in several respects, both physical and other, reminds me of the late Lord Kitchener.' He also commented on the low voice in which Piłsudski habitually spoke.

Paderewski, on arrival in Warsaw, had been greeted by large and enthusiastic crowds. Not long afterwards, on 23 February 1919, the British Government formally recognized Poland as an independent sovereign state. The United States Government had already done so. Paderewski's presence certainly contributed to the timing of the recognition by both countries. His personal acquaintance with Herbert Hoover helped to bring about the huge exercise in famine relief associated with Hoover's name. But his political passage in Poland was not easy.

Piłsudski was determined to get rid of Paderewski. He made life very difficult for him as Prime Minister. Like all conspirators he loved intrigue. He made trouble for Paderewski by fixing demonstrations against him. The Poles then loved demonstrations, which they had been unable to enjoy for a hundred and thirty years.

In November 1919 Paderewski told Rumbold in the course of a long and frank talk that Piłsudski had advised him to resign. Paderewski had decided that he would do so if he could not command a working majority in the Polish Parliament. At the same time he warned Rumbold of the dangers presented by secret societies of officers who were preparing for a dictatorship under Piłsudski.

Rumours were spread that Paderewski had in fact resigned, and to quash these he went down to the Parliament building and demanded the resignation of other ministers in his Government, but he had only a short respite.

At that time Madame Paderewska held regular receptions on Saturday evenings in the Zamek Palace, which, as Bentinck put it, were *crowded by rank and fashion and those who wanted to get on*. Rumbold, being indisposed, instructed Savery and Bentinck to attend one of these. They did so and found the only other guests on this occasion were the American Minister, Hugh Gibson, an American secretary and Paderewski's *chef de cabinet. Madame Paderewska was in tears. The regime was changing.*

A day or two later, early in December, Paderewski did resign. Soon afterwards he left for Paris after a stay in Poland of almost exactly a year. He had been defeated by a shrewder and much more single-minded politician. Rumbold commented: 'Of the two General Piłsudski is more indispensable than M. Paderewski. But there is room for both in this country which is so poor in statesmen.'

The Legation was only one of a number of British missions sent to Poland immediately after the first world war. In Czechoslovakia a well-organized state came into being fairly rapidly, largely because many Czechs had been employed in the civil service of the Austro-Hungarian Empire and could provide both continuity and professional skills. In Poland the supply of such people was more meagre, and there was virtually no administrative tradition. Britain and France tried to make good some of the deficiencies.

Gordon Macready, a soldier, who was to play an important role in the military government of Germany after the second world war, was sent to Poland in October 1919 to help train a Polish police force. This he did with considerable success. Another mission was charged with organizing the railway service. When the railway mission was thought to have completed its task Bentinck was called upon to wind up its activities. For this he had, for the only time in his life, and at the age of twenty-three, a special train permanently at his disposal.

There were also military and naval missions whose duties were primarily advisory. The head of the military mission was Adrian Carton de Wiart, holder of the V C and a man who seemed to have been created a size or two larger than life. *I knew Carton quite well. I was very fond of him. He had great success with women. His father had been a Belgian judge in the mixed courts in Cairo. He was sent to Cambridge and from there volunteered to go to the Boer war and become a British subject. Before 1914 he was in Somaliland, where he lost an eye. The brother officer who took him back was Pug Ismay. He did brilliantly commanding troops in 1915, 1916, 1917 and 1918, was wounded repeatedly and lost an arm.* Carton de Wiart was later to resign from the British Army and become the non-paying tenant of a half-million-acre estate on the Pripet Marshes belonging to Prince Charles Radziwill. In the course of time he transferred his affections from one female member of the Radziwill family to another.

One of Carton de Wiart's first actions after his arrival early in 1919 was to recommend the immediate despatch to Poland of the three Polish divisions formed in France under the command of General Haller together with their equipment and reserve ammunition.

The presence of Haller's legionaries was to make the difference a year later between survival and annihilation to the Polish state, but one British official disapproved strongly of their arrival in Poland. This was the future Sir Lewis Namier, the eminent historian, who served in the Foreign Office from 1917 to 1920. Namier rarely missed an opportunity, while working in the Northern Department, of castigating the Polish Government, often supporting his arguments by a wealth of erudition. When he went on leave it was noted on a Foreign Office file that there was nobody else in the Northern Department who could read a Polish newspaper. Namier's minuted comment on the transfer of Haller's troops was: 'General Haller openly flouts the Peace Congress, as the Poles seem to have no scruple in doing. But by sending Haller's army to Poland the Allied Powers have given the Poles the means to do so freely.'

Another British mission which came to Poland late in 1919 was investigatory rather than advisory in purpose. This came about because the British Board of Jews had read alarming reports of the continuation of pogroms in the Polish territories formerly under Russian occupation. The leader of the mission, Sir Stuart Samuel, was a man of great piety. He caused Rumbold, who had invited him to dinner, some surprise by arriving with his cutlets, suitably prepared, wrapped in news-paper. He also insisted that the train which conveyed his mission around Poland must be halted throughout the Jewish Sabbath. Rumbold reported to the Foreign Office that he had had two very interesting talks with Samuel, adding, quite correctly, that the mission was 'very unpopular in Poland'.

The Secretary to the mission, Peter Wright, had been attached to the British Delegation to the peace conference in Versailles. The reports he drafted for Samuel's approval were stimulating, and the conclusions reached were more en-couraging than might have been expected. 'Three-fifths of the world's Jews,' it was pointed out, 'live in what was once the Kingdom of Poland . . . If a plebiscite were taken today in Warsaw, the capital of Poland, as to whether Warsaw should be Polish, yes or no, the answer might quite easily be no.' It was conceded that, 'a great quarrel has arisen in the present generation between Jews and Poles, each in their millions', and that this had been stimulated because 'not only have the Jews grown modern in the nineteenth century, but the Poles have too'. Nevertheless, the authors attributed the so-called 'exces-ses' perpetrated against Jews almost wholly to the military. 'All these excesses,' they concluded hopefully, 'will cease on demobilisation.' Among the recommendations contained in the final report were that the British Government should assist Polish Jews who wished to emigrate to Palestine, Canada or South Africa, and that a Yiddish-speaking secretary should be added to the staff of the Legation in Warsaw. Neither was put into effect.

Peter Wright was to become notorious not long afterwards because of a book he wrote in which he impugned Gladstone's motives for interesting himself in the fate of prostitutes. The Gladstone family sustained their attack on him until they brought him, as they had hoped, to the point where he himself brought an action. *Poor Peter Wright*, Bentinck commented, *he had a crash. A most entertaining fellow. He looked rather like Oscar Wilde. Very sad.*

After a year or two the readiness of the British Government to provide advisory and other services to the Polish nation, which had been so evident immediately after the war, began to diminish. In the change which occurred the influence of the Treasury can be clearly seen.

Early in 1921 the Polish Ministry of Finance approached the Foreign Office in London and asked for the appointment of a British financial adviser to the Polish Government, making it clear that the Polish authorities would be unable to extricate themselves from their present critical financial position owing to the lack of anyone capable of managing the finances of the country. Curzon asked Hilton Young, a banker and Member of Parliament, to take on the job. Young at first agreed, but was then appointed Financial Secretary to the Treasury, and an approach was made to the Hon. R. H. Brand, financier, Etonian and cricketer. He decided he had too many commitments in Britain.

A few further ineffectual soundings were made, but in September Rumbold's successor reported that the Polish Government had turned to the United States for the help it needed. 'Poland's fianances,' he added, 'are meanwhile going from bad to worse.'

Such changes of direction were among a number of reasons why Pilsudski and others found British policy towards Poland puzzling. They also complicated the task of those who had to present that policy to the Polish Government.

The British Government had decided at the end of the first world war to support the Russian forces commanded by General Denikin and others which were fighting against the Bolsheviks. The help given was not nearly as much as Winston Churchill wanted and consisted largely of quantities of boots and greatcoats. To Poles this all seemed wasted effort. In December 1919 Rumbold reported: 'On one point only in connection with Russia do almost all Poles seem to be unanimous, viz. that Kolchak, Denikin and Yadenich are all three doomed to failure.'

Bentinck, as soon as he came into contact with Russian soldiers, was able to see for himself why the Polish judgement was correct. *Denikin was a bit better than Kolchak, but they hadn't got the confidence of their men. I remember seeing Russian prisoners going about the streets of Warsaw with British uniforms with brass buttons on them still with the royal arms. We booted them and we uniformed them and they went over to the other side.*

I was sent on a couple of occasions to inspect the prison camps in which the Polish Army had kept Russian troops, and on one occasion I found that the Red Army orderlies in the hospital wards deprived Russian officers, who were suffering from typhus, of water, which was extremely painful and made their recovery improbable.

Once it had disposed of the Russian counter-revolutionary forces the Soviet Government made no secret of its intention to establish a workers' government in Poland and rapidly increased the number of its divisions along the line dividing the two countries, from seven to twenty. Piłsudski therefore decided on the strategy of the pre-emptive strike. He made a temporary agreement with the Ukrainian nationalist leader, the Hetman Petlura, attacked the Russians, and captured Kiev. This humiliation, Trotsky stated, was the making of the Red Army.

There were Poles, Paderewski among them, who warned Piłsudski of the folly of advancing as far as Kiev, but in military matters Piłsudski relied largely on his own judgement. Prince Sapieha, *an excellent Foreign Minister* in Bentinck's opinion, once told Loraine that 'Piłsudski's principal foible was his conviction that he was a military genius of the first order, and that while he was willing to be taxed with a political blunder, and even admit to it, the slightest criticism of his conduct of military affairs was bitterly resented.' Sapieha's own opinion was that Piłsudski's 'political talent was of a much higher order than his military attainments'.

The Polish lines were of course badly overstretched. The Soviet forces counter-attacked, the retreat began, and the newly created Polish Army was in poor shape. Carton de Wiart reported scathingly on 'the utter inefficiency of the regimental officers'.

Allied policy in response to these events in the spring and summer of 1920 was largely one of confusion. It was hampered by such events as the decision of the National Union of Railwaymen in Britain taken on 22 May not to handle any material intended for Poland which might be used against Soviet forces. There were also differences between the French and British governments.

As the Soviet forces advanced, tentative proposals for peace were put forward on both sides. The Polish Government offered to send plentipotentiaries to London to meet Soviet representatives, but the Russians replied that the venue was not suitable. The Soviet demands grew. Curzon considered that a Soviet proposal for a new frontier line, later to be known as the Curzon line, was acceptable, but the Russians then went further and demanded what was tantamount to surrender. The French Minister in Warsaw, André de Panafieu, stated that the Soviet demand was quite unacceptable to the French Government. Curzon had already instructed Rumbold to tell the Polish Government that unless it accepted Britain 'could not assume the responsibility of taking hostile action against Russia'. When he learnt what the French Minister had said he was reported to have been furious.

While these diplomatic exchanges were going on the French and British governments had decided to send yet another mission to Poland. This was a joint Anglo-French venture. The military leader on the French side was General Maxime Weygand, Foch's former Chief of General Staff. One of the junior officers was Charles de Gaulle. The head of the British half of the mission was Lord D'Abernon, a banker who had been financial adviser to the Egyptian Government and a governor of the Imperial Ottoman Bank. A large, rather untidy, bearded, impressive figure, D'Abernon had played poker with Abe Bailey in Johannesburg before the Jameson raid for stakes which called for a cool nerve.

The members of the mission, who set off by train in July, had a discouraging start. In Paris they found Paderewski filled with gloom. In Prague President Masaryk told them that the situation of the Poles was hopeless. The outlook in Warsaw was little more encouraging. When the mission reached Warsaw on 25 July Soviet forces were only a hundred miles away, the

Poles having been driven back four hundred miles in forty days. On the same day a new Polish coalition Government was formed with the Peasant Party leader, Wincenty Witos, as Prime Minister.

In Warsaw, Kimens reported, people were storing cash in the belief that if the Bolsheviks captured the city they would close the banks. D'Abernon was struck rather by what he called 'the outstanding *insouciance* of everybody while the enemy is at the gates'. Two days after taking office as Prime Minister, Witos, as a good farmer, went off to attend to his harvest.

Piłsudski seemed unwilling to defer to Weygand and advanced the argument that the battles he was fighting were quite unlike trench warfare and the kind of experience required, he considered, was that of a British colonial general. By 1 August D'Abernon was commenting in his diary: 'The chances remain strongly against the possibility of holding Warsaw.'

The same view was taken by the diplomatic corps as a whole. Two of its members were deputed by the rest to negotiate evacuation or other procedures in the event of Warsaw being captured. One was Rumbold. The other was the Papal Nuncio, Monsignor Achille Ratti, who was later to ascend the throne of St Peter as Pope Pius XI.

As plans for an orderly evacuation were made the quality of the different diplomats became more evident. The American Minister, Hugh Gibson, made an excellent impression. *An American career man, a very good diplomat*, Bentinck said. *He had been number two at the American Legation in Brussels and had been very active in efforts to save Nurse Cavell*. The German Minister was Count Alfred von Oberndorff, of whom Rumbold noted: 'His unconcealed satisfaction during the recent invasion of Poland by the Bolsheviks could not but damage him in the eyes of the Poles.' The Swedish Minister opted for flight. *His First Secretary came to the Chancery the next morning and found his Minister had fled and left the Legation to him. Like Edward VIII and Fruity Metcalfe in 1940*. 'Rumbold,' D'Abernon recorded, 'keeps a cool head under these difficult circumstances. He has fortunately an excellent personal position here and is regarded by the Poles as a sincere friend to their country.'

By 13 August preparations were completed for a special train to take the diplomatic corps out of Warsaw. This reached Poznań the next day. From there Rumbold wrote to his wife: 'We have cut a very sorry figure in the business.' Alone of the diplomatic corps the Papal Nuncio remained in Warsaw.

On the day the diplomatic train reached Poznań a Polish army to the north of Warsaw, commanded by General Wŀadysŀaw Sikorski, launched an attack which took the Soviet forces by surprise. It was followed by attacks in the other sectors which Piŀsudski and Weygand had planned. Within four days the Soviet Army was in full retreat. The Poles captured some seventy thousand prisoners.

D'Abernon described the battle at the approaches to Warsaw as the eighteenth decisive battle of the world and wrote a book with that title. The military historian Creasy had listed fifteen, to which D'Abernon added the battles of Sedan, the Marne and now Warsaw. In a despatch dated 24 August Rumbold wrote: 'I cannot recall any parallel in history to the dramatic change brought about by this event. In my view the issue at stake was nothing less than the final ruin and possible disappearance of Poland. It is certain that if the Soviet troops had captured Warsaw a Soviet regime would have been set up in that town.'

This last statement was certainly correct. As they were to do again more than twenty years later, the Russians held in readiness 'a provisional revolutionary committee to take control' when circumstances permitted. This committee was kept in Biaŀystok, not, as in the second world war, Lublin.

Weygand's part in helping to save Warsaw was generously admitted by Poles. Addressing the Polish Parliament a month after the battle, Witos said: 'During the Bolshevik advance France was the only nation which understood the danger. In the other Western countries the elements hostile to Poland stirred up agitation and called the Poles adventurers and imperialists. In this crisis Poland found her unity. The High Command, aided by General Weygand's genius, won a striking victory.'

It was not a wholly unfair interpretation of events. When the head of the Northern Department in the Foreign Office, J. D. (Don) Gregory commented on a report: 'Presumably

Poland will one day learn sense,' Curzon added: 'A bold presumption.'

In the popular version of these events which most Poles came to accept in the inter-war years the only foreigner, other than Weygand, to emerge with evident credit was the Papal Nuncio, whose staunchness was much admired.

D'Abernon had been so favourably impressed by Rumbold that he recommended him for the post of High Commissioner in Constantinople, and on 29 September 1920 Curzon offered Rumbold the appointment. Rumbold accepted. In his final report on Poland he wrote:

'The difficulties of the agent of one of the Allied Great Powers in this country are manifold. He has to be on the alert the whole time for, given the number and complexity of the questions which this country has had to solve and which remain to be solved, he passes literally from one crisis to another.' In a letter to D'Abernon he had written: 'I think Lord Curzon ought to know what sort of post this is. It is perhaps the most trying post in the service.'

The Foreign Office clearly conceded that the post was an unusually demanding one when a letter was sent from the Northern Department to the Legation in Warsaw stating: 'In the very exceptional circumstances we are prepared to consider 1920 a "war year" in Poland and do not insist upon the production of an annual report.' Yet there was no hurry to appoint Rumbold's successor, and a question was even asked in Parliament about the delay. This was put by Sir Samuel Hoare, who described the delay as 'very injurious to this country'.

In the end the man chosen was William Grenfell Max Muller. As he was of German Jewish origin there was a suggestion that the Polish Government might not find him acceptable. *Percy Loraine was horrified. He said the only time this had happened before was when our man who had been in Pretoria at the time of the Jameson raid was to be appointed Minister at the Hague and the Dutch Government didn't like it.* The *agrément* was duly received, and when Max Muller went to present his credentials to Piłsudski he was given an escort of lancers commanded by a general.

Max Muller I liked. He was a difficult chief in a way, as he was always complaining about his staff. He was not liked in the Foreign Service, and people were unfair to him. He was never made Ambassador in Warsaw, but the minute he retired his successor was, which I thought was rather spiteful.

After the military victory at the approaches to Warsaw the Polish Government obtained the agreement of the Soviet Government to a new frontier. This was well to the east of the Curzon line, but while the negotiations were still taking place Prince Sapieha told Loraine he did not think that 'the peace about to be concluded would be of very long duration or that its territorial provisions would be of a permanent character'.

Among the weaknesses of the settlement was the lack of any consideration for the claims of the Ukrainians. *The Polish landlords came back and said they were going to get their properties back. Charles Radziwill told me that the people came out to meet him with bread and salt. He knocked it away and said: 'I don't need bread and salt when I'm coming back to my own home.' There was too much of that, and they paid no attention to any Ukrainian leader, Petlura or Skoropacki. It was the same with the White Russians.*

No less complicated was the settlement of the frontier with Germany. In this the Western Allies continued to play a major part throughout Bentinck's period of service in Poland, and he himself frequently had to act as observer and reporter.

The main area of dispute was Upper Silesia, which had a mixed German-Polish population and an important industrial district including coal-mines. A plebiscite taken indicated that the territory would have to be split but how this should be done was debatable.

Allied policy was divided. Whereas the French consistently backed the Polish claims, the British, with some Italian support, aimed rather at impartiality. This was not popular in Poland, and Max Muller, fairly soon after his arrival, reported: 'There is a widespread, though so far as I can judge, unjustified belief that His Majesty's Government have consistently adopted an attitude adverse to the interests of Poland.' It was largely knowledge of the Allied differences which led the unofficial leader of the Silesian Poles, Wojciech Korfanty, into taking action.

At the beginning of May 1921 Bentinck was sent to Upper

Silesia, where he reported to the British Commissioner at Opole (Oppeln). He had a feeling of trouble in the air, but the Commissioner told him that the French President of the Inter-Allied Commission, General Lerond, had just left for Paris, stating that all was quiet. That night while Bentinck was sound asleep, a huge explosion occurred. *The next morning when I woke up I found that a railway bridge a few hundred yards from my hotel had been blown up.*

This was a beginning of a *putsch* organized by Korfanty with the object of making Polish possession of most of Upper Silesia a *fait accompli*. Six weeks of fighting followed before the Inter-Allied Commission helped to bring it to an end.

Lloyd George continued to be sympathetic to the German claim, and the issue was referred to the Council of the League of Nations. There a fairly equitable decision was reached. In the Polish popular version of history, just as the name Curzon meant only the Curzon line, so Lloyd George came to be known exclusively as the man who wanted to give Upper Silesia to the Germans and who did not know where it was on the map. French support for the Polish claim was not forgotten.

During his stay in Poland Bentinck travelled widely and learnt much. His duties within the Legation too were varied. He learnt, for example, the accepted manner of ending a letter to the Foreign Secretary, Lord Curzon. This was: 'I have the honour to be with the highest respect, My Lord Marquis, Your Lordship's most obedient, humble servant.'

As a junior Secretary he was deputed to deal with problems arising from statements in the Polish press. In September 1921, for instance, a Polish newspaper reported that a rebellion had broken out in India and extended to a third of the country. 'As this information appeared more than doubtful,' Max Muller wrote, 'Mr Bentinck made private enquiries of the News Department of the Foreign Office.' There he learnt, first that the report had emanated from Moscow, and later that it had come from somewhere in Germany. At that time there were no Embassy or Legation officials who had the specific task of dealing with the press, although in November 1919 a somewhat plaintive minute appeared on a file of the Northern

Department stating: 'Could not some pro-British propaganda be inaugurated in Poland? The money would be better spent than on greatcoats.'

Another instructive experience Bentinck had was a conversation when he was on his way to visit Berlin. *We arrived at the frontier. I got out and spoke to the German officer there, who was a very decent fellow. The troops were miserable boys with huge helmets. He hadn't got instructions to let us through and we had to telephone back. We sat and talked, and I said to him: 'The German Army looks very different now from when I saw it in Weimar in 1914.' He said: 'That's not surprising. You made a very hard treaty with us. It will be as it was after the battle of Jena. We shall have Turnvereine, Feuerwehr and other societies, and then you will get tired of sitting on us, and we shall re-arm secretly. Then he used the words, 'Und dann wird ein Führer erscheinen,' which I've never forgotten, 'and we shall have the Revanchekrieg.' I said to him: 'Who will the leader be? A Hohenzollern?' 'No, no, no! Anybody at all. But the spirit of the army will remain.'*

Bentinck left Poland early in 1922. He had performed his duties well enough to be promoted Second Secretary in December 1920. His next assignment, a comparatively brief one, was to be in the Foreign Office.

CHAPTER 3
With Curzon in Lausanne
(1922–23)

Bentinck's Foreign Office appointment on his return from Poland was in the Egyptian section of the Eastern Department. *We were occupied by the negotiations for the future government of Egypt. Allenby was about to retire. Zaghlul was heading the nationalists. We deported him to the Seychelles, which was a very good place for deporting troublesome politicians from our subordinate territories. They invariably came back to run them. We were cheek-by-jowl with the Near East section and we shared a big room with them.*

Among those who worked in the Near East section were Eric Forbes-Adam, then aged thirty-three, who some two years later was to commit suicide, and Harold Nicolson. Of Nicolson Bentinck said: *I was very fond of him. He was very good company, a good friend. I admired his writing. He was not suited to be a diplomat. He had too much feeling, too many likes and dislikes. I once told him he was a coagulated mass of prejudices. He didn't disagree. He couldn't. He and Eric Forbes-Adam, also a very intelligent fellow, had nervous breakdowns when the Greeks were routed in Asia Minor.*

By 1922 relations between Greece and Turkey had become one of the principal concerns of British foreign policy. There was a serious danger that they could lead to a British involvement in war, and they were already causing rifts in the Franco-British alliance.

In order to induce Greece to enter the war against the Central Powers, which she eventually did in June 1917, both the British and French goverments had made ill-advised offers of territory forming part of the Ottoman Empire. The British had specifically mentioned 'large concessions on the coast of Asia Minor' and Clemenceau had even held out hopes that Constantinople might be on offer. With this encouragement Greek troops were landed at Smyrna in May 1919. The action received the sanction of the political leaders of Britain, France, the United States and Italy, though some of their military advisers were sceptical. Foch estimated that twenty-seven divisions would be needed to pacify the areas which Greece was due to occupy.

Although Turkey had been a defeated power, the new revolutionary leader, Kemal Ataturk, had already begun to revive the national spirit, and he skilfully played off the Western Allies against each other. While it was still British policy to describe him as a brigand the French made a secret agreement with him to negotiate a frontier between Turkey and the French administration in Syria. There were some eight thousand British troops in and around Constantinople, and the officer commanding them found it necessary in June 1920 to issue a proclamation stating that any attack on them, either by Greeks or Turks, would be resisted by force.

The military prospects of the Greeks steadily deteriorated, and in August 1922 a massive defeat was inflicted on them by a Turkish army under the command of Ismet Pasha. Vast numbers of refugees fled towards the Aegean Islands and Thrace. Turkish confidence grew, and the initial and punitive post-war treaty with Turkey, which had been drawn up at Sèvres, a treaty Poincaré wittily and correctly declared to be as fragile as porcelain, was repudiated.

Discussions were held in the League of Nations. The great Norwegian polar explorer, Fridtjof Nansen, who had recently been appointed the League's High Commissioner for Refugees, called public attention to the plight of the Greeks driven from their homes. A decision was finally taken to hold a major international conference to discuss problems of the Near East. The site chosen was Lausanne.

Bentinck was sent to Lausanne ahead of the British delegation to find hotel rooms and make any other necessary arrangements. That one young man of twenty-five with the rank of Second Secretary was thought capable of doing all that was required offers a curious contrast with, for example, the economic summit meeting in London sixty-two years later, when there was six months' detailed planning of security measures, special weapon-training courses were held, and the leave of 27,000 London police officers was cancelled.

The hotel which Bentinck chose for the British delegation was the Beau Rivage near the Lake. He took particular care to have the best suite, situated on the second floor, reserved for the delegation's leader. This was the Foreign Secretary, the Marquis Curzon of Kedleston.

From his undergraduate days, when he was the subject of the well-known rhyme, 'My name is George Nathaniel Curzon, I am a most superior person,' through his years as Viceroy of India, an office whose power and pomp appealed to him strongly, to his fairly long tenure of the Foreign Office under Lloyd George, Bonar Law and finally Baldwin, Curzon inspired respect more easily than love. D'Abernon, while serving as Ambassador in Berlin, wrote in his diary: 'The resentment of the Foreign Office against the haughty and inconsiderate Curzon is such that the devil himself would be welcome. Curzon's misfortune is to have the lofty manners of a minor royalty without the incapacity with which they are normally associated.' Nicolson, who wrote of Curzon's 'superb direction of foreign policy during his last years of office', described him as 'one of the most interesting, as well as one of the most perplexing, of British Foreign Secretaries'. Bentinck himself spoke of Curzon not without affection.

Curzon suffered greatly from a back. He always wore a corset, and if his back ached he didn't sleep at all. He used to work at night. If his back wasn't hurting he could be very jolly and pleasant and, if one was lunching with him, tell stories of India and elsewhere. If his back was half hurting, all foreigners were being more bloody than usual but his faithful sta-aff were protecting him. (Curzon always affected the flat ǎ rather than *ah*, in such words as 'staff'.) *If the nerves in his back were hurting like hell everyone's hand was against him.* Bentinck also noticed the affection which Curzon felt for his second wife, the former Grace Duggan, daughter of an American Consul in Rio and widow of an Argentinian, to whom he was married at the age of fifty-eight. *I remember going to the railway station with him to meet her when he'd begged her to leave St Moritz and come for a while to cheer him at this dreadful conference.*

As the train came in Curzon literally ran along the platform to greet her. I was rather struck by that.

Curzon's advisers at Lausanne included Rumbold and Sir William Tyrrell, under whom Bentinck was later to serve in the Embassy in Paris and from whom, he later said, he learnt more than from any other ambassador. As one of the most important subjects for negotiation was to be the future of the Dardanelles there was a fairly strong Royal Navy contingent. This was headed by Sir Roger Keyes and included a Captain Pound who, as Admiral Sir Dudley Pound, First Sea Lord, was to become a familiar figure to Bentinck in the second world war. *Keyes*, Bentinck said, *liked playing a role. He rather wanted to intrigue with the Russians. He was inclined to intrigue, and it was decided he should be recalled. Pound remained.*

Forbes-Adam and Nicolson were both included in the delegation. Another British subject present was Oliver Baldwin, son of the future Conservative Prime Minister and himself a Labour supporter. He attached himself to the Armenian delegation. Not the least interesting member of the British party was a valet whom Rumbold had brought with him from Constantinople. He was later to serve other British ambassadors in Turkey and under the code-name Cicero became one of the few successful spies in the German service in the second world war.

Curzon's journey from London to Lausanne in November 1922 was not an easy one. It was a time of deteriorating Franco-British relations. The Cannes conference, at which Lloyd George and Briand had hoped to solve problems of military security and German reparations, had disintegrated when Briand's Government had fallen. Briand had been succeeded by Raymond Poincaré, whose views on how to extract reparations from Germany differed widely from those of the British Government and were to be the cause of even greater dissension than the affairs of the Near East. In Paris Curzon had a meeting with Poincaré. *It wasn't very successful. Poincaré was very unpleasant and Curzon was almost in tears at his unpleasantness. They got into the train, in separate carriages, Poincaré and his staff and Curzon and his delegation, and went off to Lausanne.*

At Lausanne station, Nicolson recorded, 'Bill Bentinck came up to us, immaculate, adolescent and so reliable.' Bentinck had ordered a dinner for Curzon and his staff with some care, but learnt from Nicolson that Curzon would not be taking it. A message had been received from the Italian consul that Mussolini would not be coming to Lausanne, but hoped to meet Curzon and Poincaré at the small town of Territet beyond Montreux.

Poincaré was inclined to regard this as an insult, but the considered opinion among the British delegation was that Mussolini, in his revolutionary youth, might have committed some offence in the Canton of Vaud and that there might still be a warrant out for his arrest. *They went to Territet and there they met Musso. They had a long talk. Then they, Mussolini on the one hand and Poincaré and Curzon on the other, bade each other good night. They thought that was the last they would see of Mussolini and they got into their carriages. The train started off. Suddenly there was a bump, and that was Mussolini's coach being tacked on to the train. The train puffed off back to Lausanne, where, filled with good food and drink, Ernest Lagalle* (Bentinck's opposite number as secretary of the French delegation) *and I met them.*

The whole episode was nothing more than an exercise in theatrical showmanship by Mussolini, who wanted Poincaré and Curzon to be seen to be doing his bidding, but Curzon did not hold it against him. On 22 November he wrote in a despatch to the Foreign Office: 'In our numerous conversations during the last forty-eight hours Mussolini had struck me as a sincere and attractive and certainly a remarkable personality, though strangely immature and lacking in experience.'

Neither Mussolini nor Poincaré remained long at Lausanne. The direction of the French delegation passed into the hands of diplomats, the seventy-two year-old Camille Barrère, and Maurice Bompard who, like Rumbold, had been serving in Turkey. General Weygand was also present.

A number of countries, on the other hand, continued to be represented by their leading statesmen. Eleutherios Venizelos, the Cretan who was eight times Prime Minister of Greece, was temporarily out of power, but his international standing was already such that his presence in Lausanne seemed necessary to the Greek Government. Curzon strongly disliked him, Bentinck too had reservations. *Venizelos was a tremendous intriguer. Totally dishonest. He was not too bad at Lausanne. He always liked to wear a black cap. I knew him again later when I was Chargé d'Affaires in Athens. He'd got megalomania then. It wasn't la Grèce c'est moi, it was la Méditerranée, c'est moi.*

The Soviet Union too was represented by its Commissar for Foreign Affairs, Georghy Chicherin. *He had a very piercing voice,* Bentinck recalled, *and drank a good deal.* Although Chicherin had the skill and adaptability to remain in office for many years, he made relatively little impact on the conference. In one of his despatches from Lausanne dealing with the proposed convention on the Dardanelles, a subject of obvious concern to the Soviet Union, Curzon wrote: 'Chicherin made a series of speeches complaining that Russia had been ignored in the preparation of the convention, that an attempt was being made to impose it upon her, and that her counter-proposals had never been examined. I replied that this was because not one of the ten powers represented at the table had had a good word to say for them.'

Nor did the chief United States representative, Washburn Child (who, in accordance with the general American policy of withdrawal from Europe, was present only as an observer), play a leading part in the negotiations. Indeed from the time of the departure of Poincaré and Mussolini until the conference was adjourned early in February 1923 only two statesmen continually held the centre of the stage. One was the victorious general and future President of the Turkish Republic, Ismet Pasha. The other was Curzon.

Curzon was able to dominate the conference almost from the outset as a result of a skilful manoeuvre. He suggested that there should be three separate committees. One, over which he would preside, would deal with territorial problems. One would deal with finance and be presided over by Barrère. The third, dealing with minorities, would be presided over by the chief Italian delegate, the Marchese Garroni, whom Curzon called 'The Turtle'. This was agreed, and it was then found that the first sixteen meetings all dealt with territorial problems.

The three main concerns of the British Government were freedom of passage through the Dardanelles, the Turkish frontiers in Asia Minor, and the settlement of the Ottoman debt. The first two were dealt with under Curzon's chairmanship. The third required the attention of financial experts rather than forceful negotiators.

In confronting Ismet, Curzon had a number of advantages. One was his own mastery of rhetoric and logic. Washburn Child likened the difference between Curzon's performance and Ismet's in one debate to that between 'a Greek temple and a dish of scrambled eggs'. Another advantage was Curzon's extraordinarily detailed knowledge of the ethnic composition of the region under discussion. A third, mentioned by Bentinck, was not generally known. *Being in occupation in Constantinople, we received translations of all the instructions which Ismet was receiving from Ankara at the same time as he received them, which was quite helpful.*

Curzon's principal weaknesses were lack of agreement with the French and, to a lesser extent, the Italian delegations and lack of support from his Government at home. Bonar Law, he once stated, was 'longing to clear out of Mosul, the Straits, Constantinople, willing to give up everything rather than have a row'.

Against all this Ismet presented a front of patience and determination. *Ismet*, Bentinck said, *was very very stubborn.* Curzon went further. 'He is impervious,' he wrote, 'to argument, warning or appeal. I can find no solace in any other reflexion than that Ismet, like all other Turks, is doubtless at bottom a true-born son of the bazaar.'

In the end both Britain and Turkey obtained most of what they wanted from the Lausanne conference, but there were times when agreement seemed unlikely. An understanding had apparently been reached at the end of January 1923, but the French delegation then informed the press that this was no more than a basis for discussion. Curzon therefore tried a tactic which had succeeded before.

Curzon thought he'd do what Disraeli and Lord Salisbury did in seventy-eight at Berlin. He said he'd leave if they didn't agree by the time the train was due to go. They didn't agree and Curzon left.

The main British delegation left too, but Bentinck

remained, ostensibly to settle administrative details, but in reality to provide a listening post. Shortly after returning from Lausanne Curzon stated that Ismet Pasha had telephoned to his hotel twice to find out whether he had really left. The source of Curzon's information was a telegram from Bentinck. During the conference Bentinck had made friends with its French Secretary-General, René Massigli, and on 6 February 1923 he sent another telegram, which is one of the more interesting documents on the Lausanne conference preserved in the Foreign Office files. This stated: 'M. Massigli informs me that M. Bompard had a long interview with Ismet Pasha this morning. I hear that M. Bompard on departing stated that peace was as good as signed.'

Bentinck's information was correct. The conference was reconvened on 23 April 1923, Rumbold replacing Curzon as head of the British delegation. *We plodded on. In the end we agreed. It was a long and dreary business. Rumbold was very shrewd, very quiet.*

The degree of freedom of navigation through the Dardanelles which Britain wanted was accepted, and a compromise was reached over the frontier between Turkey and the British-mandated territory of Iraq. The main British interest here was the oil in Mosul, over which a company whose shareholders were predominantly British held the rights. A commission consisting of a Swedish diplomat, a Belgian soldier and a Hungarian geographer was appointed to decide the future of the disputed territory. Finding that its population consisted mainly of Kurds, who clearly preferred Iraqi to Turkish rule, the commission decided, as Rumbold had hoped, in favour of Iraq.

The most extraordinary achievement, if achievement it could be considered, of the Lausanne conference lay outside the area of conflict between Ismet Pasha and either Curzon or Rumbold. This was the greatest transfer ever negotiated of populations by two sovereign states. Two and a half years after the conclusion of the treaty 370,000 Moslems had left Greece and nearly all the Asiatic Greeks, apart from some in Constantinople who were given a special exemption, had left Turkey. Appalling hardships were caused, but the transfer did as least remove conflict between the two countries until a new one appeared in Cyprus. *I have a distinct recollection,* Bentinck recalled, *that at the last minute Ismet wanted us to agree that if we left Cyprus we'd return the whole island to the Turks. We said we really couldn't take this up again. We weren't going to leave.*

A number of the British delegates to the conference were specialists, whose tasks were clearly defined. Bentinck's duties were general and varied. Among them was the care of the guests whom Curzon chose to entertain. *Curzon decided that he would give a large dinner for all the delegates to the conference, and I was told to prepare this. I produced the menu for Curzon and sent out the invitations. Then I found some very good Madeira at the hotel and I told Curzon of this. I said to him: 'Would you like to have cocktails served before dinner?' He drew himself up and said: 'Bentinck, does your father have cocktails served in his house?' 'No, he wouldn't hear of it.' 'Then why should you expect me to have them served in mine?'*

Harold Nicolson in his scintillating book, *Curzon: The Last Phase*, when describing the *rapport* Curzon established with the Bulgarian Peasant Party Prime Minister, Aleksandr Stamboliski, wrote: 'The only people with whom he could not establish relations of amity were the "upper middle class."' This no doubt facilitated his relationship with Bentinck who, though he could claim a carpenter and a gipsy among his comparatively recent ancestors, was devoid of any trace of middle-class blood.

Press coverage of the conference was fairly thorough, and among the many British foreign correspondents present was one who had brought a girlfriend with him from Vienna, named Betty. On returning to the Beau Rivage Hotel one evening he learnt that Betty had last been seen having drinks in the bar with one of the Italian delegates. He went up to the Italian's room and found him in bed with Betty. He seized a lamp and brought it down on the Italian's head, inflicting considerable damage to an ear. Bentinck was deputed to arrange with the Swiss police that the journalist and Betty should leave the country: *Two or three days later Curzon was delivering a speech to the conference about Armenia, and he said: 'And you mean to tell me, General Ismet Pasha, that in those va-ast territories there is not one nook, not one cranny, where that unhappy folk may remain Armenian?' Then he finished his speech, turned to*

Rumbold and, pointing to the Italian delegation, said, 'Which of those Italians was the adulterer? Which ear was it?'

Bentinck was also involved in a successful effort, which was launched from Lausanne, to save the life of the father of the present Duke of Edinburgh. This was Prince Andrew, described by Bentinck as *the only really intelligent member of the Greek royal family.*

The Greek Government which had come into power after the humiliating military defeat in Asia Minor had decided to find a number of scapegoats. One of these was Prince Andrew, who had held an important command. *Curzon tried to get Venizelos to intervene on behalf of the ministers and Prince Andrew. Venizelos wouldn't do it. But there was a man called Gerald Talbot, who was a friend of Venizelist Greeks and had a lot of friends with influence in Athens. Harold Nicolson and Tyrrell arranged that Talbot—Curzon pretended he hadn't heard of this person—should go out there and try to get Prince Andrew out. I remember getting the funds out of the safe, and supplying Talbot.*

Shortly afterwards a telegram was received from the British Chargé d'Affaires in Athens, Charles Bentinck—a distant cousin of Bill Bentinck's—stating that Talbot had been given an assurance by the Minister of War and Colonel Plastiras that Prince Andrew would be sentenced to either penal servitude or death, but that Plastiras would then pardon him and hand him over to Talbot for immediate removal. The need for secrecy and the swift despatch of a British warship for transporting Prince Andrew were stressed. Both conditions were met, and Prince Andrew, under sentence of 'perpetual banishment', was brought to safety. *On his return to London Gerald Talbot was summoned to Buckingham Palace, where King George V knighted him on the spot.*

As any capable young diplomat should, Bentinck established friendly relations with his opposite numbers from other countries. His friendship with Massigli, who later became French Ambassador in London, was to be a long-lasting one. He was on good terms with the secretaries of the French and Italian delegations, Lagarde and Indelli. He also came to know one of the French interpreters well. *A remarkable interpreter called Camernynck, who'd been at the Treaty of Versailles. He'd interpet what was said with hardly any notes, perfectly. The minute he'd left the conference hall he'd forgotten all about it. Several times, walking with him to luncheon at the Beau Rivage and speaking to him about what had been said, I found he couldn't remember a damned thing. He was a* libre penseur. *I attended his funeral at the Père Lachaise cemetery. It was very cold, very gloomy. A* libre penseur *funeral is not at all jolly.*

In the months he spent in Lausanne Bentinck had learnt much. He had been at close quarters to some of the leading statesmen of the world. He had watched, day by day, the unfolding of a major act of British diplomacy. For a long time this had seemed to take the form of a personal encounter. Yet the outcome, once the Treaty of Lausanne had been signed and British troops withdrawn from Constantinople and the Dardanelles, was a long period of exceptionally cordial Anglo-Turkish relations. He had witnessed the virtuoso performance of Curzon, which Nicolson summed up by stating: 'The Lausanne Conference re-established his reputation and his self-confidence. His handling of that Assembly will always remain among the classic examples of expert diplomacy.' Finally he had seen the details settled under the expert professional guidance of Rumbold.

Nicolson had some grounds for implying that Curzon's reputation and self-confidence needed restoring. Relations with the French Government in particular had deteriorated during his tenure of office, and in the short Christmas and New Year break in the Lausanne conference sessions he decided to make an effort to reach an understanding. This was to be done by a meeting in Paris. Bentinck's explanation of how this ended in failure differs from the accepted version.

Tyrrell and Curzon went off. I trotted to the railway station, carrying the Marquis's green baize foot-rest, and saw them off. They got rather late to the hotel, the Ritz, and the walls between the rooms were rather thin. A Roumanian couple, who had had a very jolly time out, came back rather late and did things which you'd expect. The Marquis couldn't sleep a wink, and next day he was useless. He couldn't really act at the conference, he was feeling so bad. The conference broke up. The French walked into the Ruhr. Horst Wessel and the rest followed, and that led to Hitler. All the fault of that Roumanian couple fornicating.

Bentinck did not resume his duties in the Foreign Office after the Lausanne conference. Instead he was given an appointment which indicated clearly that he was regarded as a young man to be watched with a view to promotion, possibly in time to the highest levels. He was posted to the British Embassy in Paris.

CHAPTER 4
'A turning point in the history of Europe'
(1923–25)

After the Lausanne Conference ended Bentinck returned to his family's home in Dorset. He had a short holiday touring the Loire district with a French girlfriend, which he described as *very agreeable*. It was also in 1923 slightly daring. He then took up his duties as resident secretary in the Embassy in Paris.

The Ambassador, the Marquis of Crewe, was a Liberal politician who had served under Campbell-Bannerman and Asquith and held office as Secretary of State for the Colonies and later for India. He was seventy-one and described by Bentinck as *very quiet*.

In his report on the year 1922 Lord Hardinge, whom Crewe succeeded as Ambassador at the beginning of 1923, had begun the section on Anglo-French relations with the words: 'This section might almost be entitled "Anglo-French Differences".' 'Serious divergences of views,' he wrote, 'disclosed themselves on practically every issue of importance discussed by the two Governments.' The issues he listed were policy towards Germany generally, reparations, the Near East, Tangier, and the conference at Genoa which had been largely concerned with relations between the Soviet Union and other European powers. The French press, Hardinge reported, had attributed the differences to 'the selfishness and materialism of British post-war aims'. He himself had different views. 'The attitude of M. Poincaré,' he wrote, 'since his assumption of office in January contributed to make Anglo-French relations even less cordial than before. His uncompromising utterances, his disagreeable personality, lawyer-like and strictly logical mind, lacking entirely in imagination or wideness of vision, have been an unfortunate and mischievous factor in international affairs.'

Crewe's task was not therefore an easy one, but to support

him he had a staff of some ability. Gladwyn Jebb, later Lord Gladwyn and a future Ambassador in Paris, was for a short time in 1923 an honorary attaché at the Paris Embassy. Of it he wrote that it was 'presided over with dignity by Lord Crewe, and on the staff were some of our ablest diplomats'. Bentinck was one of those he mentioned by name in this category.

I worked as an ordinary secretary there, Bentinck stated, *and was occupied very largely with reporting on what was happening in France, in French political life and business.*

The reports produced by Bentinck and his colleagues, who included future ambassadors such as Eric Phipps and Hughe Knatchbull-Hugessen, as well as Ralph Wigram, who died young and was described by Lord Gladwyn as 'probably the ablest of them all', make stimulating reading today. They also provide some evidence of improvements in Franco-British relations.

In 1923 France was still the greatest military power in the world, and the occupation of the Ruhr, with Belgian support, in January of that year was intended as a manifestation of that power. Yet there were already signs which acute observers could see of cracks in the French economic and political structure. A long despatch sent by Lord Crewe in June 1923 told of these.

'There is discontent,' it was stated, 'in the devastated departments at the delay in reconstruction and the financial difficulties which impede progress. The powerful syndicates and unions of official *employés* might prove dangerous. Another danger lies in the lack of discipline and cohesion hitherto noticeable among the majority.'

1923 was the year in which the Secretary-General of Action Française, Marius Plateau, was assassinated in January by a female anarchist, who was acquitted by a jury in a trial in December. Demonstrations and violence followed. Embassy reports told too of disturbances organized in Paris and the provinces by the Camelots du Roy and of an incident in Montmartre when members of the ruling family of Dahomey were ejected from a restaurant to meet the wishes of an American client.

In describing Poincaré's problems Crewe's despatches showed some sympathy and understanding. Poincaré's skill in managing the Chamber of Deputies was commented on with respect, and the difficulties he faced because of the strength of anti-clericalism were emphasized. 'The prominence of the religious question is striking. Any departure from the strict path of republican virtue will be severely visited upon him by M. Poincaré's opponents and will react directly upon opinion in the provinces. M. Poincaré, although originally un "Homme des Gauches", has been able to avoid labelling himself as a partisan of either the *Bloc National* or the *Bloc des Gauches*. It is this religious question which rekindles ancient fires and divides the *Bloc National* from the *Bloc des Gauches* more than any other insofar as internal politics are concerned.'

By the end of the year Crewe was able to report 'a certain modification in the hitherto uncompromising attitude of the French Government towards proposals for solving the reparations difficulty'. This was partly attributed to the decision of the British Government to turn to the United States for support.

In 1923 the American political presence in Paris was fairly strong. Its principal figure was Charles G. Dawes, who was trained both as an engineer and as a lawyer and who became the chief supply officer of General Pershing's army in Europe in the last years of the first world war. He was later to become Vice President of the United States and American Ambassador in London and to share the Nobel prize for peace with Austen Chamberlain. His name remains known chiefly for the plans which he and Owen M. Young worked out in Paris for the payment of German debts, which eventually gained international acceptance.

He used to smoke a pipe at dinner, Bentinck said. *That rather shocked people.* Bentinck also recalled a social occasion when Dawes *thought he'd liven the thing up. He had a waiter who was a sort of clown. The dish was going to fall down somebody's neck and he just saved it, and so on. The Spanish Ambassadress said to him: 'General, these sort of people do not like those sort of jokes.'*

As resident secretary Bentinck had to deal with a variety of individuals who called at the Embassy at different times of the day. Lord Gladwyn, who described him as 'exceptionally promising and having done very well at Lausanne', said that he was 'brilliant at dealing with drunks and eccentrics'. Other recollections Gladwyn had of Bentinck were that he was 'very popular in Parisian society' and that he regularly brought his smooth-haired fox-terrier with him to his office. The dog was named Ismet Pasha.

Bentinck's social life ranged from *very smart parties, plenty of well-trained servants and so on*, to *low dance-halls*. The dance-halls he usually frequented in the company of an honorary attaché named George Sandys, the father of Duncan Sandys, wartime minister and son-in-law of Winston Churchill. It was also his social life which led to an unfortunate incident. Bentinck returned late one night to the Embassy and found a telegram waiting. *I put it on one side, intending to decipher it in the morning. I woke up late. By the time it was deciphered the Marquis of Crewe had left for the Conference of Ambassadors without his instructions. That was, you might say, untoward. I think that was the time, if I remember rightly, when Mussolini was showing off in the Adriatic and attacked Corfu. However we weathered that.*

Among those whom Bentinck met socially was a Mrs Quigley, the widow of a Kentucky lawyer, who with two marriageable daughters and a large Pierce Arrow car made something of an impact in certain circles in Paris. One of the daughters, Clothilde, was the dark, slim type, which particularly appealed to Bentinck physically. To the consternation of a number of his friends he proposed marriage to her in the autumn of 1923 and was accepted.

Both Bentinck's parents were dismayed. Lord Crewe took the fairly unusual step for an ambassador of advising him against the marriage. Sixty years later friends still expressed surprise that Bentinck, whose judgement they rated so highly, should have made the marriage he did. But he remained impervious to pleas or warnings. His was the kind of infatuation presaging disaster which ancient mythology is as ready as latter-day psychology to explain.

The marriage took place in February 1924. As a married man Bentinck could not continue as resident secretary in Paris, and he was transferred to The Hague. It was a slight setback in his career but not a serious one. Graver setbacks would follow later.

The permanent Court of International Justice had recently been established at The Hague, but in other respects it was not a capital in which Britain's representatives were expected to conduct affairs of great moment. While Bentinck was there a suggestion was put by the Dutch Foreign Minister, Van Karnebeek, during a talk in Geneva, that the British and Dutch legations in each other's capital should be raised to the status of embassies. The instructions which Sir Charles Marling, the British Minister at The Hague, received were that he should turn down the request 'in such a manner as will not give offence', at the same time making it clear that the decision was final.

During the period of a little over a year, beginning early in 1924, which Bentinck spent in the Netherlands he was less occupied than at any other time in his career. *It was a very pleasant post, but absolutely nothing to do.* The Minister, who was nearing retirement, confirmed this judgement. In his report covering the year 1924 Marling wrote: 'It must be but seldom that twelve months pass in the life of a people without the occurrence of a single outstanding event of sufficient import-ance merely to remain in the memory. Such seems to have been the case in Holland in 1924.' The national finances improved. The budget was balanced. The ex-Kaiser Wilhelm seemed to have settled down to 'the quiet pleasures of a country life', and, as Marling stated, 'no country is more determined—and with good cause—to avoid entering upon any line of action which might result in the Netherlands being involved in the disputes of others'.

Visitors from Britain provided occasional diversions, one who particularly interested Bentinck being the well-known prison administrator and reformer, Alec Paterson. *I drove him round to the Dutch prisons. I learnt that you shouldn't keep a bird or anything in a circular prison. The prison at Haarlem which we visited was circular, and that had the effect of giving people the willies. Then the prisoners in Dutch prisons wore masks, so they couldn't be seen by other prisoners and blackmailed on being let out. I suppose it had something to be said for it.*

Bentinck also had some conversations on a subject of con-siderable potential significance. These were with Prince Albert de Ligne, who was the Belgian Minister at The Hague. The

Dutch and Belgian Governments were in the process of negotiating an agreement to settle certain outstanding differences, and towards the end of January 1925 the Prince de Ligne told Bentinck there would a secret annexe to the agreement. This would not be submitted to the States-General but would commit the Dutch Government to the understanding that any violation of Dutch neutrality would be regarded as a *casus belli*.

In forwarding a report of this conversation Marling stated that he would find it 'hard to explain how the Prince de Ligne could bring himself to inform a member of another Legation, however friendly and discreet, that such a document was under contemplation except on the explicit instructions of the Government'. Marling was then told by Van Karnebeek that no secret agreement was contemplated, and a terse minute was entered on the Foreign Office file: 'I can only conclude that Mr Cavendish-Bentinck has misunderstood the Prince de Ligne.'

A few days later Marling forwarded a memorandum recording another conversation between the Prince de Ligne and Bentinck. In this the Prince said that the Dutch Government had changed its attitude slightly and was now considering violations of neutrality rather more as an issue to be referred to the League of Nations. Nevertheless the Prince added: 'If war were declared between Belgium and Germany and any violation of Dutch neutrality took place on the part of German troops, the Belgian forces would then be entitled to come to the help of the Dutch.' Bentinck suggested that the Belgian General Staff might be hoping that if war did break out again the future battleground would be either German or Dutch territory. The Prince agreed.

Bentinck concluded his memorandum with the comment: 'I think that the reason which has caused the Prince de Ligne to be so pleasantly communicative to me regarding the proposed agreement is the idea that I will report what he says and that his name will in this connection reach the Foreign Office as I suspect that his present ambition is to succeed Baron Moncheur at the Court of St James.' This time Bentinck's judgement was not disputed, and the file was minuted: 'Mr Cavendish-Bentinck has probably hit upon the true reason.'

Bentinck also had to compile a report on the Dutch colonies. Writing of the Dutch East Indies, he called attention to the rise of a society called Budi Utomo, whose purpose was to develop Japanese culture. 'The loyalty of this society,' he wrote, 'still seems unaffected.' The attitude of the local Dutch towards defence he summarized all too correctly by stating: 'The government and residents consider that neither the British Empire nor the USA are likely to lay violent hands on the archipelago, and that these powers would permit no aggression on the part of the Japanese.'

Bentinck's period of relative idleness did not last long. In February 1925 he was appointed to a post where, for the most part, he found the work as absorbing as he had found his duties at The Hague dull. This was in the League of Nations Department of the Foreign Office.

Bentinck's first home in London as a married man was a flat in Hay Hill in Mayfair. In the year in which he returned from The Hague his first child was born. This was a son, William James, who became known as Billy.

Working in the League of Nations Department of the Foreign Office was to some extent a fulfilment of an early ambition of Bentinck's. *In 1919, when I went to Paris to rub up my French, being very much affected by the fact of my generation having been wiped out during the war, I applied to join the Secretariat of the League of Nations rather than go into the Foreign Office. Fortunately Eric Drummond, who was then Secretary, had too many English people applying, and I couldn't be accepted, which, I suppose really, was a bit of luck.*

The head of the League of Nations Department was Alexander (Alec) Cadogan, who was to be the Permanent Under-Secretary at the Foreign Office during the second world war, and for whom Bentinck formed a high regard. *Cadogan's strength was his complete honesty and his excellent judgement of people. If anybody was unflappable he was. He was almost too calm for Winston. Winston thought him a slab of frozen cod. But he was very shrewd and he would never pander to anybody. His memoirs ought never to have been published. Rather like Alan Brooke he used to write in the evenings and at odd times accounts of his meetings, really letting off steam.* Cadogan's posthumously published diaries, it must be admitted, did him little credit. The most persistent feeling they conveyed was that foreigners generally, and members of Allied governments in particular, existed to irritate the British Foreign Office.

Soon after taking up his new appointment Bentinck entered into the rhythm of travelling four or five times a year to Geneva, which was to continue until late in 1928. One of his earlier tasks was concerned with the prevalence of slavery in the Arabian peninsula and parts of Africa. *I drafted a treaty about this*, he said, *and it was signed. In the Portuguese colonies there was not much difference between slavery and forced labour.*

He had been engaged on this and similar duties for only a few months when he was chosen to make the preparations for another international conference. The site selected was again in Switzerland, this time being Locarno in the Italian-speaking Ticino. In the 1920s it was the practice to hold conferences of major importance, not in capital cities where large staffs were available, facilities for reporting were good and police presence was strong, but in pleasant holiday resorts with large and comfortable hotels. Lausanne, Locarno, Cannes, San Remo, Stresa and Spa were all among the sites selected.

The agenda for the Locarno conference was to be much less complex than that for the conference at Lausanne some two years earlier, but its main purpose was perhaps more ambitious. This was to create satisfactory machinery, or at the very least a formula, for maintaining peace in Europe. Individual countries represented at Locarno had subsidiary aims.

The guiding principle of French foreign policy since 1918 had been to ensure that Germany could not start another war. Clemenceau had been persuaded of the desirability of a League of Nations only when Colonel House told him that this might be the only means by which he could obtain a guarantee from the United States and Britain that they would come to France's help if she were attacked. The idea of a defensive alliance between France and Britain was mooted several times in the immediate post-war years. Nothing was achieved, largely because of the reluctance of British governments, which represented not simply a European nation but territories in every other continent, to enter into binding new commitments.

In 1924 a new tactic was tried, through the League of

Nations. This was the so-called Geneva Protocol, which the Czechoslovak Foreign Minister, Eduard Beneš, persuaded the French Government formally to propose. Under the protocol any dispute between nations which was not submitted to the Permanent Court at The Hague, or to some other form of arbitration, would have to be brought before the Council of the League. The Council's decision, if unanimous, would be binding; if the Council were not unanimous, the decision of an arbitrator appointed by the League would also be binding. A Labour Government was in power in Britain when the protocol was first debated, and Ramsay MacDonald, who was his own Foreign Secretary, favoured it. But when a Conservative Government returned to power what was deemed to be the Dominion interest again prevailed and British policy was reversed. Edouard Herriot, who was both Prime Minister and Foreign Minister of France when the protocol was proposed, greeted this decision by saying that he looked forward with terror to Germany making war again in ten years' time. To the French Government therefore Locarno seemed to offer primarily another opportunity of ensuring that France would be safe from German aggression.

To the German Foreign Minister, Gustav Stresemann, the idea of a conference at Locarno appealed primarily as a means of striking a bargain. On the one hand Germany would recognize existing frontiers and the demilitarization of the Rhineland, and on the other the withdrawal of all occupying troops would be achieved.

British motives were more complex. The man who has the best claim to have been the principal architect of the Locarno treaty was almost certainly Lord D'Abernon, who was then British Ambassador in Berlin. From this vantage point he was continually conscious of the danger of a German-Russian rapprochement, and he used his considerable influence with Stresemann to try to steer him away from it. This, he felt, could best be done by offering Germany some positive advantages from closer co-operation with Britain and France. Briand, a much more generous man than Poincaré, concurred in this.

The basis of the conference of Locarno, Bentinck said, *was that Austen Chamberlain was very anxious, supported by Briand, to get*

Germany back into what might be called the comity of nations—she'd been a pariah—so that Germany would play a sensible role and would act with the big powers. This had been the subject of exchanges of telegrams with D'Abernon. He was strongly for that. We had several meetings in Chamberlain's room in the Foreign Office, and it was decided to call a conference.

Austen Chamberlain, who was to lead the British delegation to Locarno, would almost certainly have had the leadership of the Conservative Party, and therefore become Prime Minister, had it not been for his continuing loyalty to the crumbling coalition under Lloyd George. When Bonar Law was confirmed in power Chamberlain wrote in a letter that he considered his real political life ended. Then towards the end of 1924 Baldwin offered him the Foreign Office and he accepted. For some time past he had been critical of the conduct of British foreign policy. 'It seems to me,' he wrote to his half-brother Neville in 1923, 'that we are becoming the scold of Europe. We run about shaking our fists in people's faces, screaming that this must be altered and that must stop. We get ourselves disliked and distrusted and misunderstood. Curzon is convinced that all is well if he delivers an oration or pens a "superior" despatch.' Once he was in office Chamberlain was able to change much of this.

I have a very great admiration for Austen Chamberlain, Bentinck said. *He was highly intelligent, had good political flair, and was really a great Foreign Secretary. Very good with his staff. He had vision. People trusted him. He got our relations with the French on a very good footing.*

In dress Chamberlain was always immaculate. The caricaturists habitually portrayed him in a top hat and morning coat and emphasized his eyeglass and button-hole. In appearance he provided a strong contrast with Aristide Briand, the leader of the French delegation, who was ungainly, untidy and a chain-smoker. Yet there was an excellent rapport between the two men.

Bentinck had no less admiration for Briand than he had for Chamberlain. At Locarno *the outstanding figures,* he said, *were Chamberlain and Briand for personality, oratory and intelligence. They were statesmen.* Bentinck also quoted the saying in which Poincaré, Briand and another French Prime Minister of the inter-war years, Georges Leygues, were compared with each other: *Poincaré lit tout et comprend tout. Leygues lit tout et ne comprend rien. Briand ne lit rien mais comprend tout.*

The third most important figure at Locarno was to be Stresemann, also a man of unusual ability. The son of an innkeeper, he could quote without difficulty long passages of German poetry and prose. He enjoyed good music and had a taste for brandy. To many people his appearance and voice were disagreeable. Bentinck remembered him as having a barking voice which was due to a throat affliction. D'Abernon stated that 'a first impression of Stresemann was that he might have been Winston Churchill's brother. The same silhouette —almost identical colouring. And in temperament and mental characteristics a close analogy.' He added that Stresemann's 'capacity for arousing animosity was quite exceptional'.

As foreign ministers Chamberlain, Briand and Stresemann all enjoyed exceptional freedom of action. The nominal head of the German delegation in Locarno was the Chancellor, Hans Luther, whom Bentinck recalled as *a very minor personality*. The French Prime Minister, Paul Painlevé, was perhaps more distinguished in the field of mathematics than in that of politics. Chamberlain, for his part, could be certain of minimal interference from Stanley Baldwin. *Baldwin didn't like foreign affairs. He didn't like foreigners, and except for hotel-keepers and the waiters at the hotel in Aix-les-Bains, to which he went every year with Mrs Baldwin, had no use for them. So Chamberlain was able to run things.*

In coming together to plan the future security of Europe the three foreign ministers had therefore virtually plenipotentiary powers.

Bentinck engaged rooms for the British delegation in Locarno's Grand Hotel. This is a magnificent structure completed in 1876 and suggesting all the opulence of the Swiss hotel tradition associated with such names as Henri Ruhl and César Ritz. The entrance hall, with its magnificent chandelier, is three floors high. Spacious grounds lead down to the lake, along whose shore palm trees, tamarisks and magnolias mingle with beeches, willows and chestnuts. The backdrop of the mountain is superb when it is not shrouded in mist.

The German delegation was housed rather more modestly in an albergo near by.

Bentinck also hired a large silver Mercedes car with a horn which sounded like a trumpet, whose recent owner was reported variously to have been a maharajah and a film star. On the morning on which he had to meet Chamberlain and the rest of the British delegation, Bentinck again overslept. (As a young man this seems to have been his principal diplomatic weakness.) *I had to run to catch the train which went from Locarno to Domodossola. I ran very hard. I got to Domodossola unshaven and had to go to a barber there. I hate having to be shaved by somebody.*

The delegation was a small one, numbering seven in all. It was accompanied only by a few shorthand-typists and cipher clerks. Bentinck was the most junior of the seven. Chamberlain's principal advisers were Miles Lampson, later to be for many years British Ambassador to Egypt, and Cecil Hurst, the Foreign Office's chief legal expert, who had played a major part in drafting the terms of the constitution of the League of Nations. A photograph still to be seen in Locarno shows the whole delegation with Chamberlain seated between Hurst and Lampson. Bentinck is standing at the back, a tall, slim young man with a slightly peering or puzzled look, attributable perhaps to short-sightedness. He is, as he always was, impeccably dressed.

The delegation was to work in total harmony, as Chamberlain generously acknowledged in a letter to Sir William Tyrrell, then Ambassador in Paris, shortly after the conference ended. 'As I look back,' he wrote, 'it all seems so simple. Only once did I hesitate and nearly go wrong—when I thought of leaving the first drafting of the pact to the French —and then Lampson saved me. I admit it would have been a crucial error. Everyone has done his part here. I believe Hurst spoke the decisive word in the German-Polish negotiations, and everyone—Hurst, Lampson, Selby, Bennett and Bentinck—has done the right thing, spoken the right words and helped the cause.'

In addition to the British, the French and the Germans, there were delegations from Italy, Belgium, Czechoslovakia and Poland. The United States and the Soviet Union were not represented. It was thought that problems of European security and frontiers could be settled without American help, and the Soviet Government was opposed to the holding of the conference, Chicherin regarding it as an instrument of British policy directed against the Soviet Union.

The Italian delegation was led by Vittorio Scialoja and the bearded Dino Grandi, but, as at Lausanne, Mussolini decided to make a brief appearance, staying two nights in a nearby villa. *At Lausanne*, Bentinck recalled, *he'd been rather the actor, Napoleon, the big man. At Locarno he appeared in a bowler hat and a dark suit, looking like a head waiter. He went about as if the Holy Ghost was up above directing him.* Chamberlain, as Curzon had done at Lausanne, welcomed Mussolini's visit and immediately after the conference telegraphed to the British Ambassador in Rome: 'Please renew to Mussolini the expression of my high appreciation of the value of his personal presence.'

Beneš headed the Czechoslovak delegation. The Poles included Skrzyński, the former emissary of the Austro-Hungarian Government. In the French delegation there was a future winner of the Nobel prize for literature. This was the Foreign Ministry official, Alexis St Léger, who became known to connoisseurs of esoteric literature as St John Persse.

Almost the first step Chamberlain took was to have cards left on the German delegation. This, he afterwards wrote in his rather modest memoirs, was 'a civility which I believe had not been paid at any of the previous conferences'.

The conference itself, which was held in a hall in the Palais de Justice, opened on 5 October. Chamberlain was asked by the French, Italian and Belgian delegates to preside, but he said he would do so only if the Germans agreed. The Germans did not agree, and it was decided that the presidency should rotate. This called for a round table, but there appeared to be no round table in Locarno large enough for the purpose. Bentinck was deputed to solve the problem and set about finding carpenters. *They sawed a round table, and I got some green baize, and the conference started.* Briand suggested that no verbatim record should be taken in order to allow free discussion. This was agreed.

Largely because much of the ground had been prepared through earlier diplomatic exchanges, the conduct of the

Signed menu of a luncheon given by the Press corps for the delegates to the Locarno Conference, 15th October 1925. The signatures of the Ministers can just be seen in their wings. Austen Chamberlain appears top left.

meetings was mostly smooth. The atmosphere was cordial and, in contrast with the practice at earlier conferences concerned with making peace, the terms 'allies' and 'enemy' were never used. Progress was also made at informal gatherings. Briand and Luther once lunched almost surreptitiously together at an inn at Ascona a few miles further south along the shore of Lake Maggiore. Bentinck also recalled having useful discussions in the evenings with the German delegates, though the comment which remained most clearly in his mind, and which was made by von Schubert, the principal German Foreign Ministry official present, did not relate directly to the conference. *One evening we were talking, Stresemann, von Schubert, myself, and a few others. They were talking about future politics in Germany. I said: 'What about this fellow Hitler?' Hitler had just got out of jail, where he'd been put after his putsch didn't come off in Munich in twenty-three. Von Schubert laughed and said: 'Ach, was für ein Narr!'* (What an idiot!')

By 16 October, which happened to be Chamberlain's sixty-second birthday, the business of the conference was completed, and the treaty was initialled. The inviolability of the frontiers between Germany and Belgium and Germany and France was guaranteed. The three countries undertook never to wage war on each other except in 'legitimate defence' or as a result of a League of Nations obligation. All the contracting parties agreed to come to the help of any one of them adjudged by the League of Nations to have been attacked. Provision was made for any frontier adjustments between Germany and either Czechoslovakia or Poland to be settled by arbitration.

It is interesting to compare Curzon when principal delegate at the Lausanne conference with Chamberlain at Locarno. Curzon was quite determined that there should be no doubt whatsoever that he was the principal Allied delegate vis-à-vis the Turks and insisted on having a higher chair than all the other delegates. Intellectually he was undoubtedly superior to the rest of them, but he did not inspire particularly friendly feelings amongst the members of the other delegations.

Chamberlain based his position on carefully remaining primus inter pares. He was undoubtedly the principal figure at Locarno. This was due to the fact that the conference was based on a proposal of the UK Government. Its success was largely due to Chamberlain's personality. He inspired complete trust and friendship both at Locarno and subsequently at meetings of the Council of the League of Nations. The only man who was difficult at the latter was the Swedish Foreign Minister, Unden, a most tiresome fellow. As a diplomat Chamberlain was certainly superior to Curzon.

The treaty was greeted with acclamation in the streets of Locarno. *After the treaty had been initialled*, Bentinck recalled, *I remember the Belgian delegate holding it up to the window to tremendous applause.* In the world's press the term 'spirit of Locarno' had come into use while the conference was still in session. When the treaty was initialled the *New York Times* reported it under the headline: 'France and Germany Ban War for Ever'. In London the headline in *The Times* was 'Peace at Last'.

The chief negotiators were no less enthusiastic in their assessment. Chamberlain wrote to D'Abernon on 17 October: 'I am convinced that the agreements which have been initialled here will mark a turning point in the history of Europe.' Briand announced that 'les États-Unis d'Europe commencent'. Such attempts as were immediately made to undermine the achievements of the conference were unsuccessful. The day after the initialling took place D'Abernon reported that Chicherin had come to Berlin 'confident of being able to sow such distrust in the mind of the German Government that the latter would find some plausible pretext for not signing the proposed pact of guarantee'. After a week Chicherin had discovered that the German Government was not willing to be persuaded and, furthermore, would not follow his suggestion that 'they should refuse to join the League'.

The formal signing of the treaty took place in London on 1 December in Chamberlain's room in the Foreign Office. A banquet followed.

At no other time during the period between the two world wars was the feeling so widespread and so strong that a lasting peace had been achieved. The historian A. J. P. Taylor summed up the significance of the Treaty of Locarno succinctly when he wrote: 'Its signature ended the first world war; its repudiation eleven years later marked the prelude to the second.'

CHAPTER 5
League Diplomacy
(1926–28)

During the years 1926 to 1928 Bentinck saw the workings of
the Council, the Assembly and the Secretariat of the League of
Nations at close quarters and when dealing with complex and
contentious issues. This gave him an increased respect both for
the concept of the League and for the way in which, during
those years, its machinery was used.

The League of Nations, he said, *was a wonderful idea. One of the
principal architects was Smuts, and it worked. It would have been of
incomparable importance for good if America had joined.* Looking
back on his diplomatic career, he also said: *I don't think I
was given to enthusiasm, but I was enthusiastic about the League
of Nations when it was formed in 1919.* Of the Council of the
League he said: *The Council meetings took place about four
times a year. They lasted about three days. It was a really efficient
body.*

At Locarno, and during the negotiations which preceded the
conference, Chamberlain and Briand had accepted the need,
not only to bring Germany into the League of Nations, but to
treat her there as a great power. This meant in practice giving
her a permanent seat on the Council.

The Council had been designed originally to consist of the
five 'principal allied and associated powers' of the first world
war, i.e. the United States, Great Britain, France, Italy and
Japan, which were to be permanent members, and four other
member states, which would have temporary seats. When
the United States refused to join the League her seat on the
Council was kept open, and in practice membership of the
Council was limited to eight. To have added a ninth member
might have been relatively simple but for the attitude of the
Brazilian Government.

Brazil was then a temporary member, and the instructions
her delegate, Afranio de Mello Franco, received were to vote

in favour of a permanent seat for Germany only if Brazil were given one too.

This, not unnaturally, did not appeal to the other temporary members, and Mello Franco himself made no attempt to disguise his opinion that the instructions were unwise. But, as Bentinck recalled, when the other delegates tried to persuade him to ignore or circumvent these instructions, he was forced to say: *C'est impossible. J'ai cinq filles et pas de fortune.* Brazil left the League and never returned.

This was a serious setback. With the continued abstention of the United States, the loss of an important Latin American country served to add weight to the criticism that the League was too much concerned with Europe and too much controlled by European powers. Before long it was to be its failure to deal effectively with a conflict outside Europe, that in Manchuria, which began the League's decline.

In Europe at least the spirit of Locarno was for a time carefully maintained. At Chamberlain's suggestion the so-called 'Locarnites', consisting of himself, Briand, Stresemann, Mussolini and Emile Vandervelde of Belgium, met in Geneva in March 1926 for a round-table discussion. This was followed by other similar meetings, and before long the 'Geneva tea-parties', as they were called, became regular and friendly gatherings of the leading statesmen of Europe.

Agreement was not always complete. With the wide divergence of view between France and Germany on what armed forces Germany should have, this would have been impossible. *I can't forget*, Bentinck said, *the scene at the League of Nations Assembly. Briand's speech, a wonderful speech, great oratory. And then Stresemann getting up and barking about Germany's right. I could see all wasn't going to be easy.* By July 1927 Briand was already describing the Locarno treaty as 'un bien relatif', and Lord Crewe reported that French public opinion 'believes that Locarno was good as far as it went. But it does not necessarily wish the policy of Locarno to be developed further for the moment.'

Nevertheless the opportunities for discussing differences were abundant and the machinery for monitoring adherence to agreements fairly satisfactory. Bentinck was among those who did the monitoring. In March 1927, for instance, he reported on discussions which had taken place in Geneva on how the League could be given some knowledge of what Germany was doing in the field of civil aviation and the construction of civil aircraft. Von Schubert, Sir Cecil Hurst and Dr Beneš, who was the *rapporteur* to the Council on the question, had reached a provisional agreement. This was that, 'subject to Dr Stresemann securing the concurrence of the competent authorities in Berlin', the Council should adopt a resolution calling for the information when required. Shortly afterwards, Bentinck reported, von Schubert had called to say that 'certain administrative difficulties had been pointed out in connection with business or manufacturing secrets'. He had gone on to cite an instance of Britain also refusing to divulge manufacturing secrets to an international authority. 'This statement,' Bentinck concluded, 'seemed to me ominous.'

Mussolini had tested the competence of the League and the patience of the members since the occasion in 1923 when, as a reprisal for the murder of the Italian General Tellini on Greek territory, he had ordered the bombardment and then capture of the town of Corfu. The next year he complained to the British Ambassador in Rome, Sir Ronald Graham, that the British and French dominated the League, which had become 'a sort of insurance for the powers which had satisfied their own needs'. Nevertheless it was, in Bentinck's opinion, during the period of League diplomacy that Mussolini was most effectively handled. *Chamberlain and Briand managed Musso far better than was done later by that dreadful Simon. Lawyers make bad foreign secretaries as a rule. Then there was the Hoare-Laval agreement. We made a great mess of our relations with Italy.*

In the early days of the League Arthur Salter, later Lord Salter, the economist who became one of the most valuable members of the League's Secretariat, had written a thoughtful and prescient paper on how the League might develop. One possibility was that it would become a body dealing with 'a mass of non-contentious business—postal conventions, supervision of waterways etc.' Alternatively it could become 'an integral factor in the determination of the policy of every national government in the world'. The likelihood was, Salter thought, that it would 'go beyond the first conception and for many years fall far short of the second'.

Bentinck's duties in Geneva and in London arose from both kinds of League activities envisaged by Salter. *The committees,* Bentinck said, *were very good. There was an economic conference to which I was sent as an observer. Non-governmental supposedly. It did have an effect on world business. Then there was the committee on international health. It was an admirable body. We did a lot about drugs, stopping the traffic in drugs, which we did very successfully, preventing the traffic in hashish. In those days it was smoked by low-class Egyptians. Nowadays the King's Road stinks of it.* In between such activities he was frequently in contact with the political leaders who were trying to use the League to advance their countries' major interests as they conceived them to be.

Soon after assuming office Austen Chamberlain had said at a banquet given by the Lord Mayor of London: 'The first thoughts of any Englishman on appointment to the office of Foreign Secretary must be that he speaks in the name, not of Great Britain only, but of the British Dominions beyond the seas, and that it is his imperative duty to preserve in word and act the diplomatic unity of the British Empire.'

In Geneva Chamberlain and those who served under him were repeatedly and rightly conscious of this duty. Though the dominions were self-governing and their representatives appeared in Geneva, they still looked largely to Britain for the detailed application of foreign policy. Australia, for example, did not create its own Department of External Affairs until 1935. For the sub-continent of India too the representative voice in Geneva, for better or for worse, was that of Britain. *The Indian delegation,* Bentinck recalled, *had an ex-Viceroy, who was Willingdon, as the head man. The number two was always a maharajah. When they were going into a function Willingdon used to say: 'Well, Maharajah Sahib, shall we go forward?' And he used to go forward a few inches ahead of Patiala or whoever the Maharajah was.*

A young politician, who was appointed Chamberlain's Parliamentary Private Secretary in 1926, was to inherit and develop the policy of adherence to the League of Nations while trying to use its machinery to promote the interests of the British Empire. This was Anthony Eden, with whom

Bentinck became friendly in Geneva, where they would sometimes go for walks together. In a speech which he made in Edinburgh in 1935 Eden, looking back over the recent past, said: 'The balance of power was no longer our foreign policy. Our foreign policy was based on the League of Nations and on the maintenance of a collective system.'

Certain ministers hoped that the League would in time override the policies and practices of individual nations. Prominent among these was Lord Robert Cecil who, at Smuts's request, had attended the first Assemby of the League in 1920 as a representative of South Africa. After appointment to a ministerial post by Baldwin he acted as Chamberlain's deputy at a number of meetings of the Council of the League. He also became the principal British representative on the Disarmament Commission in Geneva, with whose secretary, Walter Roberts, Bentinck worked closely.

Cecil found the British Government's relative lack of enthusiasm for the League irksome. 'Unless my colleagues,' he wrote to Chamberlain in March 1927, 'pretend to take an interest in our proceedings here the foreigners will conclude that I have not any real support at home.' Shortly afterwards he resigned on grounds of principle, but remained President of the League of Nations Union. Before leaving the Government he wrote to Chamberlain: 'There is one pleasant part of the situation, and that is that all my delegates are personally charming and most of them very helpful. So that, out of school, we have a very pleasant time.' Cecil's enthusiasm gave rise, after his departure, to a Foreign Office minute, which read: 'It is rather pathetic and possibly even dangerous that he should suggest and imply that it is up to us to set an example.'

Another dedicated supporter of the League was Philip Noel-Baker. Bentinck recalled how he played a part of some significance in securing the acceptance of Ethiopia as a League member. For admission to the League, nations had to adhere to certain standards of government, and there was much debate following Ethiopia's application to join because a League committee had produced damning evidence about the prevalence of the slave trade.

Bob Cecil, Bentinck said, *had Philip Noel-Baker as his P A. Noel-Baker was fanatically pro-League. Everything must be done to*

*strengthen the League and so on. He was a nice fellow. He had been
an Olympic runner, and he had also been very gallant in the war. He
drove an ambulance because he was a Quaker. There was a meeting of
the Council in Paris. They didn't always go to Geneva then. The
question of the entry of Abyssinia into the League came up. The
Foreign Office in their wisdom had sent a telegram to Lord Robert
Cecil telling him that the question of the entry of Abyssinia to the
League of Nations should be postponed. Philip Noel-Baker put that
telegram on one side until after the decision had been taken.*

Both the idealists and the advocates of Realpolitik, to whose
camp Bentinck, with his measured enthusiasm for the League,
clearly belonged, had cause in the late 1920s for reasonable
satisfaction. Until the effects of the crash on the New York
Stock Exchange in 1929 were fully felt *Europe*, Bentinck said,
was on a really even keel. The future looked rosy.

That the hopes were not fulfilled was due, in his opinion,
not to weaknesses in the machinery of the League, but to its
composition. The machinery had proved adequate for preventing at least one war, that which was threatened between
Greece and Bulgaria in 1925. It provided acceptable government in areas of contention such as Upper Silesia and Danzig,
where a League high commissioner remained in office until
1939. The legal protection afforded to refugees by the so-
called Nansen passports issued under the auspices of the
League was the kind of humanitarian measure which only an
international agency could have brought about. What the
League disastrously lacked was American participation.

*If the League had been backed by the United States, the Japanese
wouldn't have dared to go into Manchuria and do what they did
to China, the French would have been more reasonable with
the Germans in the early days over reparations and so on—the
Americans would have had an influence there—and Mussolini would
certainly not have got up to the antics he did. The guilty men, the
people who have the biggest guilt, are the American Senate, who
would not ratify the Treaty of Versailles and would not enter the
League of Nations. It was most unfortunate that Wilson got ill with
strokes, that he couldn't exercise any influence on the Senate, that his
wife wouldn't let anybody come near him, and the thing went by
default.*

The absence of another large power, the Soviet Union, was

in the 1920s much less important. Soviet policy was consistently hostile to the League, and when Soviet delegates did attend conferences sponsored by the League their contributions were seldom helpful. In a despatch to the Foreign Office on the work of the economic conference, which he attended as an observer, Bentinck reported the Soviet delegate as having said that the USSR 'did not consider the League satisfactory for the maintenance of peace but rather as an instrument of the imperialists'. Bentinck added: 'Abuse of the League by a delegate of a non-member state was generally considered ill-mannered, and the Soviet delegates have made a distinctly unfavourable impression.'

Both the USA and the USSR were founder members of the League's successor body, the United Nations, but it would be difficult to point to any other respect in which the new body compared favourably with the old. Burdened from the outset with a manifestly absurd name, it was to arouse minimal enthusiasm among experienced diplomats with first-hand knowledge of the workings of the League. To Bentinck it was *this bouillabaisse.*

Bentinck generally found his visits to Geneva agreeable. *Geneva*, he said, *was a much nicer place than it is now. There were no neon signs.* Those officials who were part of their countries' permanent delegations, and some members of the League's own Secretariat, tended to regard Geneva rather less benignly, particularly because of its climate. In January 1929 an experiment was tried, at Stresemann's suggestion, of holding a week's meeting in Lugano in the hope that there might be some sunshine. 'For the first three days,' Cadogan reported, 'it was not evident that the climate of Lugano was an improvement on that of Geneva, but it must be admitted that the last three days justified Herr Stresemann's choice.' In his report on the fifty-third session of the Council of the League Cadogan wrote: 'It would certainly be a relief if Council sessions could be held more often elsewhere than at Geneva, especially in winter. Unfortunately the cost has to be reckoned.'

The arrangement whereby Bentinck travelled regularly to Geneva, while being based in London, in addition to being personally agreeable, was continually stimulating. The experience also greatly broadened his knowledge. A diplomat in the normal course of his assignments is posted to a relatively small number of capitals. During periods in the Foreign Office he may deal with the affairs of several nations, but this is done as it were by remote control. In Geneva Bentinck regularly met representatives of other powers, often when they were dealing with matters of grave moment and not engaged merely in the verbal sparring which later characterized so many international gatherings.

He also acquired a first-hand knowledge of the Secretariat of the League. The Secretary, who largely created it and who remained in office until 1933, Eric Drummond, later Lord Perth, had been sent to Versailles in 1919 as Balfour's private secretary. Balfour, being rather bored by discussions about the form the League should take, left Drummond to deal with most of the details. From a modest beginning at a temporary headquarters in London at 117 Piccadilly, Drummond gradually built up the organization in spite of continual financial restrictions, until it had a highly professional staff of 750. Among the committees it served was one dealing with intellectual co-operation, which had Henri Bergson as its president and Einstein, Lorentz and Marie Curie among its members. *Eric Drummond*, Bentinck said, *was very intelligent. He did the correct things quietly, but he didn't have an outstanding personality.*

Bentinck was twenty-eight when he attended the Locarno conference. He was thirty-one when he was transferred from the League of Nations Department to take up his next assignment. Those years were probably the most valuable of any in preparing him for the formidable responsibilities with which he was to be confronted a dozen years later.

Meanwhile his next assignment meant a return to Paris.

CHAPTER 6
Paris Years
(1928–31)

During his second appointment in Paris Bentinck enjoyed, or at least experienced, a social life of the kind which is sometimes described as brilliant. *My wife*, as he succinctly put it, *saw a lot of people socially. One heard all the gossip, and so on.*

The Ambassador, Sir William Tyrrell, who was elevated to the peerage in 1929, was married, but led what seemed to the outside world a bachelor existence. *(Lady Tyrrell hardly appeared. She was rather dotty, a little pixillated.)* Bentinck, who combined the duties of number two in the Chancery with those of private secretary to the Ambassador, organized all Tyrrell's entertaining, and for this reason alone he and his wife were frequently invited out. Bentinck was wise enough to learn from an experienced private secretary to the distinguished Spanish Ambassador, Quiñones de Leon, the intricacies of *placements* at Paris social functions, to which much importance was attached. In time he became so skilled in this himself that he was able, by taking advantage of Tyrrell's bachelor way of life, to bring together at the same function two women, neither of whom was willing ever to cede precedence to the other. These were the Princess Murat and the Duchess de la Trémoille. Bentinck placed one of them opposite Tyrrell and the other on his right, and neither objected.

When Bentinck first arrived Paris seemed full of Americans. It was the period of which Simenon wrote in *Maigret's Memoirs*: 'Americans used to light their cigars with thousand-franc notes. Montmartre was teeming with negro musicians, and rich, middle-aged ladies let themselves be robbed of their jewellery by Argentinian gigolos at *thés dansants*. A whole social set, in full view of the masses, lived a life of sophisticated leisure, and the newspapers reported all the doings of these people who had no other preoccupation than their own pleasures and varieties.'

When the Wall Street crash occurred in October 1929 Americans left in large numbers. The Hotel Ritz seemed to have been suddenly emptied, but in other respects Paris social life was, for some time at least, little affected. The franc remained stable. Taxation relief in 1930 amounted to 2,656 million francs, and in January of that year the Finance Minister was able to describe the French financial position as 'extremely satisfactory'. A year later a British Foreign Office minute stated: 'France is beginning to feel the general depression but of course to nothing like the extent to which we are. France continues to enjoy and increase a favourable balance of trade with her own colonies and protectorates.'

One of the most colourful figures in the diplomatic and social life of Paris whom Bentinck saw frequently was Charles Mendl. Lord Gladwyn, recalling his own experiences in 1923, described Mendl as 'particularly kind to young members of the staff'. *Charles Mendl's father*, Bentinck said, *came to England from Bohemia, I think in gabardines. He had three sons. The eldest one was called Sigismund, and he became head of the London Corn Exchange and highly respectable. Then there was Charles and a younger one called Tops, who, I think, went into the stockbroking business. Charles Mendl was a bit of a freelance. He went out to South America for some arms deals. There he met Grace Duggan, later Marchioness Curzon. He was also friends with George Graham, who was a Counsellor there. In the first war he went back and was badly wounded. Then he was put in naval uniform as, I think, part of C's business. Then George Graham got him the job of Press Attaché at the Embassy, which he did wonderfully well. He knew how to get hold of people, and he was well-informed.* Mendl was a pioneer in the new diplomatic post of Press Attaché. It was through him that Bentinck had first met his wife.

Opinion was still divided in Paris social circles on the reception to be accorded to the representatives of Germany. The Ambassador, Leopold von Hoesch, was described in a British Embassy report as 'a quiet and experienced diplomatist of excellent manners who has carried out his difficult duties in Paris with a dignity which has earned him the respect of the French officials with whom he has to deal'. The report went on: 'The majority of the French "monde" still rather dislike meeting the German Ambassador, but in industrial and political circles this feeling is rapidly dying down. The members of the German Embassy do not yet belong to a French club.' Von Hoesch was later posted to London, where he died. *Some people say the Nazis killed him here*, Bentinck stated. *Maybe they did, maybe not.*

The Soviet Chargé d'Affairs, whose name was Bessedovsky, caused something of a stir in September 1930 when he escaped over the wall surrounding his Embassy after being questioned by a member of the Cheka, as the Soviet security organization was then known, who had been sent to Paris to report on his conduct.

The Chinese representatives made little social impact. In a British Embassy report sent in January 1931, in which the hand of Bentinck can perhaps be traced, it was stated: 'Mr Kao Lou speaks some French, but Mrs Kao Lou speaks only Chinese. The only social entertainment which so far as I know they have given was a *thé dansant* on Good Friday, which seems an eccentric day to choose in a Roman Catholic country. The entertainment appeared to be chiefly attended by minor members of the Diplomatic Corps and large numbers of Asiatic students with their lady friends from Montmartre and Montparnasse.'

Behind the social façade, and to some extent because of it, the British Embassy was extremely well informed, just as it had been a few years earlier under Lord Crewe. *Far better informed*, Bentinck said, *than it was later. They weren't properly informed in thirty-eight and thirty-nine. What a disaster!*

Tyrrell, who was of partly Indian origin, was a professional diplomat. He had served as Private Secretary to Sir Edward Grey, when, Bentinck said, *he had been very much the* éminence grise. *He was very small. He always wanted to be rather in the background. I was fond of him.* The Counsellor, by contrast, Nevile Henderson, who was later to be an ill-judged choice as Ambassador in Berlin, was *a man of whom Tyrrell had rather a low opinion. He was far from intelligent.* Ralph Wigram, *a remarkable fellow*, was still in Paris. He was now Head of Chancery and the author of a number of penetrating reports.

About the end of the decade of the 1920s several of the outstanding political and military leaders in France died in fairly rapid succession. Clemenceau died in 1929 at the age of eighty-eight. Foch died in the same year and Joffre two years later. Briand died in 1932 and Poincaré in 1934.

Of the new figures beginning to take the centre of the stage, one on whom the Embassy reported with some care was Pierre Laval. The son of an Auvergnois innkeeper, Laval had become a left-wing deputy in 1914 and three years later had enthusiastically welcomed the Russian revolution. He first headed a government on 27 January 1939. By then he had already amassed a considerable fortune. He was still at that time regarded as a protégé of Briand.

On the day he took office the Embassy reported: 'Laval is a man of great strength and very ambitious, but with few principles.' A week later Tyrrell analysed the reactions in French political circles to Laval's accession to power. 'M. Laval,' he wrote, 'seems on the whole to have made a good impression on the Chamber. Many people drew attention to his long-standing friendship with M. Briand and claim that his supple nature and conciliatory attitude make him the natural successor to the great advocate of peace and goodwill at home as well as abroad.'

By 1930 Briand had held the office of Minister of Foreign Affairs in different governments for five years. This had served to maintain continuity in French foreign policy, but early in 1930 new trends began to be evident, which Tyrrell brought to the Foreign Office's attention. On 28 January he wrote a private letter to Sir Robert Vansittart passing on confidential information he had received about plans for 'a Franco-German economic agreement to the exclusion of England'. Two days later he added a report that 'the French Government is now working very hard for a better understanding with Germany'. This, he stated, was partly due to 'the desire to cut out Italy with the Germans'.

Tyrrell was asked to comment further on this apparent new direction in French foreign policy. The result was a despatch which gave a remarkable preview of what that policy was to be nearly twenty years later. The despatch was dated 17 February 1930.

'The ultimate political organisation of Europe for which France is apparently working,' it stated, 'is a general system of compulsory arbitration and mutual guarantee such as is defined by the Geneva protocol of 1924. In this would be included the French network of alliances, assistance and arbitration treaties. Just as she believes a complete agreement respecting security to be the first step to a politically organised Europe, so she considers a series of agreements respecting specific industries and types of production to be the surest procedure towards economic organisation. There seems to be a certain opinion in Paris which realises that the economic organisation of Europe through industrial agreements may constitute a difficulty for British production. It is stated that the organisation of the latter is generally less advanced than on the continent. Almost every reasonable person in France would welcome our cooperation politically as well as economically. It is considered that our cooperation would strengthen Europe as a whole, and that it would tend to strengthen France in the Franco-German discussion. On the other hand French opinion has grave doubt as to our ultimate participation.'

No less prescient were some of the reports on military matters. In a despatch sent fairly soon after Bentinck's arrival in Paris, for instance, it was stated: 'Taking into consideration the fact that the army is undergoing a period of transition the French army is as efficient as can be expected, but it is behindhand as regards mechanisation and armament. It is of interest, however, to note that the average Frenchman of today, contrary to his habit of praising French institutions (other than political) considers that the army is in an unsatisfactory condition morally and as regards armament and training. Nobody knowing the French army of 1928 could conceivably look upon it as a militaristic or imperialistic instrument.' In a later report it was stated that the British peacetime army was generally regarded in France as 'une armée de parade' and that little interest was shown in it 'except from the point of view of our progress in matters of organisation'.

Relations between the staffs of the British Embassy and the French Ministry of Foreign Affairs were for the most part, as Tyrrell pointed out on one occasion, 'of the most cordial character'. This of course enabled Tyrrell, Wigram, Bentinck and others to obtain semi-confidential information about French foreign policy. A similar relationship existed with the secretariat of the Ambassadors' Conference. This body had remained in being since the Peace Conference at Versailles as a medium for discussing policy. Its Secretary-General was René Massigli, whom Bentinck had known since the Lausanne conference.

That it still discussed matters of some moment was shown in the instructions sent from London about the attitude to be taken to a German proposal in the later 1920s to develop pilotless aircraft. 'Pilotless aircraft,' it was stated, 'are at present in a very early experimental stage, and any foreseeable application for this form of flying must be purely for military purposes. The proposal should therefore be "resisted".'

Bentinck's duties in Paris were more varied than ever before. Some of the duties were ceremonial. An event, for instance, which was to be a test of the cordiality of Franco-British relations was the celebration in February 1929 of the fifth centenary of the entry of Joan of Arc into Orléans. The French Government had decided to treat this as an occasion of major importance, and Tyrrell recommended active British participation. In a Foreign Office minute the opinion was expressed that there was *prima facie no reason why we should help the French celebrate our defeat by a lady whom we subsequently captured and burnt at the stake*'. Nevertheless Tyrrell's recommendation was accepted, and he chose Bentinck to accompany him to the celebrations. As a result, Bentinck said, *I expiated the sins of my ancestors by going through Orléans in full diplomatic uniform in pelting rain holding an umbrella over my head.*

For both Tyrrell and Bentinck the form of the celebrations threw an instructive light on the relations between Church and State in France. *It was*, Bentinck said, *la république laique et sociale, and to get advancement you were handicapped if you went to church. Foch was always a straightforward Catholic. Pétain, I think, saw the divine light after the German onslaught in 1940. When I went to Rouen and Orléans – two separate trips – with my chief, Willie Tyrrell, in connection with the five hundredth anniversary, there was a mass in Rouen. The only people who knelt down when the host was raised were the President of the Republic, Doumergue, a Protestant, Willie Tyrrell, who was a Catholic, very much a Catholic, and myself, who had been trained always to do obeisance: shoes off in a mosque, hat on the head at a service in a synagogue, and kneeling down when the bells tinkle in a Catholic church. Pétain was bolt upright, as were all the other officers, civil servants and politicians.*

Tyrrell, after mentioning that at no time since 1905 had so many French cardinals and prelates bowed to the head of the French lay State, described the celebrations in Orléans as another step towards establishing reasonable relations between Church and State in France. He added: 'From certain observations made to Mr Cavendish-Bentinck by a well-informed member of the French diplomatic service, I understand that this is also the view taken by the Ministry of Foreign Affairs.'

A no less spectacular event was the funeral of Marshal Foch in March 1929, when again Bentinck found himself marching through the streets. Whereas Clemenceau was, as he had asked to be, buried in privacy in the Vendée, Foch was buried in the Invalides after a funeral procession which included a number of crowned heads and Edward, Prince of Wales. This was one of two occasions on which the Prince visited Paris while Bentinck was there.

King George V was ill, and the Prince of Wales had been in East Africa and was summoned back by air. It had been announced in the press that the Prince of Wales would be passing through Paris. At that time there were several ladies who thought they were the Princess of Wales. One looked exactly like a respectable French governess with wire spectacles. She appeared at the Embassy saying he was her husband and he was going to meet her and discuss things on his way through. I put her in a room and told a footman to watch. I telephoned to the Sécurité and they sent two people round. Meanwhile she'd smelt a rat and slipped out.

The next day at the military airport at Le Bourget Senegalese sentries were there and security people. The plane was coming down. 'God Save the King' and the 'Marseillaise' were being played. I looked round and there she was. I told the Sécurité: 'Voilà la princesse.'

Other duties ranged from the harrowing to the slightly

absurd. On October 5 1930 the British airship R 101 crashed into a hill near Beauvais with the loss of forty-six lives. This effectively brought to an end British construction of airships and plans for linking different parts of the Empire by a new means of transport. The response of the French Government was both helpful and sympathetic. The Air Minister personally supervised salvage operations, and the day of the funeral of the victims was declared one of national mourning.

I was staying the weekend that happened, Bentinck said, *with the Edouard Rothschilds. I came back to the Embassy. The next day we went off. An awful shambles. When the coffins were being put in the train I stood beside the first Lord Stansgate, who was called Josiah Wedgwood Benn. The Government were keen on the Empire and Empire links. He said to me: 'Very sad, very sad, but I don't think it will do the Government too much harm.'*

The Air Attaché came to me and said: 'A woman's shoe has been found in the wreckage.' What was he to do about it? I said: 'Say nothing. Put it in a dustbin. If the press get hold of it, families in Glasgow and Belfast and Birmingham will think it's their daughter's, gone to Paris to practise the oldest profession.'

Among the various fields of activity in which the British at that time sought the help of the French Government, one which occupied an inordinate amount of time was the despatch to Britain of books deemed to be obscene.

In 1929 the Society of French Publishers and Libraries made a formal request for some enlightenment on the standards which the British were applying. In particular they wanted to know whether works by Rabelais and Zola were to be banned. The upshot was a conference in Paris attended by the British Director of Public Prosecutions, whose name was Bodkin. Further meetings followed, but progress was slow.

The Home Office were very keen on stopping books like Lady Chatterley's Lover. *A copy was sent over, which I read. I used to say I had a copy of* Lady Chatterley's Lover *provided for me by the Home Office. Scotland Yard had a liaison officer in Paris. He came to me and said: 'Well, Mr Bentinck, this business about publishing pornographic books. We shan't get anywhere until the French Minister's Chef de Cabinet gets what he wants, which is a British decoration. It needn't be very much, but he'd like a decoration.' I reported this to London in a letter to the Department. This evoked a* reply sent to Tyrrell expressing surprise that a member of his staff should suggest that His Majesty's decorations might be used as bribes.

In April 1929 Bentinck was promoted to the rank of First Secretary. Not long afterwards his second child was born. *My wife was expecting a child, who turned out to be our daughter, and didn't want to go to England because she didn't get on with my parents. She liked sunshine. So we went to Cannes.* Cannes was at that time barely developed as a summer resort, 1929 being the year in which the summer casino, named under American influence Palm Beach, was opened. *In those days you could walk along the beach without treading on bodies. I remember thinking if I only had some money I'd have bought land on that coast and built a house.* On their return to Paris Bentinck and his wife were able to surprise their friends, who were in the habit of visiting Deauville or Biarritz in the summer, by telling them that the Côte d'Azur was also habitable at that time of year.

Beneath the surface glitter of Bentinck's social life there were difficulties, and these were becoming increasingly known to other people. From time to time gossip columnists even paid him some attention. In June 1929 it was reported in the *Daily Express* that 'Mr Cavendish-Bentinck startled attachés in Paris by renting Mlle Spinelli's flat with a large sunken pool of goldfish in the hall'. Another report told of Mrs Cavendish-Bentinck giving 'the visitor an overpowering sense of wealth'.

The report of the goldfish pool in the hall was correct. *I had a rather uncomfortable flat*, Bentinck said, *very showy in a building paid for by a rich Central American gentleman for Mlle Elise Fournier* autrement dit *Spinelli, the French actress. She owned the building. She was very tiresome. We had Tonkinese servants. They were excellent.*

The overwhelming sense of wealth was illusory. *I speculated on margin in twenty-eight and twenty-nine*, Bentinck said, *and I lost £2000, which was a lot of money in those days.* To meet his commitments Bentinck had to turn to his parents for help.

Bentinck's wife, who was little liked by his colleagues, had an unfortunate propensity for quarrelling with their wives. She also quarrelled with Tyrrell's daughter, and Tyrrell, who had great influence in the Foreign Office, was aware of what was going on.

At that time the Foreign Office expected its representation in Paris, whatever might happen elsewhere, to be of the highest order. Although poor appointments were occasionally made, it had enough men of ability with wives who could perform their duties satisfactorily to ensure that in general its requirement was met. Occasional quarrels conducted by a diplomat's wife could be tolerated. But in a city where so much importance was attached to the social life as the means whereby a diplomat could learn what was happening and report accordingly, a persistent and known tendency to quarrel was clearly a liability. When staff changes were made therefore it was decided that Bentinck should not remain in Paris.

Bentinck's hope had been to succeed Wigram as Head of Chancery. This did not happen, and Oliver Harvey, whose political judgement could hardly be compared with Bentinck's, was offered the post instead.

In January 1932 Bentinck was transferred, not on promotion, but at best in a sideways move, to the Embassy in Athens, where he was to replace Harvey. It was the first serious setback in his career.

CHAPTER 7
Greek Interlude
(1932–33)

In the early 1930s no country had a greater interest than Britain in the financial stability of Greece. Two-thirds of Greece's foreign debt was owed to British concerns, and there was even a guaranteed loan made in 1832 which was still being serviced. An International Financial Commission operated in Athens, to which the revenue from certain Greek taxes was paid and which the Commission used to meet the requirements of foreign creditors. The Commission had been established under the terms of a treaty of 1898 and consisted of representatives of the British, French and Italian governments. In the first world war Britain advanced roughly twice as much money to Greece as did the USA. France and Italy advanced virtually nothing.

Politically it was important to Britain that governments of a liberal persuasion, such as those of Venizelos and his associates, who had traditional pro-British sympathies and worked closely with the League of Nations, should remain in office. Their likeliest replacements were men to whom Italian fascism was by then a powerful magnet.

Unfortunately the quality of British diplomatic representation in Greece was for the most part manifestly inadequate. Until he arrived in Athens Bentinck had consistently served under heads of missions or departments for whom he had a professional respect or a personal regard or both. What he learnt in Athens showed the Foreign Service in a rather different light.

The man who was Minister when Bentinck arrived, the Hon. Patrick Ramsay, had had a shattering experience in childhood, when on board the family yacht in Cannes his father, Lord Dalhousie, had first shot his wife in an access of apparently unwarranted jealousy and had then committed suicide. *Ramsay*, Bentinck said, *was very dotty and he had rather a violent temper. He had a habit of walking down the Chancery corridor and saying: 'Any news?' or 'I think I'm going off my head.'* I refrained from saying this wasn't a question for the future.

Ramsay's successor was named Waterlow. *Sidney Perigal Waterlow*, Bentinck said, *entered the Foreign Office before World War I. He was divorced for nullity. Then just before the war he reappeared in the divorce court as a co-respondent. Instead of patting him on the back and saying, 'Well done, my boy, you've re-established your reputation,' the Foreign Office insisted, as they had to then, that he should resign.* Waterlow returned to the Foreign Service via a wartime appointment in the Department of Overseas Trade and in time he was posted to Sofia. From there he went to Athens. *He was very difficult. He didn't hit it off with the Greeks. Ramsay didn't either. When Waterlow arrived he complained: 'On mange beaucoup mieux en Bulgarie,' which didn't please the Greeks.*

Waterlow had meanwhile acquired another wife. *A Parliamentary delegation came out and he didn't want to give an expensive meal for a lot of Greeks. He thought it would be a good thing if the delegation had luncheon with him and his staff and they could explain the situation. His wife was there as hostess. They sat down and the first course was served. Lady Waterlow took up a glass, looked at her husband rather severely at the other end of the table, and said: 'Sidney, why the best claret?'*

When Bentinck arrived in Athens at the end of January 1932 Venizelos was in power as a result of an overwhelming electoral victory in August 1928. In a major speech which he made about a fortnight before Bentinck's arrival Venizelos summarized some of the achievements of his Government. His first task on assuming power, he said, had been to ensure external security by a series of treaties of friendship with neighbouring powers. He had then given the country stable government. The budget had been balanced, social services had been extended and taxes had been reduced. The problems of the refugees from Turkish territory had been largely solved, and major works of land reclamation had been carried out in Macedonia. The principal problems which Greece now faced were, he said, caused by the international monetary crisis.

He dwelt particularly on Britain's abandonment of the gold standard.

Venizelos's rule was not uninterrupted during the period of Bentinck's appointment. An election held in October 1932 produced a result which enabled Panayoti Tsaldaris, who was described in a British legation despatch as 'a moderate, timid and well meaning man', to form a coalition Government with Venizelos's benign approval. Venizelos told Ramsay shortly after the election that he was prepared to allow Tsaldaris to govern for six months. In fact he withdrew his tolerance after three months, and in January 1933 Tsaldaris was defeated on a vote of confidence. Venizelos then returned to office.

Efforts were made to remove Venizelos by force but they were all unsuccessful. In March 1933 a coup d'état was staged by Plastiras, the man who had released Prince Andrew during an earlier period of military rule and who had now risen to the rank of general. Martial law was proclaimed, but it lasted only fourteen hours. Plastiras escaped on board a small sailing ship to the Italian Dodecanese. Three months later there was an attempted assassination. On this Bentinck reported at some length to the Foreign Office.

'I am informed by a reliable person in Venizelist circles,' he wrote, 'that at 9 p.m. yesterday evening he received a visit from a former police officer, who told him that he had seen some ten people wandering about in the vicinity of M. Venizelos's house who appeared to be contemplating some nefarious deed. Amongst these ten persons he had recognised a former brigand and a plain-clothes police officer. My informant telephoned to M. Venizelos's son, who at once telephoned to the house where M. Venizelos was dining.'

Venizelos decided to return home. A green car came out of a side road and apparently without difficulty inserted itself between Venizelos's car and that of his bodyguard. Shooting began.

Recalling the incident later, Bentinck said: *Venizelos's car drove on and they tried to pot him. He fell on the floor and Mme Venizelos fell on top to protect him and got shot in the behind.* In his written report he concluded: 'M. Venizelos owes his life more to his presence of mind in lying flat in his car than to the efficiency of his bodyguard.'

Bentinck was to leave Athens in November 1933. From the time of his arrival until then the principal concern of Venizelos, and therefore in practice that of the Greek Government, was the state of the national finances.

One of the first indications the British Foreign Office had that the Greek Government might be seeking a loan abroad came, perhaps surprisingly, in a private letter which Bentinck sent from Paris shortly before his departure for Athens. This was addressed to Jock, later Sir John, Balfour. Bentinck's information came in the first instance from a Greek shipping man named Embericos. 'The head of the European Department at the Quai d'Orsay,' Bentinck wrote, 'says that he knows nothing of a proposed loan to Greece, but Francis Rodd of the Bank of England, whom I saw yesterday, thinks that the French might give the Greeks a loan to keep them on the gold standard.' On 19 January, the day after Bentinck's letter was written, Ramsay reported from Athens that Venizelos would be going to Paris and Rome to seek help for his programme of public works. On the following day he added the information that Venizelos would be going to London, that he wanted to see the Foreign Secretary, Sir John Simon, and that he would be asking for a five-year suspension of repayment of existing loans.

Venizelos did go to London at the end of January 1932 and had a rather discouraging reception. Simon offered him nothing better than a lunch at the United Services Club, and Neville Chamberlain, as Chancellor of the Exchequer, sent him a coldly worded and negative reply to his financial proposals. On his return home Venizelos wrote to Chamberlain: 'What has mainly encouraged me to approach the British Government was the communication made by His Majesty's Minister in Athens to the Greek Government at the moment when Great Britain has been compelled to abandon the gold standard. The British Minister has assured me that his Government were willing to do everything in their power for assisting the countries which used in the past to deal with the London market for their finance.' This elicited a reply from Chamberlain: 'I can assure you that my Government view the difficulties of Greece with the most cordial sympathy.' But nothing more positive was forthcoming, and Venizelos therefore decided to try other tactics.

In February 1932 the Greek Government imposed restrictions on currency exchange as an emergency measure. This immediately affected British firms operating in Greece, which were owed appreciable sums of money. The Financial Committee of the League of Nations had sent the British banker, Sir Otto Niemeyer, as an independent observer to report on Greece's finances, and in March Venizelos announced that he would resign if the Financial Committee did not reach a decision favourable to Greece on the strength of Niemeyer's investigations.

The threat of resignation brought support from an important quarter. This was the Bank of Greece, which had a British adviser named H. C. F. Finlayson. On 9 March Finlayson wrote to Niemeyer that it was 'essential in the interests of British holders of Greek stocks that every effort should be made to enable the Greek Government to carry out its programme and remain in office'. The alternative, he warned, might be chaos.

About a week later the Foreign Office received a report from Cadogan at Geneva that Niemeyer was recommending to the League of Nations that a loan backed by governments should be made to Greece. Further investigations by bankers followed before Greece received the help she needed.

Meanwhile the state of the Greek national finances deteriorated sharply. On 20 March Ramsay reported that 430 drachmas could be obtained privately for a pound note, the official rate being 280 to £1. The next month the Greek Government defaulted on certain loan repayments which were due. In May Finlayson reported: 'The Treasury position is such that they cannot pay salaries and carry on unless they resort to the printing press or unless the International Financial Commission hand over surplus revenue of 200 million drachmas and abstain from piling up extra revenue to meet the substantial deterioration of the drachma.'

Once Greece had defaulted on her loan repayments the British Government became concerned, not only with the stability of Greek finances, but also with the protection of the interests of British bondholders. On the initiative of the

Governor of the Bank of England a formidable committee was set up to represent these bondholders. Among its members were Sir Austen Chamberlain, Sir Otto Niemeyer and Sir Arthur Salter. Negotiations on behalf of the committee in Athens were conducted largely by Bentinck.

Venizelos's Finance Minister, Andreas Michalakopoulos, tried an interesting tactic when he reminded Ramsay of Palmerston's dictum that 'Investors who place their money abroad for gain, without consulting Her Majesty's Government, have no right to call upon them to intervene if they lose their money.' But this did not satisfy a British government of the 1930s, and Bentinck was expected to produce results.

From his discussions with financial experts and Greek ministers and officials Bentinck came to the conclusion that the most that could be extracted from the Greek Government in 1932 was thirty per cent of the interest due to the bondholders. He therefore recommended acceptance of this figure. *The British representative on the International Financial Commission said to me: 'Aren't you rather sticking your neck out?' I told him that was what I was there for.*

Bentinck's estimate was soon shown to have been right. In September 1932 it was officially announced that an agreement had been reached in London between the Council of Foreign Bondholders, the League Loans Committee and the Greek Finance Minister, whereby Greece undertook to pay thirty per cent of the interest due that year.

Negotiations continued with the object of achieving longer-term settlements. On 2 June 1933 Bentinck wrote to Ralph Wigram, who was now at the Foreign Office: 'An imposing and far too numerous Greek delegation is leaving here today to attend the forthcoming meeting of the Finance Committee of the League of Nations in London, subsequently to negotiate with the League Loans Committee, and to assist at the beginning of the World Economic Conference. The Greek Government would like to make an agreement with the bondholders covering a number of years, but they realise that the League Loans Committee are unlikely to agree to this proposal. I suspect that the Greek delegation will cry out "poverty" and "ruin" and, to begin with, offer the bondholders twenty per cent of the interest due during the financial year April 1933

–April 1934. They will easily come up to twenty-five per cent and, if pressed firmly may agree to thirty per cent. I doubt, however, whether the present Government would be prepared to pay more.'

A month later Robin Hankey at the Foreign Office received a letter from the Treasury official, David Waley, stating: 'The bondholders have asked for forty per cent of the interest and the Greeks have offered twenty per cent. I believe that the Greeks are in fact willing to go up to twenty-five per cent and I strongly suspect that the bondholders would come down to thirty per cent.' The haggling continued with the foreseeable result.

The settlement of the Greek debt was only one of a number of financial subjects on which Bentinck had to negotiate. On several occasions he did so as Chargé d'Affaires either because Ramsay was on leave or in the interim period between Ramsay's departure and Waterlow's arrival. At other times he was deputed to act by Ramsay.

In November 1932 Ramsay reported that he had directed Bentinck and the Commercial Attaché, A. N. Cumberbatch, to discuss 'the position of the Ottoman Bank, which has advanced large sums in foreign currency with the Finance Ministry'. A month later he was able to state that the Greek Government was likely to indemnify both the Ottoman and the British-French discount banks.

On another occasion Bentinck had a meeting with two ministers and the political director at the Ministry of Foreign Affairs. From this he came away with assurances that foreign exchange would be made available immediately for the payment of small debts owed to British firms, and that restrictions would be raised to allow payment for Greek goods exported to the United Kingdom. In August 1932 he obtained a personal assurance from Venizelos that the settlement of all commercial debts would be speeded up, and he recommended that this should be pointed out to the Greek Minister of Finance, who was due to visit London shortly.

Finance was not a field in which Bentinck had had much training or experience, yet his conduct of negotiations in Greece was as deft as it was successful. This was largely because of his ability to spot, and then come to know, those financiers and officials who could give the best advice or information. In reporting the forthcoming visit of a Greek delegation to London, for instance, he was able to state: 'If M. Massovinos of the Ministry of Finance should call upon you, I think you may be interested to hear what he has to say, as he is by far the most capable official in that Ministry.'

Unfortunately none of this success could mitigate in the official view the effects of events in Bentinck's private life. Sir John Colville wrote discreetly of Bentinck's wife: 'She chose Athens to display her contempt for the conventions.' Bentinck said simply: *My former wife took a strong dislike to Ramsay's wife.* There were in fact some distressing public scenes, so many and so public that Bentinck was removed from Athens after serving there for less than two years.

The capital chosen for him was almost as far removed as was possible from the main centres of political power and influence. This was Santiago in Chile.

CHAPTER 8
In the Outer Circle
(1934–37)

For Bentinck the years he spent in Chile, from early 1934 to mid-1937, provided a test of character of a rather sterner nature than superficial appearances might have suggested. Among the qualities he revealed were patience and a refusal either to complain or to be diverted from the task in hand. They were qualities he was to show again later in other circumstances.

I liked the Chileans very much, he said. *They were easy to get on with, and I got on with them well. I was lucky there. I had a very nice house, rather like a large Californian bungalow, and the best roses I've ever had. There were two palm trees, and if you stood outside in the evening you would see nothing but the palm trees and the Andes, probably snow-capped, which I used to call my garden wall.* Bentinck suggested that the Foreign Office should buy the house and keep it furnished for members of its staff rather than incur the cost of transporting furniture to and fro. *I got an answer: 'My dear Bill, you've surely been long enough in the service to know that His Majesty's Government does not speculate in real estate.' You have to remember that the Duke of Wellington, in spite of having won the battle of Waterloo, got into hot water for buying what is now the Embassy in Paris plus the contents.*

The inhabited area of Chile stretches further from north to south than that of any other country in the world. Yet the population, when Bentinck was there, numbered only about four and a half million. Some three-quarters of the people were thought to be at least partly of Araucanian Indian blood, but a significant number of them had British or Irish names.

There had been strong ties between Chile and Britain almost from the time when Francis Drake reached Valparaiso and opened up the west coast for plunder. The colourful Scottish admiral, Thomas Cochrane, Earl of Dundonald, who also served in the navies of Greece and Brazil, became the first commander of Chile's naval squadron. It was by his residence on the island of Juan Fernandez off the Chilean coast that Alexander Selkirk provided the inspiration for *Robinson Crusoe*. Loans raised in London in the nineteenth century enabled railways to be built in Chile and the guano deposits to be exploited. The national hero and liberator, Bernardo O'Higgins, was initiated into radical politics in London. When Bentinck was in Chile there were fourteen British schools there. The playing of cricket in Chile dates back to the 1820s.

A number of the principal merchant houses engaged in importing and exporting in Chile in the 1930s were still British-controlled, but already by the outbreak of the first world war both Germany and the United States had begun to overtake Britain as Chile's principal trading partners. In the 1930s, as German trading became more and more aggressive, Britain's share of the Chilean market continued to decline. This was to be one of Bentinck's principal concerns during his period of service in Chile. Another, by a curious coincidence, was the difficulty the Chilean Government had in paying debts owed to British bondholders.

In June 1934 the British Ambassador in Santiago, Sir Robert Carminow Michell, sent a despatch to the Foreign Office reporting a conversation which Bentinck had had with an English broker named H. J. Tanner, who was the head of a local issuing house for loans and whose services the Chilean Government had often used. Tanner told Bentinck that 'the Civilian Government do not consider that they will be in a position to pay even a portion of the interest on their external debt for a long while to come'.

The Chilean Finance Minister, Don Gustavo Ross, who wanted a settlement to be made, was attacked in the Chilean press for being in the service of foreign usurers. Sir Otto Niemeyer was sent out on a tour of inspection, and a Council of Foreign Bondholders became active on behalf of auditors. In short, Bentinck found himself replaying a familiar scene.

Michell seems to have had some difficulty both in presenting the British case to the Chilean Government and the Chilean case to the British Government. In March 1934, shortly after Bentinck's arrival in Santiago, Michell wrote to the Foreign Office: 'I found it almost impossible to make the Chilean situation comprehensible during my personal discussions in London last summer.' His manner of communicating was not always well received in the Foreign Office, and one telegram of his elicited four different minutes from four members of the American department. These were: 'Not very satisfactory.' 'This is not only not very satisfactory: it indicates that Sir R. Michell has not appreciated the misleading nature of his reports.' 'I entirely agree that we should protest against the tone and the substance of this telegram.' 'A little too hasty in his conclusions as in his language. He deserves a gentle rebuke.'

Michell, Bentinck said, *had been the Consul and was married to a Chilean wife, who, when he'd been made an Ambassador, became very pompous. A rather irritating female. Michell wasn't a bad fellow. He had to retire at sixty. He tried to get himself prolonged, but they wouldn't hear of it.*

The experience which Bentinck had gained in the settlement of the Greek debt was appreciated by Michell, who wisely gave him the task of conducting most of the negotiations. In these Bentinck had the support of the Commercial Secretary, Arthur Pack, whose wife was later to become notorious as a secret agent with the code-name Cynthia.

Arthur Pack, Bentinck said, *had been before World War I an employee in the General Post Office. He joined up and was wounded. He had a commission and he was sent to help to drill American troops. There he married a very pretty girl called Betty, the daughter of a marine officer, and they came out to Chile. Then he got taken in to the Department of Overseas Trade. He wrote good reports, but he had chips on his shoulders, and he didn't like the fact that I, being the Head of Chancery, insisted on things being sent up to the Ambassador through me. That led to friction.*

He had trouble afterwards with Betty. She was employed during the war by Bill Stephenson in Washington. She lured a French officer to make love with her and she got hold of the key of his safe.

The negotiations for bringing about a debt settlement were prolonged, just as they had been in Greece. In July 1934

Bentinck and Rothschild's representative, David Blair, wrote a report giving their estimates of Chile's capacity to pay. In August Michell reported that the Government might be willing to pay up to £250,000 towards serious debts. Rothschild's figure was £500,000.

At the end of August Chilean newspapers announced that Ross would shortly seek the sanction of Parliament 'to begin negotiations for an agreement with representatives of the holders of Chile's long term external debt'. An extraordinary session of the Chilean Parliament was held in October, when Ross put forward a plan for using Government revenue from nitrates and copper to service debts. The Council of Foreign Bondholders considered his proposals inadequate, and negotiations continued.

The culmination came in December 1935, when the British Foreign Secretary, Sir Samuel Hoare, announced, in answer to a question in Parliament, that the President of the Chilean Republic had promulgated a law providing for 'the partial resumption of service on the Chilean external debt'. State revenues from nitrate, copper, iodine and certain other sources would be used for this purpose. 'The law was passed,' Hoare said, 'with the utmost difficulty, and if the provision had been any more favourable to the bondholders it would certainly have been rejected.'

Among the reasons for the success of the negotiations was the friendly relationship which had grown up between Bentinck and Gustavo Ross and his wife. *I could lunch with them any time I wanted*, Bentinck said. Two months before Bentinck's arrival Michell had been complaining that he could not even obtain acknowledgments of his letters to the Minister of Finance.

Gustavo Ross had been an enterprising speculator, who had made and lost more than one fortune. At a time of low ebb in his finances he won the Buenos Aires Christmas lottery, but he kept this fact secret for a year. In 1927, being politically out of favour, he spent some time in Argentina and in Europe. He returned to Chile at the end of 1932 after the military regime of Colonel Ibañez had come to an end, and the Liberal-Conservative Arturo Alessandri had become President. Alessandri appointed him as his Minister of Finance. In one

British Embassy report Ross was described as 'without doubt the wiliest and most capable Finance Minister that Chile has ever had'.

I became very good friends with Don Gustavo Ross, Bentinck said. *He was the man who really ran things there. I used to provide his wife with orchids and things like that. He had a fine new swimming pool which he was very pleased with, and I thought it would be nice if he were to have a couple of penguins. Unfortunately penguins are filled with oil, and in fresh water the oil comes off. One should learn more natural history.*

Bound up with the settlement of outstanding debts was that of the unfreezing of credits. When negotiations on this subject also ended satisfactorily Michell reported: 'The Embassy has particularly prided itself on the success which has been attained in liquidating frozen credits as a result of all the perseverance and attention that have been dedicated to this matter in the course of the last three years, whereas our United States and French colleagues have large amounts dating back several years that are still unliquidated.' A Foreign Office minute a little earlier had stated more laconically: 'The Embassy seems to have handled this matter very well.'

After some two years in Chile Bentinck returned to England for two months' leave. *The Foreign Office hadn't got anywhere else for me to go, and I went back to Chile. My wife didn't go back with me. She wanted to stay in England as the boy had to go to school.* By this time the marriage was clearly doomed. *I thought I had to remain married because of the children. It didn't do a bit of good. Nothing is worse for children than to have two parents who don't get on.*

For the last year of his service in Chile Bentinck acted as Chargé d'Affaires. The man who had been chosen to succeed Michell, Joseph Addison, was serving in Prague and managed to avoid being posted to Chile by announcing that he could not find the country on his map. Some time elapsed before Sir Charles Bentinck arrived to take over as Ambassador.

I'd given up the lease of my house, and I had a small garçonnière *flat in Santiago. I also had a bedroom, sitting-room and bathroom in the Hotel O'Higgins at Viña de Mar. It was the only time when my life was well organized. I used to go down to Viña de Mar on the Friday evening train, about two hours' journey, and come back on the*

Monday night or the Tuesday morning. I did my entertaining at the local clubs.

During Bentinck's last year in Chile Hitler's Government exercised steadily increasing pressure in order both to capture Chilean markets and to enlist the political sympathies of the many Chileans of German origin. In one of his numerous conversations with Ross, of which Bentinck reported the substance to the Foreign Office, Ross told him that 'German exports to Chile are increasing in a most remarkable manner owing to the system employed by the German Government and German exporting firms, which practically amounts to dumping. His Excellency said that Germany seemed to be making an effort to capture the Chilean market for all classes of goods, especially motor cars.'

The counter-action which Ross recommended was a commercial treaty between Chile and Britain. This idea was coldly received by the British Government, chiefly because it did not seem that any special concessions could be made for Chilean goods without interfering with the system of imperial preference.

In one of his last reports from Santiago Bentinck gave his impressions of the prestige enjoyed in Chile by some of the leading powers and of the effects of their propaganda.

'Germany,' he wrote, 'is generally respected in Chile and her prestige is high. Her propaganda is based on the large, patriotic, highly organised and comparatively well-to-do German colony in Chile. There is an excellent German school at Valparaiso, two schools at Santiago, one at Concepción, and various others throughout the southern provinces. The German Government invited, at the beginning of 1937, thirty Chilean university students to visit Germany, all expenses paid by that Government. They have also arranged for an exchange of professors. Large quantities of German propaganda material of all kinds are distributed to the press.

'In intensity Italian propaganda comes some distance behind that of Germany. The Italian colony is smaller and poorer, being chiefly composed of grocers and minor shopkeepers. Those who were born in Italy are as a rule highly patriotic, but those born in Chile seem to lose all enthusiasm for the land of their forefathers. The news reels from the United States for exhibition in Chile generally seem to contain items of Italian propaganda, which is perhaps due to the fact that the theatrical antics of the Duce provide first class material for the cinema.'

After stating that French prestige in Chile was not very high Bentinck went on: 'Whilst the Chileans are impressed with the military and naval strength of Japan, no amount of propaganda will persuade the Chilean Government to allow the entry of Japanese emigrants.'

The spread of United States influence was to some extent hampered by the quality of its official representatives. Of one American Ambassador it was stated in a British Embassy report that he owed his appointment to the political activities of his wife, 'a forceful lady in a red wig'. The Ambassador himself 'at first gave the impression of being a courtly old gentleman, anxious to do the right thing in strange and exotic circumstances, and likely to impress by the dignity of his bearing. Subsequently, however, it was noticed that His Excellency behaved on several occasions a trifle queerly, and the sad truth leaked out that he is in fact a dipsomaniac. In the Ministry of Foreign Affairs it is said that he had not been seen inside there after his first formal visit, but that the bars in the town know him well.' When a career diplomat was eventually appointed to the post it was stated in another report that he followed 'a heterogeneous line of nondescripts whose representation has done their country more harm than good'. The top German diplomats, by contrast, were described as being of high quality, suspected by their Government of being insufficiently Nazi, and 'anxious to be on the best of terms' with the British Embassy.

Soviet influence was exercised mainly through the Communist Party, which was strong and well organized. Its most popular figure, who was named Marmaduke Grove, had been head of the Chilean Air Force and in that capacity had authorized the arming of the population and encouraged them to seize bourgeois property. His attempted coup failed, and he was banished to Easter Island, but he was allowed to return on the fall of the Ibañez regime. In a British Embassy report it was stated: 'It is widely alleged that Grove is not mentally balanced.' Nevertheless he contested the election for the presidency, received some sixty thousand votes and came second to

Alessandri in the poll. Although under the regime of Alessandri and Ross material conditions did improve in Chile, it was still a fertile ground for advocates of communism. In a report which he wrote early in 1935 Bentinck stated: 'The standard of life of the poorer classes in Chile compares unfavourably with that of the Greek refugees from Asia Minor or that of the lower classes in the large towns of Poland in 1919.'

In the mid-1930s British diplomats, when competing with representatives of the new totalitarian powers, were hampered by a lack of forceful salesmanship and a lack of propaganda material. They were also limited by a tradition of gentlemanly conduct. To attain their ends their best course was often to exploit that tradition by establishing friendly relations with a few individuals, through whom they could hope to influence events. This Bentinck did, not without success.

When proposals were put forward within the League of Nations to restrain Italy after she decided to attack Ethiopia, not merely by the formality of sanctions, but by force, Bentinck was given an undertaking by the Chilean Government that it would provide a cruiser and a battalion of troops for this purpose. In the event neither the cruiser nor the battalion was needed, but as an exercise in persuasion Bentinck's effort was impressive.

Bentinck left Chile in June 1937. The next month the Chilean Ambassador in London wrote to Anthony Eden, who was then Foreign Secretary: 'Mr Victor Cavendish-Bentinck, who for three years held the appointment of Counsellor to His Majesty's Embassy at Santiago, has, upon transfer to another post, just left Chile. My Government desires me to leave on record before Your Excellency what pleasant recollections he has left in my country. During his stay there and in his constant dealings with the Ministry of Foreign Affairs he never spared any effort to strengthen the good relations between our respective countries. My Government highly appreciates these friendly endeavours and has seen with regret the departure of Mr Cavendish-Bentinck from their midst.' The Ambassador went on to state that the President of the Republic would have bestowed on Bentinck the order *Al Merito* had British Foreign Office regulations permitted.

In the Foreign Office file which contained the Ambassador's

letter a minute was added: 'This is another remarkable tribute to Mr Cavendish-Bentinck, who should, I think, be shown this paper.' He never was. The first he heard of it was when I told him of the Ambassador's letter nearly fifty years later. *The Foreign Office*, he said, *did extraordinary things*.

Bentinck's efforts, however, had not been unrecognized, and it was decided that he should be found suitable employment within the Foreign Office. For a time this was to be in dealing, principally, with the affairs of Egypt and of Ethiopia.

CHAPTER 9
The Coming of War
(1937–39)

In the first world war Egypt had been proclaimed a British protectorate. A few years later a degree of independence was granted by a treaty which made special provision for 'the security of the communications of the British Empire'. This meant in practice ensuring freedom of passage through the Suez Canal against the danger of any form of enemy attack.

In 1936, the year before Bentinck took up his new appointment in the Foreign Office, a further treaty was signed. It had been negotiated largely by Sir Miles Lampson, with whom Bentinck had served in Locarno, and Nahas Pasha, the undisputed leader of the nationalist Wafdist party, which had once been led by Zaghlul. The treaty removed various controls which the British had continued to exercise, changed the status of the British Residency in Cairo to that of an embassy, and generally increased the appearance of Egyptian independence. At the same time it provided for close co-operation between Egypt and Britain in the event of war and allowed a twenty-year period for the gradual withdrawal of British troops.

The principal British interests in Egypt were therefore the effective functioning of a government which was relatively friendly to Britain and, as war became increasingly likely, time and opportunity to strengthen the defences of the country. The problems of how best to promote these interests were complicated by the coming of age of the young Egyptian King, Farouk, in July 1937, about the time when Bentinck began his new duties. The King made it clear at once that he intended to exercise a number of the privileges of his position.

Broadly speaking, there were two schools of thought among British officials concerned with executing policy towards Egypt. One favoured considerable intervention in Egyptian internal affairs. The other believed that such intervention should be kept to a minimum consistent with the safeguarding of essential British interests. Lampson, as Ambassador in Cairo, tended to favour intervention. Bentinck before long became of the other persuasion.

Soon after the new treaty had been signed Lampson sent a revealing report on the standing of the British Embassy in Cairo. 'One or two incidents lately,' he wrote, 'have given me a definite impression of the intention in some quarters to belittle the position of the Embassy. Naturally, with the change of status, a great many of the special facilities and privileges accorded to the Residency have disappeared. This is quite natural. But in regard to certain minor matters affecting the Embassy and also in regard to the Military Mission I have noticed a tendency to "rub in" the change of status. I therefore asked Amin to tell Nahas that I was definitely on the watch and, if necessary, would hit out. Amin said that he was very glad that I had authorised him to give the Prime Minister this warning.' In a departmental minute on this report the comment was made: 'Sir M. Lampson is no doubt right in his conclusion that the Wafd should not be allowed to get away with any attempts to belittle the status of the Embassy or to overemphasise Egypt's new independence.'

These observations were made in January 1937. Almost exactly a year later Bentinck wrote a lengthy memorandum, in which he set out his own opinions on how the Egyptian authorities should be handled.

'We should,' he wrote, 'as a rule only intervene or speak out if
a) The terms and spirit of the Treaty of Alliance are not being loyally and wholeheartedly observed;
b) The Egyptian Government try to reinsure themselves by negotiating a treaty of non-aggression or some similar instrument with Italy or another power;
c) The Government do not take the necessary measures to improve the defence of Egypt;
d) The maintenance of law and order deteriorates to such a degree that the lives and property of foreigners are affected;
e) A danger becomes apparent that the Egyptian Government may be unable to fulfill their international obligations;

f) The Government of King Farouk should begin to support Arab elements hostile to His Majesty's Government.'

Bentinck was not the head of the department when he wrote this memorandum but was serving immediately under David Kelly, who had first-hand knowledge of Egypt, where he had been Counsellor. Nevertheless the memorandum was accepted *in toto*, and its contents were sent to Lampson in the form of an instruction. Bentinck liked and admired Kelly.

Shortly afterwards, commenting on a report by the Chief of the British Military Mission in Egypt on a conversation he had had with the Egyptian Prime Minister, Bentinck wrote: 'I am a little frightened by the excessively blunt and frank expression of opinion on the part of General Marshall-Cornwall in his conversations with and letters to Egyptian Ministers.' He added: 'However, if Sir M. Lampson thought that these were dangerous, he would presumably say so.'

Bentinck had a fairly high regard for Lampson. *I'd known him from the days when I was first in the Foreign Office, when he was head of the Central Department. He was able, intelligent and was much better when his first wife was alive*—that was to say, before his appointment as High Commissioner in Cairo. Nevertheless he remained ready to question Lampson's judgement, particularly on the subject of the Egyptian King.

'Sir Miles Lampson,' he wrote on one occasion, 'foresees that either King Farouk will be an outstanding success or an abysmal failure with grave results to the whole constitutional regime. The odds seem to be on his being a failure, as, apart from his irresponsibility, capriciousness, irregular habits and frivolity, he appears not to have a very nice character and to be as vindictive as his father.'

Less than three months after coming of age Farouk chose a chief political adviser named Ali Maher Pasha against strong Wafdist opposition, and some two months later appointed a new Cabinet, which was presided over by Mohammed Mahmoud Pasha and which did not contain a single Wafdist minister. Mohammed Mahmoud Pasha wrote a friendly letter to Cadogan 'as one Balliol man to another', but this was not enough to persuade Bentinck that the new Government would be either desirable from a British point of view or popular in

Egypt. Commenting on a report from Cairo, he wrote in May 1938: 'I would draw special attention to the statement that the vast majority of Egyptians dislike Palace rule more than any other form of regime and that sooner or later an anti-Palace front is likely to be formed.' A few days later he wrote: 'I hope that Sir M. Lampson will keep in touch with Nahas Pasha and Makram Pasha in spite of their present anti-British attitudes as it is possible that one day they may return to office.'

The anti-British stance of the Wafd was, Bentinck believed, largely tactical. In April 1939 he wrote: 'I suspect that if and when the Wafd come back into office, or if Egypt should suddenly find herself at war on our side, they would cease this anti-British campaign.'

It was a judgement that was to be vindicated by events nearly three years later. By then the threat from Rommel's army was apparent, even though not yet immediate, and King Farouk was known to be in contact with the Italians. With British tanks surrounding the palace, Lampson compelled the King to appoint a new Government. It was Wafdist in composition and headed by Nahas Pasha. Massively corrupt though it was, Nahas Pasha's Government was the most satisfactory which could have been formed for the further prosecution of the war by Britain and her allies.

Much of the work of the Egyptian Department in the years 1937–39 was concerned with military matters. Some of this arose from the evident need to strengthen the defences of Egypt. Some was a consequence of the 1936 treaty. In February 1938 the Committee of Imperial Defence reported with some satisfaction that an anti-aircraft brigade, a searchlight company and a light tank battalion would shortly be sent to Egypt, and the R A F squadrons in the Middle East were being equipped with up-to-date medium bombers. But it admitted that it still had to deal with urgent requests from Lampson for armaments, vehicles and stores, signalling and anti-gas equipment, hospital and mobile ambulance units, and reserves capable of reaching Egypt in fourteen days. Among the tasks assigned to Bentinck was the setting up of a committee to advise on the development of the harbour of Alexandria.

The 1936 agreement reached with the Egyptian Government provided for a redistribution of forces which would not necessarily be of benefit to the defence of Egypt. British troops were, for instance, to be moved from the Cairo area to the canal zone. *There were endless departmental meetings about this*, Bentinck said. *There was a lot of argument about the cost and so on*.

Bentinck remained sceptical of the outcome, and in April 1939 he wrote: 'In previous minutes I have alluded to the idea which I knew was at the back of the minds of a number of Egyptians that a Maginot line should be constructed in the western desert to guard Egypt against attack from Libya. I think that the money would be far better spent for all concerned in constructing this defensive line than in making expensive barracks and cantonments on the desert banks of the Suez Canal. My belief that these barracks will probably never be built remains unshaken, in spite of the voluminous correspondence that has taken place and the lengthy legal arguments to which this matter has given rise. Little progress seems to have been made during the last six months, and the Egyptian Parliament has not yet considered the draft law. In a month's time the weather will be getting warm in Egypt, the building committee will adjourn until October, and no progress will be made.

David Kelly, the head of the Egyptian department, commented on this that the General Officer Commanding in Egypt had made no suggestion for such a Maginot line and that at present there would not be enough troops to man it. The proposal does not seem to have been pursued further.

By the autumn of 1937 Italy had gained effective military control over the whole of Ethiopia, and such guerrilla activity as continued served little immediate purpose. Yet it was apparent to the British Foreign Office that, in spite of the commitment of large numbers of men and large quantities of money, the Italians were having little success in the development of their new colony. In a report presented in January 1938, to which Bentinck contributed, it was estimated that Italian-controlled forces in Ethiopia consisted of 56,000 white troops, 60,000 native troops and 95,000 white labourers, including settlers. Yet, the report concluded, 'up to date the only material advantage accruing to Abyssinia from the Italian occupation has been an improvement in communications'.

One of the recommendations which Bentinck made was that 'it would surely be to our advantage not to be in a hurry to grant *de jure* recognition and thus help to bolster up Mussolini's prestige'. Another was that a firm line should be taken in disputes over where the frontiers between Ethiopia and Kenya and Ethiopia and the Sudan lay. Representations should, he suggested, be made to the Italian authorities by the British Ambassador in Rome. 'If these representations do not bring them to reason, or if a rude reply is returned, then I submit that the next step is to place Sudan and Kenya police (not troops) beside the Italian posts in order that there can be no doubt that we are just as much in occupation as the Italians.'

The question of the frontiers did in fact reach Cabinet level, and Bentinck was required to be in attendance at a Cabinet Committee meeting at which it was discussed. *The chair, he said, was taken by the Prime Minister, Neville Chamberlain. Maps were shown and everything was explained to him. 'Oh no, I don't like that,' he said. 'The British public won't understand that. The British public and the House of Commons are used to frontiers with straight lines in Africa.' I ventured to point out that a party of officers had spent months finding out which was the most suitable frontier for the various tribes, for watering their cattle, and so on. This had no effect. 'I can't help it. A straight line.' After luncheon I went to do the minutes of the meeting with Edward Bridges, the Cabinet Secretary, who said to me: 'Well, Bill, the only thing that matters about this operation is that the Prime Minister should not appear to have talked balls.'*

As the threat of war increased the policy of accepting the Italian occupation of Ethiopia as a *fait accompli* was modified surreptitiously, and certain quantities of arms and money were smuggled into the country. The nature of the supplies sent was decided largely by Hastings (Pug) Ismay, who was then Deputy Secretary to the Committee of Imperial Defence. *Pug Ismay had been out there before the first war. He said the one thing you must have is a bandolier for cartridges—very useful—and the only money to send is the Maria Theresa dollar. So Maria Theresa dollars were minted here.*

It was one of the earliest and least well documented operations of the kind for which the Special Operations Executive was later created. It was also in line with an instruction which

Bentinck issued on 24 August 1939, when he wrote in a minute: 'Telegrams containing information on the situation in Abyssinia should be sent to Lieut.-Colonel J. C. F. Holland, D.F.C., M.I.(R), c/o Room 47.' Holland was the head of a small section in the War Office concerned with guerrilla warfare. This was one of the principal roots from which S O E was to grow.

In February 1938 Lord Halifax succeeded Eden as Foreign Secretary, Eden having resigned partly on grounds of policy and partly because of concern about his health. *Halifax*, Bentinck said, *was very good. He was very much the grand seigneur. Also very trustworthy. The important thing for a Foreign Secretary and for a diplomat is to be trusted.*

Changes took place too among the senior permanent officials, Cadogan replacing Sir Robert Vansittart as Permanent Under-Secretary and Vansittart being edged aside into an indeterminate post as diplomatic adviser. *Van was very good in many ways, but he was too highly strung. He had a great deal of ability. He could write plays and he knew French literature. Unfortunately his advice wasn't always couched in the best way and he was thought to be too radically anti-German. He always had been, largely because he'd had a brother killed in the first war. He was also thought to have too many likes and dislikes, one thing a diplomat shouldn't allow himself.*

How far such changes in personnel affected policy is debatable. Certainly there was a widespread awareness in the Foreign Office both of the seriousness of the German threat and of the inadequacy of British defences. This underlay much of the thinking which led to the fragile agreement which Neville Chamberlain brought back from Munich.

I was convinced, Bentinck said, *that Munich was the right thing. People who weren't alive at the time have no idea of the atmosphere. Munich was welcomed by a large proportion of the population, including the House of Commons. The Labour Party pretend now they were so bellicose and they would have saved Czechoslovakia. What with?* It is certainly true that when Chamberlain announced in Parliament that he had been invited to go to Munich cheering broke out in all parts of the House.

While accepting the Munich agreement as a necessity,

Bentinck was under no illusion about German intentions. He had known the German Ambassador Dirksen in Warsaw and liked him, and he maintained social contact with the German Embassy. Dirksen was then replaced by Ribbentrop. *I thought he was an awful bounder, a very second-rate German. I remember a cocktail party at the German Embassy. There was Ribbentrop talking to Frankenstein, the Austrian Ambassador, and walking up and down with him with his arm round him most affectionately. I knew that the S S and the German Army were greasing their boots to march into Austria in about a couple of days.*

I was asked to go to Nuremberg to see the great rally—I didn't think I'd really enjoy that. I didn't go.

One action which the Foreign Office took in response to the threat of war was to strengthen its representation in Berne, the post in which Rumbold had operated in the first world war. The man chosen as Minister was David Kelly, and Bentinck was offered the chance to succeed him as head of the Egyptian Department. *I was rather reluctant to take it on as I had never been in Egypt.*

Then another opportunity arose when Ralph Stevenson was appointed Private Secretary to Lord Halifax. Stevenson had for a short time been the Chairman of a little-known body called the Joint Intelligence sub-committee of the Chiefs of Staff. Bentinck was asked to take over from Stevenson, and he accepted the post. He did so with the rank of First Secretary and Acting Counsellor.

There has long been a widespread belief that before the second world war Britain had a powerful and effective secret service which was concerned with all aspects of intelligence. This is largely a fallacy. The secret service, which had a number of cover-names but is most conveniently known by the initials SIS, was formally established as a separate entity in 1909. In 1921 it was made exclusively responsible for espionage, which it carried out under Foreign Office control. Although its duties were defined as being 'inter-service', its funds were limited, and senior officers in the armed forces complained that it was better at obtaining political than military intelligence. It did however control the Government Code and Cipher School, which was later to operate in Bletchley, whose importance was to become evident before long to those who knew what it was doing.

In addition the Royal Navy, the Army and the Royal Air Force each maintained its own intelligence directorate, and contact between them was slight. Each made its own appreciations, nearly always with little reference to those of the others.

The Joint Intelligence Committee, or JIC as it came to be known, was created in 1936 at the suggestion, it seems, of Sir Maurice, later Lord, Hankey, who was then the Secretary of the Committee of Imperial Defence. This was an attempt to provide some co-ordination in the collation and appreciation of intelligence. Unfortunately the scope and powers of the committee, both before and shortly after the outbreak of war, were so limited that it achieved little of value. It was available to assist the Joint Planning Staff of the Chiefs of Staff, but, as the authors of the Official History of British intelligence in the second world war wrote, the JIC was for the first three years of its existence 'a peripheral body'. They added: 'The Planners did not call for its views except on topics on which intelligence was either of a routine nature or hard to come by. Nor did the JIC itself show any initiative in volunteering appreciations on more important questions like the intentions and military thinking of foreign states.'

Early in 1939 the Deputy Director of Military Intelligence put forward the novel suggestion that the JIC might have a Foreign Office chairman, ostensibly on the ground that this could make it a more effective body. *I suspect*, Bentinck commented, *that the War Office supported this idea in order to ensure that the chairman should not be a sailor.* Certainly the DDMI, in making his proposal, stressed the importance of not 'interfering with the liberty of action of the individual departments'.

The Directors of Intelligence of the three armed services were all members of the JIC, but in the early months of the war, while paying lip-service in this way to the concept of joint intelligence, they rarely attended the committee's meetings. Deputies were sent instead, and it was not until February 1940 that all three Directors of Intelligence were present at a JIC meeting.

To begin with, as Bentinck put it, *I found the situation a little*

Victorian child

Edwardian boy

Schoolboy

Guards Cadet Officer

Locarno, October 1925

(*Photograph: University of Birmingham*)

Young diplomat

Paris Embassy

Intelligence chief extraordinary

Visiting Auschwitz
(*Photograph: L. H. Massey*)

The Ninth Duke of Portland   (*Photograph: Allan Warren*)

difficult, as I was lower in rank than the Directors of Intelligence, who all thought that a war was no matter for a civilian. Nor was he provided with a staff which could be expected to cope with the problems likely to arise. *There was a major and a typist, and that was that.*

In short, although there was a Joint Intelligence Committee in being, there was hardly any product which could be classified as joint intelligence. Britain had in fact no equivalent to the efficient and well-organized French Deuxième Bureau.

Within a year of the outbreak of war, the JIC was to function as its name implied. Before this happened intelligence failures occurred comparable with and related to the major operational disasters of the time.

While working at the Foreign Office Bentinck was living just off Park Lane. *An uncomfortable flat, expensive and uncomfortable. What you might call a penthouse.* He and his wife were still maintaining the façade of a marriage.

Then one day, when he was in Stevenson's office in the process of taking over the duties of chairmanship of the JIC, the telephone rang. The caller was Stevenson's wife, from whom he was separated, announcing that she was returning to England. Stevenson was appalled. *Then the telephone rang again, and a rather incomprehensible Hungarian maid, whom we had to look after the children, rang up from the country to say that my wife had left. She didn't say where she was going, but she'd gone off with the children. She rather thought she'd gone to take a boat at Glasgow for America. It was like a French farce, one wife coming back and the other going off.*

The Hungarian maid's understanding was right. Bentinck's wife had, without warning, removed herself and their two children to the United States.

It could at least be argued that by leaving when she did Bentinck's wife rendered her principal service to her country of adoption. Relieved of a marriage which now offered little but emotional stresses, he was able to devote all his mind and energies to the task facing him.

CHAPTER 10
Failure of Intelligence
(1939–40)

The proper function of an intelligence service is to bring the right information to the right people in the right way at the right time. During the second world war the British War Cabinet, the Chiefs of Staff and those in direct command of operations received information on which they could base their decisions from a wide variety of sources. But in the first months of the war nearly all parts of the machinery for obtaining information were deficient to a greater or lesser extent. The machinery for processing it was even more unsatisfactory.

SIS was neither as effective at the time of the outbreak of war as its international reputation implied nor as weak as a few widely publicized instances of failure have led many people to suppose. Much of its reputation was based on the skill with which the British secret service had been portrayed in works of fiction, and this in itself had a certain effect on the enemy in wartime. Both Himmler and his equally ruthless associate, Reinhard Heydrich, were addicts of British spy fiction, and Heydrich even signed some of his internal correspondence with the letter 'C', the well-known symbol of the head of the British SIS. Admiral Canaris, the professional head of the Abwehr, by contrast, was much less respectful of SIS. He described its members as amateur and considered them inferior in calibre to those of France, the Soviet Union, Japan, Italy and Poland.

One of the strengths of SIS has derived from the fact that Britain had a world-wide empire and trading interests almost everywhere. In consequence there was no shortage of patriotic British citizens in foreign capitals and ports who were able and willing to supply information when called upon to do so. But neither these nor other sources of information could be exploited fully because throughout the inter-war years the

Treasury consistently starved SIS of funds. In 1935, two years after the advent of Hitler to power, when new cuts were imposed on the service, Admiral Sir Hugh Sinclair, the head of SIS, pointed out that its entire annual budget amounted to the cost of maintaining one destroyer in home waters.

A number of the senior officers in SIS had seen service in India, where for the maintenance of rule over a large territory, with small armed forces and a mere sprinkling of British civil servants, good intelligence was a necessity. There were also a perhaps surprising number of Armenians and other former citizens of the Russian Empire. *I had dealings with SIS continually*, Bentinck said. *I could really say daily. I did not think very highly of a number of its members.*

When Admiral Sinclair died of cancer in November 1939, *Stewart Menzies was the next senior officer there and got the succession. He would not have held the job for more than a year if it had not been for Bletchley. He was not a very strong man and not a very intelligent one.* The outstanding officer in SIS was, in Bentinck's opinion, Claude Dansey, a veteran of the Matabele war of 1893.

SIS's control of the Government Code and Cipher School dated back to shortly after the first world war. During that war a group of naval cryptographers under the direction of the celebrated Admiral known as Blinker Hall had successfully read German wireless signals. The group remained in being as part of the Admiralty until, on Curzon's insistence, it was brought under Foreign Office control.

In the inter-war years the GCCS had a number of successes, including, for example, breaking the chief Japanese Army and Navy ciphers. But unlike the Polish Cipher Bureau it had been unable to penetrate the German system based on the machines known as Enigma.

The story has been told several times of how Commander Alistair Dunniston, the head of GCCS, Stewart Menzies and Dilwyn Knox, a member of the distinguished literary family, attended a secret meeting in Warsaw in July 1939, and of how shortly afterwards reconstructed Enigma machines were made available to SIS and the French Deuxième Bureau. The Warsaw meeting was to have consequences of invaluable importance, but before the early summer of 1940 the practical value of such Enigma messages as were deciphered was slight. This was largely because of the time lags which then occurred between receipt and deciphering.

Indeed until after the fall of France the advantage gained by deciphering enemy messages lay heavily with the Germans rather than the Western Allies. The German B–Dienst was able to read the main British naval cipher up to the late summer of 1940. Messages between the French High Command in Paris and French army groups were also read. So were Belgian ciphers.

The intelligence directorate of the three armed services received most of their information in time of peace through comparatively overt channels, particularly the reports of naval, military and air attachés. Some of them were excellent, though they varied of course according to the quality of the individual. Outstanding among them were the reports sent from Berlin just before the second world war by the Military Attaché, Kenneth Strong. These were among the factors which persuaded Neville Chamberlain's Government to introduce conscription.

Although a posting as a service attaché in an embassy could be regarded as a pleasant interlude in a man's career, intelligence appointments were normally shunned by ambitious officers, particularly in the army. Haig once said that 'intelligence is rather a special kind of work and has a very small place in the Army in peacetime.' This was in line with much military thinking. Intelligence was considered of some account in the Indian Army, but elsewhere it lacked any of the traditions in which even the most modest of regiments could take pride. As a result, a problem which was to confront Bentinck throughout the war was what he called *the rather delicate one of the calibre of officer who is in intelligence*. This was evident even at the highest levels. *I think that the reason for the mediocrity of the directors of military intelligence was that officers who went into intelligence were not regarded as likely to command troops and rise to the top rank.*

The Royal Navy was rather better equipped in the early months of the war to obtain and assess intelligence than the Army. The achievements of Admiral Hall in Room 40 in the first world war had created a tradition of respect for the possibilities of intelligence. Unlike the War Office the Admiralty was an operational headquarters and there was no phoney war at sea. As a result naval intelligence officers were directly concerned with operations from the outset. Yet in the Navy too intelligence had been regarded as a backwater in the inter-war years, and there was really no such being as an intelligence officer on board HM ships.

Being less bound by tradition, the Royal Air Force might have been expected to be readier than the other services to take advantage of modern methods of obtaining information. In fact, in a branch of intelligence in which it was later to make a contribution of major importance, that of photographic reconnaissance and interpretation, its record before and shortly after the outbreak of war was lamentable.

The possibilities of photographic reconnaissance had been recognized in the first world war, yet the Air Ministry took no part in aerial photography between 1918 and 1935, when a certain number of pictures were taken of territories bordering on Ethiopia. The revival of photographic reconnaissance for intelligence purposes was due to private enterprise or, as Bentinck put it, to *a buccaneer called Cotton*.

Sidney Cotton was an Australian, the son of a rich sheep farmer, who bought an aircraft out of his inheritance and was recruited to work for SIS. Even after war was declared the most successful early sorties for photographic purposes were for some time carried out by Cotton. Similarly, of a Swiss machine then found indispensable for certain kinds of photographic interpretation only two specimens could be found in Britain when war broke out. One belonged to the Ordnance Survey and the other to a private company in Wembley. At the outbreak of war the Navy had no officers trained in photographic interpretation, the Army had one, and the RAF half a dozen. Not until April 1940 was it found possible to take an aerial photograph of the German naval base at Kiel.

Reports from British embassies and legations abroad were the kind of intelligence which Bentinck had long been trained to assess. Yet for a time he, like others, was misled by information, or lack of it, emanating from the British Embassy in Paris, particularly when it concerned the French Army. *In the phoney war we did not realize the state of the army.*

We would have realized if Charles Mendl had been functioning and there'd been more wide-awake people at the Embassy. They just hadn't got on the right wavelengths. A different picture emerged when two generals whose judgement Bentinck respected visited the French Army. *Pug Ismay came back from a visit to France in the latter part of the winter of 1939–40 very pessimistic about French morale. The same applied to Dallas Brooks, who expressed the view that sitting in idleness in the Maginot line was undermining French morale.*

Information from prisoners of war had long been recognized as a major source of intelligence, and a Combined Services Detailed Interrogation Centre under War Office administration was ready to operate as soon as war broke out. It was no fault of those in charge that, because there was so little action involving British forces on land or in the air in the first six months of war, the number of prisoners interrogated was small and the information obtained from them slight. Similarly there was a paucity of captured enemy material from which conclusions could be drawn.

A Ministry of Economic Warfare was also established, one of whose tasks was to be the assessment of economic conditions in Germany. It had to rely largely on published information, and some time elapsed before these assessments were much more than pointers to matters of possible future interest. Of more immediate value as a source of intelligence was a new service provided by the B B C. This was based on the work of a multilingual body in Evesham, whose members recorded news bulletins and commentaries broadcast from all parts of the world. A daily digest was then compiled of what had been taken down.

Among the early shortcomings of the intelligence services was one which was to be rectified with much success later. This was the lack of topographical information. It was apparent even at the highest levels. Recalling events in 1940, Churchill wrote: 'We had not the admirable map rooms of more coherent periods.' The shortage became more alarmingly clear when British forces went into action. For planning raids on Norwegian airfields occupied by the Germans in 1940 Bomber Command had to rely on a 1912 edition of *Baedeker.*

In the early months of the war Britain was not without allies who had well-developed intelligence services. Kenneth Strong, who was to become General Eisenhower's chief intelligence officer and, after the war, the first Director-General of Intelligence in the Ministry of Defence, considered that shortly before 1939 the French Deuxième Bureau was 'the most competent intelligence organisation in the world'. This was an opinion to be respected, for Strong wrote with more authority and insight on the subject of intelligence than perhaps any other senior British officer of the second world war. That the Deuxième Bureau was not as successful in practice as it might have been was, Strong believed, largely because the excellent analyses made by Colonel Gauché, its head, did not always reach the highest quarters, where decisions were made. Nevertheless it was recognized in the British War Office that much could be learnt from the Deuxième Bureau, and Strong himself, when preparing for a visit to France in 1940, was told to accept French estimates and information where they differed from British ones, as they were more likely to be correct.

Shortly after the Munich agreement Colonel František Moravec, the head and virtual creator of the Czechoslovak intelligence service, transferred thirty agents and all his files to Britain, where he worked closely with Claude Dansey. From Britain he continued to control a high-grade agent inside the Abwehr named Paul Thummel, who, until he was caught, was able to provide information of considerable value, particularly on the German order of battle.

Poland had organized her military branches on lines similar to the French, with a Second Bureau responsible for all intelligence. When the country was overrun in 1939 separate organizations were left behind to promote active resistance and to provide intelligence. The value to Britain of the intelligence sent from Poland was to grow appreciably from the time when Hitler began in earnest to plan an attack on the Soviet Union.

These various sources of information could and, as happened in most cases, would be improved in time. For Bentinck the more immediate task was to manage the JIC in such a way that, in contrast with what had been happening hitherto, it could begin to carry out the task assigned to it. This had been defined in a directive as

i) The assessment and co-ordination of intelligence received from abroad with the object of ensuring that any Government action which might have to be taken should be based on the most suitable and carefully co-ordinated information obtainable;

ii) The co-ordination of any intelligence data which might be required by the Chiefs of Staff or the Joint Planning Sub-Committee for them;

iiii) The consideration of any further measures which might be thought necessary in order to improve the efficient working of the intelligence organization of the country as a whole.

That the directive was not carried out for some time was due mainly to the continued resistance of the other committee members to the very concept of joint intelligence. *The various services and their intelligence divisions*, Bentinck said, *each thought they were the best informed, and this applied also to the Foreign Office. Consequently the JIC received no encouragement to make appreciations, and the Directors of Intelligence did not urge that the JIC should volunteer them.*

In adopting the attitude they did, the Directors of Intelligence were reflecting the views of their own superiors. In 1940 'the leaders of the three Services,' Churchill wrote, 'had not yet got the conception of the war as a whole, and were influenced unduly by the departmental outlook of their own Services.' To break down this resistance required, on Bentinck's part, an understanding of the personalities involved. It also needed what Captain Charles Drake RN, a seaman-cum-stockbroker, who worked closely with Bentinck during the war, called 'subtle handling of his committee members' and 'patience and diplomatic scepticism which helped the Directors to weather some dangerous gusts of inter-service disagreement and personal dislike'. As Bentinck himself put it, *occasionally I had mildly and as tactfully as possible to assert my position as chairman.*

The outstanding character among the Directors of Intelligence was, by common consent, Rear-Admiral John Godfrey. Ewan Montagu, a distinguished barrister who served under him, stated that Godfrey was the only man to whom he would 'give the accolade of genius, certainly as regards intelligence work'. He added: 'In most ways I disliked him as a person.' Godfrey, who was appointed Director of Naval Intelligence early in 1939, received much guidance from Admiral Hall, who urged him to act on his own initiative. He knew how to delegate authority and was able to take a broad view. He had a wide range of contacts, including bankers and newspaper proprietors. One of his sources of information was Lord Tyrrell, the former British Ambassador in Paris, who warned him that Admiral Darlan was not the simple sailor he was sometimes thought to be, but a man to be distrusted. He had an imaginative and able personal assistant in Ian Fleming, the future creator of James Bond, who had worked with Reuter's before the war and had been recruited for intelligence work by Sir Robert Vansittart on the recommendation of the Governor of the Bank of England.

John Godfrey, Bentinck said, *was highly efficient, an excellent organizer and very intelligent, but a difficult character who did not get on with the other Directors of Intelligence.* As Patrick Beesly, Godfrey's biographer, put it, 'He made little attempt to conceal his contempt for colleagues of lesser mental calibre.'

The Director of Military Intelligence, Major-General P. C. (Paddy) Beaumont-Nesbitt, was a very different character. An Etonian, a Guards officer and a future Gentleman Usher to the Queen, he was a man of considerable charm, but certainly of lesser mental calibre than Godfrey. *A very nice fellow*, Bentinck said, *a dear fellow, great fun, but he assured us on one occasion that the French had five generals just as good as Foch.* Beaumont-Nesbitt had been Military Attaché in Paris from 1936 to 1938.

The Air Ministry was represented for a time by A. R. (Archie) Boyle, but when he left to become the director of intelligence and security at the newly formed SOE he was replaced by Charles Medhurst, *a most able fellow*, in Bentinck's judgement. Professor R. V. Jones confirmed this view. 'He understood intelligence,' he wrote, 'and was excellent to work for.'

There was also a representative of the Ministry of Economic Warfare named Noel Hall. *He was rather touchy, and the military were inclined to snub him occasionally.* Hall was later replaced by Geoffrey Vickers, who was accepted more readily. No doubt the fact that he had won the V C in the first war contributed to this.

The blending of these varying personalities with their distinct sectional interests into a cohesive and effective committee was achieved only slowly, and with the exercise of patience. This was a quality which Bentinck had shown before but it was one for whose exercise wartime conditions do not normally allow much scope. In Bentinck's own words, *it wasn't till after the fall of France that the JIC really came into being.*

Although the JIC was one of their own sub-committees, the Chiefs of Staff made little use of it during the first six or seven months of the war. The Chairman of the Chiefs of Staff Committee when war broke out was Air Chief Marshal Sir Cyril Newall. The other members were Admiral Sir Dudley Pound, whom Bentinck recalled from the time when they had both attended the Lausanne conference, and General Sir Edmund Ironside. Two of the three, Pound and Ironside, were already, in Bentinck's judgement, *played out.*

On 6 September these three service chiefs met and made certain decisions on 'the dissemination of important information'. The first was 'to inform H M the King of the situation daily'. The others established the method of bringing 'vital information' to the War Cabinet. This was to be done 'via the Departmental War Rooms to the Central War Room and thence to the Cabinet Office', which in turn would be responsible for passing the information to the ministers concerned.

Arrangements were made as soon as war broke out for the Joint Planning Staff to be in a neighbouring room when the Chiefs of Staff met. No such arrangements were made for the JIC. In the later years of the war the JIC as a body would attend Chiefs of Staff meetings every week. Up to the time of the fall of France it did so only once. The JIC's own meetings were held, not in the vicinity of the Cabinet Offices, but in a house in Richmond Terrace, *my Uncle George's house*, as Bentinck put it.

On 14 September 1939, when the Chiefs of Staff decided to call for 'an appreciation of the possible future course of the war', the task of preparing it was given to the Joint Planning Staff. At a meeting early in October Ironside took it upon himself or, in other words, the War Office to provide 'an intelligence map' of the situation on the western front for the benefit of the other Chiefs of Staff at future meetings.

Almost the only papers called for from the JIC in the early months in which the Chiefs of Staff showed much interest. were one on 'reports of a German secret weapon' and one on 'measures to be taken in the event of the overrunning of Holland or Belgium or both'. In the first the JIC, which was still under Stevenson's chairmanship, had concluded that Hitler, when referring to a 'weapon in which we are unassailable', was referring to the power of the Luftwaffe. The point was made that 'waffe' in German meant a weapon. The second report, which was approved by the Chiefs of Staff, called for co-ordination of policy with the French, who, the Chiefs of Staff added, 'might themselves have thought of similar action'.

One consequence of the lack of co-ordination of intelligence was a proliferation of reports. The official history of British Intelligence described the Cabinet in the early months of the war as being 'deluged with summaries'. Churchill in *The Gathering Storm* described how the Chiefs of Staff, having reached their decision, reported them to their respective ministers, who met at the Military Co-ordination Committee. At this 'there was a copious flow of polite conversation, at the end of which a tactful report was drawn up by the secretary in attendance'. Then came a meeting of the Defence Committee of the War Cabinet, when 'all had to be explained and re-explained'.

As Prime Minister Neville Chamberlain did institute an inquiry into the intelligence services. This he entrusted to Lord Hankey, but nothing much came of it. One reason for this was that Hankey was expected to concentrate on the relationship between SIS and the security organization, MI5. This was not a particularly profitable field of inquiry. Moreover Hankey, after a career of great public service as official and administrator, had briefly become a minister. As such he was an enthusiastic supporter of Chamberlain, and when Chamberlain's Government fell he fell too.

The first serious test in action which the British intelligence service as a whole faced in the second world war came in the spring of 1940 when Hitler decided on the occupation of Norway and Denmark. This test it comprehensively failed. The British Government as a whole had no foreknowledge of German plans, and the occupation of Denmark and the landings in Norway in April came as a total surprise. One of the daily reports issued by the JIC did suggest the likelihood of a German landing in Norway. This was based on information from the British Naval Attaché in Stockholm, Captain Henry Denham, who drew his conclusions from conversations he had had with Swedish staff officers. But with a lack of any corroborative evidence the report was understandably given little credence. An officer who took the report to Churchill later quoted him as saying: 'I don't think so.'

When British forces were sent to Norway to oppose the Germans, the movements of HM ships were generally made known to the German Navy by the reading of ciphers. By contrast the British, once they had landed, operated with little knowledge either of the terrain or of the strength of the forces opposing them.

Hitler did, it is true, decide on the Norwegian campaign with little more than a month to prepare for it, being influenced by the very real threat of Allied landings in Norway. This made the task of the intelligence services harder than it might otherwise have been. There was also a reluctance on the part of the British operational command to ask for intelligence assessments because of a mistaken belief that to do so might widen the circle of those in the know, and thus jeopardize the security of operations. But this was in itself a condemnation of the way in which intelligence services were then expected to function.

A month after the invasion of Norway the German High Command launched its main offensive in the west with attacks on the Low Countries and France. Once again the Allied intelligence services failed badly.

That the Germans should move on to the offensive in the

west was not in itself unexpected. There had indeed been much speculation on the form the attack might take. The JIC, after considering various possibilities, had come to the reasonable, but not very satisfactory, conclusion that 'which of these courses Germany will select will depend less upon logical deduction than upon the personal and unpredictable decision of the Fuehrer'. Nevertheless the Germans repeatedly achieved almost complete tactical surprise.

Worst of all, perhaps, was the lack of any effective co-ordination between the Allied intelligence services. Churchill later recorded that when General Gamelin informed him that there was no strategic reserve to counter the German breakthrough, 'it came as one of the greatest surprises I have had in my life'. 'Why,' he asked reasonably enough, 'had the British Government, and the War Office above all, not known more about it?'

Certain successes were achieved in the field of intelligence. When a liaison officer on von Brauchitsch's staff, while escaping capture, left documents in a staff car giving details of the German order of battle, action was promptly taken. The information was passed to the War Office, and two divisions were transferred to plug a gap. This, it has been claimed, played a major part in saving the British Expeditionary Force from almost total destruction.

The JIC was now called upon, for the first time, to make strategic assessments of immediate consequence. On 15 May 1940, for instance, it reported: 'Germany is in control of Holland except Zeeland. The most serious attack at the moment is that on the Sedan sector. The next twenty-four hours should show whether this attack is likely to have very serious consequences for the Allies. The complete German plan has not yet been disclosed. It seems possible, however, that it may comprise two major movements, one in the South to envelop the Maginot Line on both flanks and the other to sweep North East towards the Channel ports.'

Unfortunately such appreciations were almost out of date by the time they were issued, and, given the German superiority in arms and strategy, it is questionable whether, even with the best intelligence, the breakthrough and subsequent defeat of the Allied armies could have been long delayed. What is certain is that better co-ordination of intelligence would have prevented tactical surprises from being achieved. A curious incident which occurred some weeks before the German offensive was launched served to illustrate this.

Shortly after the German campaign in Poland Admiral Canaris made the acquaintance of the wife of the former Polish Military Attaché in Berlin. Her name was Halina Szymańska, and for reasons which were not apparent to her at the time Canaris arranged for her and her children to settle in Switzerland. Her mother remained in Warsaw, and for a time mother and daughter communicated through Canaris. In Switzerland Halina Szymánska knew a Pole named Count Horodyski, who was working for SIS.

In early March, Bentinck said, *I noted amongst the SIS reports on my desk one which purported to be through a delicate source—if I remember right—and said that the attack would come between 7 and 13 May and that the main thrust would be through the Sedan area. I thought this interesting, but did not attach any particular value, as no source was indicated, which was usual with the SIS reports. If the source was thought to be important, this was indicated, but without any names.*

After the war Count Horodyski told me the origin of this report. Horodyski was an Austrian Pole, who had been very useful to us in the first war and had remained in contact with Colonel Dansey between the wars. He told me that the wife of the Polish Military Attaché in Berlin was friendly with Canaris and had received a message from him to meet him at the restaurant of the railway station in Lausanne, as he would be passing through there on his way to Rome. It was in this restaurant that Canaris was said to have passed on the information about the future attack.

Had I known the origin of this report, Bentinck said, *I would have paid more attention to it. I believe that Admiral Canaris and certain other German officers would have liked the war to end in a stalemate which would have enabled the army to get rid of the Nazi Party and the Führer. Canaris probably calculated that if there was a stalemate between the Anglo-French and German forces neither would wish a repetition of the trench warfare of 1914–18, and that peace could be concluded once Hitler had been disposed of.*

Dr Józef Garliński, the Polish historian, who had the remarkable distinction of obtaining his PhD at the age of fifty-nine with a thesis based on his first-hand experiences in Auschwitz concentration camp, talked to Halina Szymańska of this event many years later. By then she was living in England under another name, having remarried. She told him that her last meeting with Canaris had been in a restaurant in Milan and that information about the German attack was brought to her by Hans Gisevius, the German Vice-Consul in Zurich, who was later to be heavily involved in the plot to kill Hitler in 1944.

The differences between her account and Bentinck's were of detail, understandable in recollections of events which had occurred more than forty years earlier. Whichever was the correct version, it is clear that information about where and when the main German attack would take place was available to the British intelligence services and was neglected.

This was not the fault of any individual. The Germans were at the time skilfully spreading misleading reports about their intentions, with Canaris himself playing a leading part in this. It was the fault of a system which, partly because of excessive concern with maintaining the secrecy of sources, did not properly serve the true purpose of intelligence, that of bringing properly analysed information to those who had to make the crucial decisions.

CHAPTER 11
Will Hitler Invade?
(1940)

The total defeat of the Allied armies and the overrunning of the Low Countries and France produced a nation-wide shock in Britain, whose intensity it must be difficult for anyone who was not adult at the time to appreciate. Millions of people who had been lulled by the gentle rhythms of the phoney war, and had come to regard the fighting as something happening to other people and at a comfortable distance away, were brought to a new realization that the war was their concern and that they themselves were immediately threatened. Those who had been in action, or directly concerned with it, were aware that Britain's conduct of the war had up till then resulted in a series of disasters. If capitulation and total humiliation were to be avoided new measures and new men were clearly needed. Churchill as leader and the new all-party Government, which took office in May 1940, were greeted with trust and hope. In the new climate of opinion almost any decision or change, provided it was thought of benefit to the war effort, was found acceptable.

Changes in the organization of the intelligence services at the highest level were immediate. Churchill instructed the Chiefs of Staff 'to review the system by which intelligence was related to the Government's procedure for taking operational decisions'. As a result the JIC received a new directive on 17 May. It read:

'The Joint Intelligence Sub-Committee are responsible for taking the initiative in preparing, at any hour of the day or night, as a matter of urgency, papers on any particular development in the international situation whenever this appears desirable to any member, in the light of information that may be received from time to time in the Foreign Office or in the Service Departments. The members of the Joint Intelligence Sub-Committee, who are in the closest touch with the intelligence situation, are in a better position than anyone else to decide when such papers should be prepared, and it is for this reason that the responsibility is placed on them.

'The object of these papers, *which should be as brief as possible*, will be:

'i) To draw attention to any information received in the Foreign Office or in the Service Departments which appears to be of special importance, to assess its value, and to supplement it with any other information available so as to present the broad deductions which are to be drawn.

'ii) To summarise broadly the available evidence regarding the intentions of the enemy or developments in any of the "danger spots" in the international situation, and to set out the conclusions which may be drawn therefrom.

'The utility of such papers will very largely depend upon the rapidity with which they can be prepared and issued.'

An additional point made was that 'nothing in this directive is intended to change in any way the other duties of the Joint Intelligence Sub-Committee in regard to the preparation of reports and memoranda on specific subjects, either on their own initiative or as directed by the Chiefs of Staff'.

The very phraseology of the directive, with its use in the first sentence of such terms as 'urgency', 'initiative' and 'any time of day or night', implied a new approach to the problems of intelligence. The directive conferred on the committee the authority and responsibility it had needed. Confidence was indicated, and it was made clear that from now on the fullest demands would be made on the committee's resources and ability.

The directive was issued within a week of the new Government being installed in office. It was Churchill's first major contribution, as Prime Minister, to the reorganization of British intelligence and one which was to be of lasting importance. As an immediate measure it was an expression of the requirement which he was shortly afterwards to sum up with the words: 'Simplify, shorten and reduce.'

One of the government's new measures which made an immediate and wide appeal was the formation of a volunteer body for home defence, known at first as the Local Defence

Volunteers and later as the Home Guard. A unit was formed within the Foreign Office, and Bentinck, loaded down though he was with his new responsibilities, volunteered his services. So, among others, did Roger Makins, later Lord Sherfield and a future British Ambassador to the United States. Makins was the head of the Central Department which was concerned with Germany and most of the countries then under German occupation.

Recalling this episode some forty-five years later, Lord Sherfield said: 'One of our duties was to help guard the Foreign Office at night. That meant four hours on and four hours off, sleeping in the Foreign Office. We were issued with American 300 rifles, a consignment of which had just arrived from the United States, and bayonets. We had with us one security officer, who was armed with a revolver. We would march up and down the Foreign Office passages at night with our fixed bayonets.'

After a time both men began to have doubts about the utility of these proceedings.

Lord Sherfield went on: 'One night I said: "Look, Bill, this is the most ridiculous nonsense. What could we do supposing there was an assault on the Foreign Office? We couldn't fire our rifles. We're incapable of using our bayonets. The only person who could do anything would be the security guard with the revolver. You're certainly the busiest officer in the Foreign Office. I'm probably the second busiest. We're perfect fools to stay up every night carrying out this performance."'

They therefore resigned, and Bentinck was able to sleep rather more often in his parents' house in Harley Street. From there he would come to the Foreign Office, immaculately dressed as always and accompanied by his dog. This was a Kerry Blue, who had been with him in Chile and who came to be known as the Intelligence Dog. Before long, as the pressure grew, Bentinck was unable to sleep as far away as Harley Street. *I migrated and lived in the War Cabinet offices underneath the ground. I had a room there. The air conditioning was very bad. It was run by marines who used to bring you tea in the early morning.*

That the man who was principally responsible for informing the Government, on the basis of all the intelligence available, whether there would or would not be an invasion of Britain should spend a high proportion of his nights as an ineffectual private soldier in a voluntary and still largely useless army was characteristic of much that happened in Britain during the months immediately following the retreat from Dunkirk.

The possibility of a German invasion and the form it might take were the principal preoccupations of the JIC throughout the summer of 1940. In a paper issued on 30 May the committee listed six main sources of information which had to be considered. The first of these was described as 'wireless intelligence sources'. This of course was a reference to the deciphering of Enigma messages or, as the process came to be called, Ultra. The priority given by the committee to this source was indicative of the importance which Ultra was now beginning to acquire.

The next three sources were shipping preparations, military concentrations and 'actual sailing'. The fifth was described as 'actions and movements of enemy agents in the United Kingdom'. This had become a possibility because the British intelligence services had already begun to achieve one of their greatest triumphs of the war, the capture and control of German agents in Britain. On the sixth source, agents in enemy countries, the committee commented: 'Their reports are unlikely to be received in time.' The day when there would be a supply of agents parachuted or otherwise infiltrated into occupied territories with radio sets with which they could communicate with Britain had not yet arrived.

The committee concluded its report with two recommendations. One was that 'The Admiralty and Air Ministry should, at once, formulate plans to establish a regular and systematic air and photographic reconnaissance of all parts of the enemy and occupied coastlines from which an invasion might be launched.' The other was the immediate establishment of 'an inter-Service Intelligence Sub-Section to weigh up all relevant information' on the possibilities of invasion. This, it was stated, could be accommodated in the Admiralty.

Both these recommendations were put into effect. The regular surveillance of the enemy-controlled coastline and of what came to be known as 'invasion barges' was the effective beginning of a vast programme of aerial photography, whose value became increasingly apparent as Britain moved over to the offensive. The formation of the new intelligence sub-section was the beginning of the permanent staff which the JIC needed to carry out its duties properly.

The idea of forming special inter-service units of officers whose full-time job would be to deal with particular problems of intelligence assigned to them by the JIC, had emanated from John Godfrey. Later there were a Future Operations (Enemy) Section formed on the same lines and an Advanced Enemy Planning Section. Both of these were presided over by the same man, a former Naval Attaché in Berlin. Out of all this grew the Joint Intelligence Staff, the permanent body which, it could be argued, the JIC ought to have had from the outset.

On the question of whether an invasion was or was not to be expected the JIC expressed an opinion as early as 21 May. 'The example of the successful German seaborne invasion of Norway,' it stated, 'should not hold good for an invasion of this country unless Germany had obtained complete air superiority. Our defending naval forces would have some protection from our fighter forces operating from their home bases and enemy transports would be objectives for our bomber forces also operating from their close home bases. Provided our air forces are in being the reverse of Germany's advantageous air situation in Norway would apply to a certain extent, though not to the full extent, owing to the superiority in numbers of the German Air Force.'

Evidence did however accumulate that the Germans were making extensive preparations for an invasion, and the results of a comprehensive study of the possible forms and scale of an attack on the United Kingdom were summarized in a paper issued on 6 June. Reports of a possible sea-borne landing in Ireland from Spain were dismissed because of lack of supporting evidence. If landings did take place it was thought that they would be in an area between the Wash and Newhaven, although feints and diversions in other places were to be expected. But, it was emphasized, 'Germany has a large number of divisions available for invasion, but she will be unable to move them across the North Sea after the first wave until, through naval and air action, she has succeeded in reducing our fleet to impotence.'

Early in July the committee stated that Germany was 'making active preparation for raids in force or for invasion of the British Isles', but that these were unlikely to take place before the middle of July. To justify this assertion it quoted reports from a wholly dependable 'secret source' that the majority of the units of the German Air Force would not have completed their refitting before that date.

The assembly by the Germans of large numbers of small craft was considered closely, but on 16 July the conclusion reached was that 'there is, as yet, no reliable evidence to show that such small craft have been assembled on any large scale for an invasion'. By September German preparations were further advanced, and on 5 September the JIC stated: 'The available intelligence has shown and still shows that invasion or raids against the United Kingdom may be attempted in the near future.' But it added emphatically: 'Successful invasion of any sort depends upon sea and air superiority, and there is no indication that this superiority is or can be obtained by the Germans. It is our opinion that the Germans, while having brought to a high pitch of preparedness their plans for invasion, will not run the risk of a major defeat and consequent loss of prestige until they obtain air superiority.'

The committee then made another unambiguous forecast. This was that German efforts 'during the next two weeks will consist of intense air attacks on military and other targets.' It went on: 'It is also our opinion that the public should be warned to expect an increased scale of air attack in the immediate future.'

A fortnight after this report was issued Hitler ordered the dispersal of the invasion fleet in tacit recognition of the fact that Germany had lost the battle of Britain. The next phase of the attack, which came to be known as the Blitz, then began.

The authority and consistency of the JIC reports up to this point concealed wide divergences of view within the committee. Bentinck remained unshaken in his belief that the Germans would not invade without first obtaining air superiority. Beaumont-Nesbitt did not agree. *I remember*, Bentinck recalled, *an occasion in September 1940, when Paddy Beaumont-*

Nesbitt said: 'Anyone who thinks the Germans are not going to invade is mad.' To which I replied: 'Well then, you'd better telephone for a padded waggon to take me off to the lunatic asylum.'

The reports of the JIC had to be unanimous. The Chiefs of Staff would have accepted nothing else. To persuade Beaumont-Nesbitt to accept his judgement on military matters, Bentinck needed both powers of persuasion and carefully marshalled facts. *I always had to produce overwhelming evidence*, he said, *in arguments with my service colleagues*. How much the committee owed to Bentinck, and also to Godfrey, for their exercise of judgement was revealed by a single report which was almost wholly at variance with all those which the committee had issued up to then.

Early in September Bentinck had a short holiday. On 7 September, contradicting what it had stated two days earlier, the JIC issued a report, which contained the words: 'Our evidence of German preparation points to an intention to invade the United Kingdom. It is considered that these preparations are so advanced that invasion could be attempted at any time.' The report was signed neither by Bentinck nor by Godfrey. The three signatories were Beaumont-Nesbitt, Boyle and a deputy standing in for Godfrey named Roger Bellairs.

This *volte-face* by the JIC brought it briefly into line with much of the thinking to be found at the highest military levels. On 13 September General Brooke, later Lord Alanbrooke, then responsible for the military defence of Britain and before long to become Chief of the Imperial General Staff, wrote in his diary: 'Everything looks like an invasion starting tomorrow from the Thames to Plymouth.' Churchill was to write afterwards that in the late summer of 1940 'The Chiefs of Staff were on the whole of the opinion that invasion was imminent, while I was sceptical and expressed a contrary view.' In forming the opinions they did the Chiefs of Staff were certainly running counter to the advice given to them by their own intelligence sub-committee on every occasion except one.

A question closely related to the threats of invasion on which the JIC had repeatedly to pronounce judgement in the summer of 1940 was that of home security. In this it had the help of

MI5, for on 24 May 1940 representatives of this body, of SIS and of the Ministry of Economic Warfare were made full members of the JIC.

The Director-General of MI5 at the outbreak of war, Major General Sir Vernon Kell, had been in control of the organization for more than thirty years. During that time, within the limits which a democracy very properly imposes on such a body, he had formed it into an efficient force.

There were thousands of German citizens living in Britain when war broke out. Many were of course Jews and others bitterly opposed to the Nazi regime, but their very presence in large numbers offered the German Government an obvious opportunity to infiltrate its own agents.

Some eleven thousand Germans were interned shortly after war broke out. This served as an effective measure, but further problems of security were created, when refugees began to stream into Britain after the overrunning of the Low Countries and France, and again when Italy entered the war.

Kell was dismissed early in the war and replaced for a time by an executive committee. A Ministry of Home Security had also been formed, one of whose tasks was, in conjunction with the Ministry of Information, to make the general public aware of the threat posed by enemy agents. This was done to considerable effect.

The main problems of security which the JIC had to consider were therefore the handling of known German agents, internment policy and the co-operation of the general public.

In the summer of 1940 Britain was gripped by a form of spy-fever. Agents and lights flashing signals to enemy aircraft were suspected almost everywhere, and when reports circulated that German soldiers had been parachuted into the Netherlands dressed as nuns, any British nun going peacefully about her business was liable to be stopped and searched for hand grenades.

The JIC considered that a halt ought to be called to this, and on 3 July 1940 it reported: 'We recommend that the attention of the Ministry of Information should be directed to the danger of a state of nervousness and suspicion regarding parachutists and other enemy agents reaching such a point as to constitute a danger to the efficient working of the machinery of Home Defence.' It went on to recommend the issuing of orders that 'the unit originating a report of this nature should in all cases take steps to verify the report before passing it on'.

On the subject of internment the committee, in the face of a certain amount of public criticism, recommended strongly that there should be no relaxation of the general principles which had been adopted. 'There is abundant evidence,' it stated in October 1940, 'that in recent months the Germans have been troubled by a marked diminution in the amount of information derived from this country. That this is seriously exercising the minds of the German High Command is shown by recent activities on their part to endeavour to plant agents. It is surely more than coincidence that this lack of information dates from the time when large-scale internment of enemy aliens took place.'

Acting on the JIC's recommendations, the Chiefs of Staff agreed that there should be no relaxation of principles and regulations under which the internment of aliens was originally carried out; that the number and categories of aliens at large should be periodically reviewed 'with the object of putting every possible obstacle in the way of the establishment by the enemy of agents in this country'; that censorship of mail should be more thorough; and that conditions of internment 'should be ameliorated so far as possible so as to remove any possible grounds for public criticism'.

The policy was to be modified later. It has also been found easy to criticize in retrospect. There were indeed people interned in the Isle of Man who would have been able and willing to support Britain's war effort. But, given the circumstances of the summer of 1940, suggestions that any government responsible for the defence of the country would have acted much differently from Churchill's, or would have accepted advice other than of the kind offered by the JIC, lack realism.

The agents despatched by Germany who were captured in Britain in 1939 and 1940 often surprised the British intelligence services by their ineptitude. Their documentation and training were on the whole remarkably poor. One agent, for instance, had an identity card with six mistakes in it. Another was supplied with indifferently forged bank notes. Even more encouraging was the fact that several showed themselves ready to abandon any loyalty they may have had to Germany.

One of them, Arthur Owens, whose task was to recruit saboteurs among Welsh nationalists, seems to have put forward the suggestion himself that he should continue to communicate with Hamburg, but to do so under British control. This he did with considerable success, beginning in 1939 and continuing for some years. His value was enhanced in September 1940 when a new agent was picked up immediately after his arrival. This man had been instructed to contact Owens and gave the names of two more agents who were to be parachuted in shortly.

Once such a channel of communication with the German intelligence services had been opened up the choice of the material to be transmitted clearly called for policy decisions. For a time this was done under the direct control of the JIC, but as the work grew a new body came into being, under whose guidance the section of MI5 concerned continued to operate. This was the so-called Twenty Committee, whose name was derived from the double cross and whose chairman was the Oxford don and distinguished athlete, J. C. Masterman. The Twenty Committee met weekly and retained its close links with the JIC. *My concern with MI5 throughout the war*, Bentinck said, *was mainly in feeding stories to the enemy via the people who had been picked up.*

When it became clear that the Germans would be able to overrun France the JIC was called upon to give an assessment of Italy's intentions. On 25 May it reported: 'All the intentions point to the fact that Signor Mussolini has made up his mind to enter the war on the side of Germany, but there is no evidence available from which the date of such entry may be deduced.'

This was not a difficult forecast to make. More complex was the question of the intentions of the Spanish Government. On 15 June the JIC attempted to analyse these in a report which stated: 'Spain has not yet recovered from the effects of the Civil War and her internal conditions are extremely bad. Until recently Franco and a considerable majority gave the impression of being sincerely resolved to remain neutral.' There had however been reliable reports of the arrival of large numbers of Germans, including young men of military age, in Spain, and these seemed 'to point either to Franco having lost his control of the situation or to his having moved further towards the Axis Powers'. The committee did not find this evidence decisive, and cautiously, and perhaps wisely, concluded by stating: 'We would wish to defer any final pronouncement as to the future intentions of Spain until such time as HM Ambassador has submitted his views.' The Ambassador was Sir Samuel Hoare, whose appointment had been greeted in the Foreign Office with dismay but who was to fill the post with much competence. *He did well in Spain*, Bentinck said, which was certainly more than Cadogan expected.

On the subject of relations with France Bentinck's views were somewhat unorthodox. *Looking back, he said, I thought at the time and still think it was a pity that when leaving France the Ambassador, Sir Ronald Campbell, did not detach a member of his staff to be Chargé d'Affaires at Vichy. He would probably have had to go before long, but it would have shown that we did not wish to cut ourselves off from France.*

He was opposed to the ill-organized expedition to Dakar carried out in conjunction with the forces of General de Gaulle in September 1940. *The JIC maintained that the appreciations and reports coming through the French were too optimistic. I believed it had been called off when I went to rest at home for those few days in September. I was distressed when I heard what was taking place.*

He also questioned the desirability of promoting what might prove to be premature active resistance in France and elsewhere. *After the fall of France Churchill decided that we must foment revolt and sabotage in the occupied territories. I was summoned to see Hugh Dalton, the Minister who had been placed in charge of this work. He told me that the Prime Minister had said that Europe must be set on fire within three months. I said: 'I believe the time is not yet ripe. It will flicker shortly, and a lot of unfortunate people will be shot.' Dalton countered: 'These are the Prime Minister's orders and must be carried out.' That ended our conversation.*

Preoccupied though it was with Europe, the JIC was called upon by the Chiefs of Staff on 6 September 1940 to prepare a paper on 'how soon the Japanese could develop an attack against Malaya'. This had to be produced by 5 p.m. on the following day and in Bentinck's absence. The answers given were twelve days for mobilization, nine for passage and forty-five for capturing and consolidating bases and moving through Indo-China and Siam or alternatively, forty-eight for consolidating bases if the move was made through other parts of the British and Dutch East Indies.

As the JIC's responsibilities grew it improved its procedures and widened its resources. It had a very competent full-time secretary named Denis Capel-Dunn, of whom Bentinck thought highly. *He was a barrister with a not very high medical category, who'd been posted to the War Cabinet offices because of his ability in drafting.* It had too in Godfrey a fertile source of ideas for change and innovation.

One of Godfrey's suggestions which was adopted was a strict classification of the reliability of sources of information from A1 downwards. This helped the process of decision-making and also served to conceal, by the simple use of symbols, the nature of such a source as Ultra.

Another of Godfrey's proposals was put forward by the JIC to the Chiefs of Staff on 30 May. This was for an 'overhaul of topographical intelligence'. Additional staff was asked for and the request granted, and the JIC undertook to 'supervise the collection, collation and distribution of information'. The sources listed from which such information might be obtained were diplomatic and consular missions and offices, business firms, travel agencies, the AA and the RAC, the Royal Geographical and other learned societies, and British residents abroad.

The JIC was also required to examine and pronounce judgement on an early and tentative proposal for simulated operations designed to mislead the enemy. The suggestion was that a number of barges and other vessels should be assembled in a Scottish port, ostensibly for the purpose of invading Norway.

The JIC was unimpressed. It was already October, and the committee pointed out that 'in view of the impracticability of an invasion of Norway at the present season of the year and of our limited resources available for such an operation, which

139

are known to the German High Command, they would be unlikely to be deceived by such dummy preparations.' The committee added: 'The essence of such plans is that they should leak out, and, from the point of view of home morale, it would be unfortunate if, in view of the abortive preparations for the Finnish Expeditionary Force, the former Norwegian operations and the more recent operation at Dakar, the impression was given that preparations had been made for another expedition which had to be abandoned.'

The project was dropped, but the concept fitted ideas which Bentinck was then forming. *Quite early on in the war I had an idea that the Germans were putting out stories with a view to deceiving us and said: 'Two can play at that game.' I do not boast that I was the creator of deception, which was at first done in an uncontrolled way by SOE and SIS.* Before long the necessary control was imposed and a clear relationship established between the body responsible for deception and the JIC.

During the summer of 1940 there were times when those in the highest positions of authority in Britain believed that the nation's prospects were even worse than they were. *At the time of the evacuation from Dunkirk,* Bentinck said, *the War Cabinet offices were gloomier and more depressed than at any other period of the war. Pug Ismay told me that the Chiefs of Staff believed that we should only succeed in evacuating one third of the number that we actually did bring away.*

From time to time the JIC reports may have served a little to lighten that gloom. Realistic though they were and based on information which was nearly always discouraging, they maintained an equable tone throughout and had a reassuring air of authority.

By October a faintly sanguine note had even crept in. 'Great Britain,' the committee reported on 10 October, 'has gained three valuable months in which to strengthen her defences, has destroyed a large number of German aircraft, impaired the morale of the German and Italian people to some extent by successful air attacks, secured a greater measure of American co-operation and material help, and enhanced her prospects of successful resistance and ultimate victory.'

It was an expression of faith and hope of the kind which among the ill-informed public at large had long been widespread.

CHAPTER 12
Germany's Options
(1940–42)

The outcome of the battle of Britain had induced the German High Command to abandon one of the courses of action open to it. Many others remained. In a paper issued on 2 July 1940, when it had been still largely preoccupied with the threat of invasion, the JIC had considered some of these.

'Now that France has fallen,' the report stated, 'Germany's military superiority is such as to enable her to move in any direction she pleases with little or no warning. Germany may decide, as her next step, to undertake one or more of the following:

'a) a peace move coupled with proposals for the reorganisation of Europe;

'b) operations against the British Isles;

'c) operations against Russia;

'd) an advance into South East Europe;

'e) an attack on Africa.

'Germany's superiority in Europe is now such that she may profitably undertake more than one of these courses at the same time (with the exception of simultaneous operations against Great Britain and Russia).'

In the winter of 1940–41, and in the spring and early summer which followed, the principal task of the JIC was to forecast the directions in which Germany was likely to move. This required, as before, the assembly of facts and the preparation of analyses. It also called, increasingly, for an understanding of the personalities of the individual Chiefs of Staff and of how to present to them the results of the committee's deliberations.

Sir Cyril Newall had been succeeded by Sir Dudley Pound as Chairman of the Chiefs of Staff Committee, it being then the Royal Navy's turn to provide the committee chairman.

Pound, Bentinck said, *had been a very bright officer at Lausanne. He had aged tremendously since then.* He was no longer a fit man, yet he was to continue in his post long after he ought to have been retired on medical grounds. One of his future colleagues, Sir Alan Brooke, was to note in his diary: 'He is asleep seventy-five per cent of the time he should be working.' Pound was in fact suffering from a tumour on the brain of which his doctors were not aware.

Ironside had been succeeded as Chief of the Imperial Staff by General Sir John Dill, who remained in office until he was replaced by Brooke on 1 December 1941. *Dill was very able,* Bentinck said, *and I had a higher opinion of him than of his successor.* The Chief of Air Staff was Sir Charles (Peter) Portal, who took over from Newall on 20 October 1940. Bentinck described him as *the best of the Chiefs of Staff, the most intelligent and the calmest.* Dill was on record as having said: 'Churchill regarded Portal as the real strategist among the Chiefs of Staff.'

The members of the JIC would appear before the Chiefs of Staff every Tuesday morning at 10.30 in the Cabinet War Room in Great George Street. *I had to lead this little choir,* Bentinck said. *I gave an* aperçu *of the position as we saw it. Then they questioned us.*

In his dealings with the service chiefs Bentinck had a source of support for which he always remained grateful. This was General Ismay, whom Churchill had appointed as his principal staff officer. In this capacity Ismay was the link between Churchill and other highly placed individuals and also between the Chiefs of Staff and various subsidiary bodies. Before long he became himself a member of the Chiefs of Staff Committee.

Pug Ismay, Bentinck said, *was a remarkable person, highly intelligent, kindly but very firm, very clever in dealing with the PM and others. He was the prop and mainstay of the War Cabinet organization.* Lord Alanbrooke's biographer, David Fraser, wrote of Ismay's unorthodox appointment: 'Such a post could have been a source of constant friction. Instead it provided an unfailing emollient.' Ismay, he went on, 'interpreted strong men to each other without usurping the authority of any'. International recognition of Ismay's qualities was to be given when, in 1952, he was appointed the first Secretary-General of NATO.

Churchill, having issued the directive which in effect established the JIC as the supreme intelligence body, did not himself rely wholly, or even primarily, on it as a source of information. *Churchill*, Bentinck said, *had a tendency to create his own intelligence*.

On 5 August 1940 Churchill sent a memorandum to Ismay in which he stated: 'I am not satisfied with the volume or quality of information received from the unoccupied area of France.' He then went on: 'I do not wish such reports as are received to be sifted and digested by the various intelligence authorities. For the present Major Morton will inspect them for me and submit what he considers of major interest. He is to see everything and submit documents for me in their authentic form.'

Desmond Morton, Bentinck said, *had left the army and been employed by SIS. He gave Churchill all the information he needed to produce facts and figures in his speeches about the imminence of war and what the Germans were doing. In 1940 a job had to be found for him. He was a curious creature. An awful lot of talk. He didn't really play an important role*. It was not long before Morton drifted towards the background, the process being accelerated by Churchill's increasing interest in Ultra as a direct source of intelligence.

Churchill's tendency to make deductions from individual items of information emanating from Ultra, without reference to intelligence from other sources, was a cause of concern and at times irritation to the Chiefs of Staff. Ian Jacob, later to become Director-General of the BBC, who worked closely with Churchill as a member of the War Cabinet Secretariat, went so far as to say: 'My impression, looking back, is that once the Ultra business got well established Churchill didn't look at anything else.' General Jacob's recollection after some forty years may or may not have been altogether correct. What is certain is that Churchill's access to other sources of information enabled him to question the conclusions reached by the Chiefs of Staff and their intelligence sub-committee, and to indulge in the probing and goading which did so much to propel the war machine forward.

One example of such probing was a memorandum issued on 5 November 1940 in which he asked: 'How is the intelligence service organised, and who is the man responsible?' He could still not be given a clear answer, but increasingly the responsibility came to lie with the Joint Intelligence Committee and, particularly, its chairman.

In late 1940 and early 1941 the JIC was at times in danger of being diverted from its main task of assessing the enemy's intentions by the already large, and steadily increasing, number of its other activities. The official history of British intelligence described it at this period as being 'burdened with too many responsibilities'. It was also the period in which everyone's capacity for work in London was limited by prolonged and repeated air raids at night.

One of the committee's tasks was to prepare a daily telegram giving information to Dominion governments and British missions abroad. *This never contained anything really secret*, Bentinck said.

In March 1940 the JIC obtained the agreement of the Chiefs of Staff for the establishment of an Inter-Services Security Board 'for the co-ordination of all projects for sabotage and irregular activities'.

The committee continued to press for more and better aerial reconnaissance and obtained an assurance from Portal that more long-range Spitfires would be made available for this purpose.

The use of German agents for deception also continued to occupy much of Bentinck's time.

The Twenty Committee and MI5 dealt with about one hundred and twenty double agents, of whom they used thirty-nine effectively for appreciable periods. Masterman, its chairman, was in most respects a highly orthodox and conformist character, whose spiritual home was an Oxford in which success was measured by firsts and blues, with both of which he was liberally supplied. He also had considerable ingenuity, which he had demonstrated in some successful detective stories. *Masterman*, Bentinck said, *I saw very often. He used to come in wearing an old forage cap from the first war. He was a most amusing character and had a mind well suited to this operation.*

He and others used to come to see me, and I would make up stories for them to send to mislead the Germans.

Among the agents with whom Bentinck dealt directly was the Yugoslav, Dusko Popov, who had never had any intention of working for the Germans, but who had persuaded the Abwehr to send him to Britain, where he arrived early in 1941. He was then sent, after briefing by the Germans in Lisbon, to the United States. He brought with him an example of the microdot, then an almost unknown means of communicating secret information, a questionnaire on the defences of Pearl Harbor and the knowledge that the Japanese were interested in the experience gained by the British in bombing naval bases.

J. Edgar Hoover of the FBI was neither impressed by Popov nor in any way helpful to him. Among the reasons he gave for his attitude was that he was running the cleanest police organization in the world and he did not care for the fact that Popov had installed himself in a penthouse on Park Avenue with a girl-friend. Whether the United States could have more successfully repelled the attack on Pearl Harbor had Hoover adopted a more liberal attitude towards cohabitation must remain a question for speculation. Certainly Hoover's approach to Popov differed strikingly from that of Bentinck who, Popov later recalled, questioned him particularly closely about a visit paid by Admiral Canaris to Spain. The main purpose of this had been to continue negotiations following the meeting between Hitler and Franco at Hendaye on 23 October 1940. Then Franco had made extensive demands as a precondition to any possible attack on Gibraltar.

Bentinck's own daily examination of information coming in was detailed and thorough. *In the morning I read religiously through the Foreign Office telegrams. I questioned the heads of departments. I read the SIS reports, and then I read some press extracts on foreign affairs.* Other information had also to be taken in, and as the deciphering process became more successful the decrypts from Ultra grew in volume and importance.

For a time the practical value of Ultra was limited by the obvious need to keep the fact that the German ciphers had been broken a heavily guarded secret. Very few people were at first privy to the secret—in the Foreign Office, for example, only Cadogan and Bentinck. Gradually the circle was widened, but at first the burden of analysing information from Ultra and making the necessary recommendations had to be carried by the very few.

One early benefit derived from Ultra was the discovery that the Germans were reading British naval ciphers. The necessary changes were introduced, and these in themselves created doubts within the U-boat command about the security of Enigma. A steadfast refusal to believe that Enigma could ever be broken served to quell all doubts, as it was to continue to do throughout the rest of the war in spite of an appreciable volume of evidence to the contrary. As a means of linking the security of British ciphers with other security precautions the Inter-Services Cipher Security Committee, which had been formed in December 1940, was made a sub-committee of the JIC in September 1941.

The principal contribution of Ultra in 1941 was certainly to the war at sea. Indeed it was the Navy's newly acquired ability to locate U-boats in the spring of that year, and so prevent an even further growth in the destruction of ships plying to and from Britain, which may justify, perhaps more than any other happening, the claim that without Ultra Britain would have been defeated. The JIC was not however directly involved in the location of U-boats through Ultra or other means, this being the responsibility of the naval intelligence and operation staffs. Similarly operational intelligence about German targets and battle formations during the Blitz was handled by the Air Ministry, although the JIC was required to give its assessment of the effects of bomb damage.

A growing concern of the JIC in 1941 was the establishment of a satisfactory relationship with the United States intelligence services. Early in the year Colonel William Donovan visited Britain as a special emissary sent by President Roosevelt to assess present and future events, including the British capacity to resist. William Stephenson, the head of the British intelligence services in the United States, had informed Stewart Menzies, in advance of the visit, that Donovan had more influence with Roosevelt than Colonel House had had with Woodrow Wilson. The British intelligence services understandably took some trouble to show Donovan everything they wanted him to see.

In May Admiral Godfrey paid a return visit to the United States, representing the JIC as a whole and being accompanied by Ian Fleming. One of the lessons which the JIC considered it had learnt and ought to pass on to the Americans was that intelligence and other clandestine activities should be the responsibility of a single body. This Godfrey was able to convey personally to Roosevelt. Bentinck reiterated it later. *I said to Bill Donovan: 'Don't you make the mistake we made of having two separate organizations, one for skulduggery and the other for intelligence. Have one simple agency. Just one.' Little did I know I was giving birth to that monster, the CIA.*

When the Office of Strategic Services, the forerunner of the CIA, came into being shortly afterwards, with Donovan as its head, it did have responsibility for both intelligence and subversive action. Ray S. Cline, a future Deputy Director and historian of the CIA, was to state later that the OSS 'might never have come into being if it had not been urged upon the United States by the British and fashioned after the British intelligence system'.

That the JIC succeeded as well as it did in handling this multiplicity of duties, while concentrating on the main question of what the enemy would do next, was made possible by the establishment of the Joint Intelligence Staff to deal with day-to-day problems. This came into being in 1941, its organization being formally ratified by the Chiefs of Staff retroactively on 18 July. It consisted of officers from each of the armed services and representatives of the Foreign Office and the Ministry of Economic Warfare, the senior officer in each service having the rank of commander or equivalent. *As a full-time chairman*, Bentinck said, *I directed the activities of the JIS to a large extent*.

The senior officers tended at first to be professional sailors, soldiers or airmen. One of these was Kenneth Strong, whose knowledge of Germany Bentinck, having never himself served in the country, found particularly valuable.

Strong was later to give a pen-portrait of Bentinck at work at this period. Bentinck, he wrote, 'was an excellent chairman, tactful, relaxed and good-tempered; he would lean back in his chair with his hands pressed together and listen, looking very wise and cunning and keeping discussion to the point.

Eventually he would intervene in a slightly bantering manner which would remove the heat from really contentious issues. He had the scepticism that any good intelligence officer needs, and a mental awareness which usually put him that vital step ahead of the other members of his committee.'

A curious diary note dated 5 February 1941 gave some indication of the regard in which Bentinck was beginning to be held. This was made by Robert Bruce Lockhart, former secret agent and gossip columnist for Lord Beaverbrook, who had become Director-General of the Political Warfare Executives. He wrote: 'Dallas Brooks tells me that question of new head of Secret Intelligence Service is again under discussion. Been offered to Cavendish-Bentinck. Dallas advised him not to take it.' Bentinck had no recollection of this offer being made, but that it was discussed in well-informed circles is significant.

Nevertheless Bentinck's substantive rank in the Foreign Service was still that of First Secretary. Although he was made CMG in the 1941 New Year Honours list, he was not confirmed in the rank of counsellor until the beginning of the next year. This was not an insuperable disadvantage, for a civilian is not obliged to display his rank on his shoulder or his sleeve. But it remained a handicap. *At one time I suggested to Pug Ismay that they should appoint somebody of higher rank than myself, but he said: 'Oh no, you soldier on.'*

On 10 October 1940 the JIC listed five possible courses of action to be taken by Germany. These were invasion of the United Kingdom; an intensified blockade of Britain and air attacks on her shipping; an attack on Egypt; an advance south-east through Bulgaria; and the capture of Gibraltar followed by occupation of north and north-west Africa.

On invasion it stated that 'the time of year, the failure to gain air supremacy and some measure of control at sea, and the increased strength of this country would render invasion hazardous.' The blockade and attacks on shipping could 'be expected to continue in the hope of stopping our trade and defeating this country'. Invasion of Egypt, it was stated emphatically, 'will be undertaken by Italy with support of German forces'. On south-east Europe the committee's forecast was: 'We may expect that military and political domination of Roumania will soon be completed. This is likely to be followed by similar domination of Bulgaria. The Axis powers would then be in a position to exert pressure on Yugoslavia, Greece and Turkey. Greece might be occupied to forestall any possibilities of the Greek harbours being used by the British Fleet.' On the fifth option the committee stated: 'The balance of the evidence does not suggest that Spain will at present willingly enter the war on the Axis side.'

Some two months later, on 13 December, the JIC reported: 'It seems likely that the original German intention was to undertake no new operations this winter, but to devote the period until next spring to preparing for operations on a large scale, possibly in the direction of the Near East. In the meantime, air and sea action against Great Britain was to continue, and pressure exerted against the Balkan countries, both by subversive action and diplomatic activity. The ill-timed attack by Italy on Greece has upset this programme. Italy is becoming, in the military sense, no longer an asset, but a severe liability to Germany.' The committee went on to consider the possibility that, in order to strengthen the block-ade of Britain, Germany might seize some of the Spanish or Portuguese ports on the Atlantic. It concluded that there was 'no definite evidence of any kind' to suggest that this would happen.

These were accurate forecasts of events as they were to occur. They did not prevent the British from suffering further defeats or even enable British forces to be adequately prepared, as experiences on the mainland of Greece and Crete were to show. But they did help the Chiefs of Staff to decide the difficult questions of where, at a time when the initiative still lay almost entirely with the enemy, Britain's limited resources of firepower and trained manpower could best be deployed.

One German venture which was not foreseen was a coup d'état in Iraq. This took place in April 1941 and brought the pro-Axis politician, Rashid Ali, into power. The failure seems to have been in Foreign Office intelligence. *The Foreign Office*, Bentinck stated, *were probably reluctant to send on SIS reports which conflicted with those received from the Embassy*. Information received through Ultra soon made it clear that intervention by

German armed forces would only be on a small scale, and the next month the status quo was restored.

In the early months of 1941 a number of reports were received of movements of German troops eastwards, north-eastwards and south-eastwards. These were brought to the attention of the Chiefs of Staff and were mentioned repeatedly in the weekly résumés which the Chiefs of Staff's secretariat issued.

On 22 January it was stated that there were three armoured divisions in Roumania and a new armoured division in Czechoslovakia. The résumé on 6 February reported: 'The number of German troops in Northern Norway, viz 3–4 divisions, is considered larger than is necessary for mere garrison purposes, but not excessive against a possible Russian move, or against a British landing which the Germans are said to expect. The number of German divisions in Roumania is now thought to be at least 15.' A week later the divisions in Roumania were estimated to number twenty-two or twenty-three. A week after that the résumé gave the number of divisions in 'Poland excluding the Corridor' at fifty-six, of which three were armoured. Attention was also called to the quality of the troops being moved. On 27 February it was stated that 'the army being assembled in Roumania contains a number of very efficient and experienced armoured and infantry divisions and some well-tried generals.'

On 27 March the Chiefs of Staff's résumé mentioned 'reports suggesting that Germany intends to attack the USSR', and a fortnight later these reports were described as 'numerous'. It was evidently felt that some comment on the reports was called for. 'The German object,' it was stated on 4 April, 'is undoubtedly to exert military pressure on Russia to prevent Russian interference in German plans in South-East Europe, and also to influence Russia's diplomatic decisions.' But a fortnight later doubt could be seen to have crept in. 'It is impossible,' the résumé stated, 'to determine whether the persistent rumours, coming from so many quarters, that Germany is intending to attack Russia, are merely being spread by Germany as part of a war of nerves or have some more solid basis in fact.'

The uncertainty felt by the Chiefs of Staff about German

intentions reflected, and to a considerable extent was conditioned by, a similar uncertainty within the JIC. Bentinck came to the conclusion fairly early that a German attack on the Soviet Union was likely. He attributed this to some extent to his instinct. *My instinct*, he said, *is better than my sense. I had at the back of my mind the French saying*: on revient toujours à ses premiers amours et aussi a ses premières haines. *I thought sooner or later Hitler would go for Russia.*

Then I got reports that the Germans had begun again to subsidize the anti-Bolshevik organizations in the Caucasus. We heard from the Poles that they were increasing the length of the runways at Warsaw airport on a very large scale. I thought to myself: they're not doing that for the Lufthansa. Then there were the troop movements. The Germans were taking troops away from the channel ports and moving divisions to Cracow.

The JIS came up with a report, and I remember Colonel Shoesmith who by then was the Secretary of the JIC—a very able officer, who later commanded troops in Korea—saying to me: 'The JIS have gone off their heads. They're suggesting that the Germans are going to attack Russia.' I said to him: 'No, I asked them to draft this report.' Of course it was very difficult to get the Directors of Intelligence to swallow it.

This difficulty continued to be formidable. One reason was an understandable unwillingness to believe that Hitler would commit an act of such consummate folly as to order an invasion of the Soviet Union when so many other lands were available for him to conquer. Another was the reasoned belief that Hitler was exercising pressure on the Soviet Union in order to obtain the kind of agreement which would suit him. The appalling consequences of such an agreement, whereby the Germans might have obtained all the economic concessions they wanted, were ably set out in an annex to a report produced by the JIC in May.

When I was on my trips in Germany after 1947 I became friendly with Helmut Wohlthat, who had been one of the chief economic negotiators for the German Government. He told me that in 1941 he was appointed German economic representative in the Far East with the rank of Ambassador. On his way to Tokyo, on instructions from his Government, he negotiated an economic agreement with the Soviet Union, of which he was extremely proud. Not long after his

arrival in Tokyo he received news of the German attack on Russia.
Subsequently he received a message from Ribbentrop, telling him not
to worry, as the German forces would soon have annihilated the
Russian armies and established communication with the Far East and
would obtain the same advantages as were contained in his agreement.

Meanwhile there were authoritative voices which cast
doubt on the likelihood of a German attack. One of these was
that of General Sikorski, the Polish Prime Minister, who was
well served by his intelligence organization, even though there
was a breakdown in secret radio communications from occupied Poland for about a month in April and May 1941. On 23
May Sikorski submitted a lengthy paper, whose concluding
sentence was: 'At present a German attack on Russia does not
seem to enter into consideration.'

The JIC was called upon to comment on Sikorski's paper.
One of its observations was: 'We do not agree that the Red
Army is grouped offensively vis-a-vis Germany, nor do we
think that any military offensive by the Soviet Government is
today within the realms of possibility.' Another was: 'We do
not agree that a war against the Soviet Union would necessarily be unpopular in Germany.' The comment on Sikorski's
final sentence went no further than to state: 'The best evidence
available does not support General Sikorski's conclusion.'

On 30 May the JIC expressed the opinion that 'Germany's
next move will be an attempt to enforce her demands on the
Soviet Union by means of a threat of force which could be
immediately turned into action.' On 12 June it went further
and stated: 'Fresh evidence is now at hand that Hitler has made
up his mind to have done with Soviet obstruction to Germany
and intends to attack her. Hostilities therefore appear highly
probable though it is premature to fix a date for their outbreak.
It remains our opinion that matters are likely to come to a head
during the second half of June.'

This could be considered a belated expression of opinion.
Aware though he had been for some time of the likelihood of a
German attack, and clearly though he had stated his own
expectations, Bentinck was not as successful as he might
perhaps have hoped in persuading his colleagues to agree with
him.

Churchill was to write later that intelligence received

through Ultra 'illuminated the whole scene in a lightning flash. The sudden movement to Cracow of so much armour could only mean Hitler's intention to invade Russia.' This was an understandable exercise in dramatization. In fact the evidence of movement of armour to Cracow and elsewhere had been available for some months. The difficulty, which few succeeded in overcoming until a comparatively late stage, was to discern just what it meant.

The appreciations made by the British intelligence services were certainly superior to any which the Soviet Government accepted. Some ten days before hostilities began the Foreign Secretary, Anthony Eden, called Bentinck in to his office to talk to the Soviet Ambassador, Maisky. *I spent twenty minutes*, Bentinck said, *trying to convince Maisky that a German attack was imminent. I remember saying that the attack would take place either on 22 or 29 June and that I would put my money on the 22nd.*

It was in fact on Sunday 22 June that the German armies invaded Soviet territory and a new dimension was given to the war.

CHAPTER 13
Decisions which Lost the War
(1941–42)

In a paper which it issued nearly a month before the German invasion of the Soviet Union, the Joint Intelligence Committee stated: 'A war forced by Germany on the USSR would be likely to have the effect, so far from disintegrating the Soviet Government, of strengthening its hold upon those parts not actually occupied by the Germans.' The committee also expressed the opinion that to be successful 'a military campaign in the USSR must be over by November'.

At the end of July 1941, by which time the German armies had been moving forward relentlessly for nearly six weeks, the JIC was called upon to produce a further report. Its title was 'The effects of a Russian collapse', but the title did not accurately reflect the committee's opinions.

'We consider,' the committee stated, 'that the conclusion of an armistice or peace treaty between Germany and Russia is improbable.' It reported 'signs (of which we await confirmation) that the Soviet Government have a plan to move the seat of government', and called attention to 'evidence that the Soviet Government's economic plans envisage a long war'. It also drew encouragement from early evidence of what came to be known as the 'scorched earth' policy. 'Germany's difficulties,' the committee stated, 'in controlling and administering territory would be increased by the efficacy of the steps taken by the Russians to destroy communications, buildings and crops. There is evidence that the Russians are acting accordingly.'

Germany's plans for the areas overrun by her armies seemed less clear to the committee. 'There are signs,' it reported, 'of Germany's reluctance to commit herself as to her intentions for dealing with the Soviet territory she may occupy.' The likelihood seemed to be that Germany would create a number of states with puppet governments. 'In the Ukraine the Germans would be able to use Ukrainian separatist feelings to their advantage. Skoropadsky himself [Hetman during the German occupation in 1918] would be a poor tool, but there are other Ukrainian quislings with the Germans who might prove useful.' Encouragement of Cossack independence also seemed likely. 'Since the German invasion the Moscow wireless has been careful to emphasise the patriotism of the Cossacks—perhaps a sign of nervousness.'

In expressing in the summer of 1941 confidence in prolonged and effective Soviet resistance to the German invaders the JIC was out of tune with the Chiefs of Staff. Sir John Dill, Chief of the Imperial General Staff, was on record as stating that 'The Germans will go through the Russians like a knife through butter.' Bentinck himself was also out of tune with some members of his committee. Kenneth Strong was to write later: 'On one important point Cavendish-Bentinck differed from his colleagues. He thought that the German invasion would end in failure, while other members of the committee felt that the Russians would last less than six weeks.' The only other prominent and well-informed individual whom Strong could recall as having shared Bentinck's confidence was Lord Louis Mountbatten.

In believing that the Germans might set up nominally independent governments in the Ukraine and elsewhere, Bentinck and his colleagues were committing the error, which all those whose task it was to forecast German policy in the second world war had at some time to guard against, of assuming that reason and common sense would prevail over crude ideology. The example of an apparently independent Ukrainian state could have been of immeasurable benefit to Germany. Yet when a German General, Kurt Zeitzler, proposed the creation of such a state to Hitler he was told that it would be tantamount to jettisoning the war aims of national socialism.

For at least a year JIC forecasts of developments on the Russian front continued to be rather more hopeful than the Chiefs of Staff thought justified by the evidence. On 1 June 1942 the JIC produced a report on the likely outcome of the huge German summer offensive. 'The German troops,' it stated, 'will no doubt recover from the trials of the winter and will still be an efficient fighting machine. From the economic point of view, the Russians can, if necessary, withdraw several hundred miles.' Politically, the committee considered, the Stalin regime would be able to withstand even the loss of Leningrad, the Moscow industrial area and the Caucasian oilfields, although it did not believe such losses likely.

'With such large forces engaged on both sides, fairly evenly matched,' the report went on, 'and with so big an area for manoeuvre, it is unlikely that a decisive phase will be reached by August. Between August and October, however, events may move rapidly to a climax.' It was in fact in August that the Germans began to invest Stalingrad, threatening repeatedly to capture the city, and in November that the Russians counter-attacked there.

The conclusion reached in the report was: 'The Russians may, therefore, initially suffer reverses, but they should be able to diminish the momentum of the German advance and bring it to a standstill on a line which might be the Tula-Voronezh-Kamensk railway, thence the River Donetz to Rostov.' At a meeting of the Chiefs of Staff it was formally recorded in a minute that the report was 'slightly over-optimistic'. Another JIC report of the same period was deemed by the Chiefs of Staff to have 'presented a picture rather too favourable to the Russians'.

The commitment of the great bulk of the German armed forces to the Russian front limited the options open to the Axis powers elsewhere in Europe and Africa. This the JIC had no great difficulty in appreciating. In the spring of 1942 reports were received of the construction of invasion craft and improvements of airfields and communications generally in Bulgaria and Roumania. 'We have considered,' the JIC reported on 26 April, 'the possibility of an attack by the Axis with the limited object of gaining control of the Dardanelles, the Sea of Marmora, the Bosphorus and the Black Sea, such an attack being part of the main drive towards Caucasia. We conclude that this operation is unlikely.' Similarly the committee decided a month later that, in spite of evidence of the regrouping of Italian forces and their training in combined operations, 'no attack is planned on either Corsica or Tunis'.

'Germany,' the committee stated, when analysing German intentions in 1942, 'is so deeply committed in Russia that no substantial change of plan this summer is open to her.' German strategy in 1942 and 1943 would therefore be
'a) to eliminate Russia this year;
'b) to beat the Allies to the post in Egypt and the Eastern Mediterranean;
'c) to consolidate her position in Western Europe by the spring of 1943 so as to render herself impregnable to invasion from the west.'

Of the seriousness of the threat to the British forces in Egypt the JIC had no doubt. On 11 July 1942 it reported: 'There are indications that the enemy's offensive in North Africa has been suspended for the time being. The present lull is only a pause, and Rommel intends, as soon as adequate supplies and reinforcements reach him, to renew the offensive.' This would 'take the form of an attempt to defeat the 8th Army and seize the Delta and the Suez Canal'. There was 'no evidence of an intended seaborne attack on Palestine or Syria in the near future'.

In one sphere of operations Britain began in the spring and summer of 1942 to move, to some extent, on to the offensive. This was in the war in the air. The JIC was called upon to assess what had been achieved to date by Bomber Command, and on 10 April 1942 it produced a paper entitled 'Effects of Bombing Policy'.

The success of the policy being pursued would depend, the committee stated, perhaps a little caustically, on 'a considerably higher proportion of the aircraft despatched bombing the target than has been usual hitherto'. No credence was given to suggestions that bombing by the R A F would seriously affect the opening phases of the campaign about to be launched in Russia. On the other hand it was accepted that long-range bombing had 'affected German morale and had had considerable effect upon the population in areas attacked'. In the absence of first-hand information emanating from Germany about the true effects of bombing the committee recommended that an independent inquiry should be made into the effects of bombing in Britain and that appropriate conclusions should be drawn.

The report was an early exercise in a kind of compromise with which members of both the JIC and the JIS would become more familiar, when dealing with the bomber offensive, as the war progressed. This was the striking of a balance between different interests and different viewpoints. On the one side were the claims advanced by the Air Ministry for the achievements of Bomber Command and the Ministry of Economic Warfare's estimates of their effects on the German economy. On the other was the scepticism of those less directly involved. The Chiefs of Staff made it clear that they were not much impressed by the compromise contained in the report of 10 April, even though it was, within its limitations, both truthful and accurate.

The JIC continued during 1941 to issue forecasts of Japanese intentions. On 13 September it stated: 'Japan has not, at present, got sufficient land forces to stage a full-scale attack against Malaya without reducing her present degree of readiness vis-à-vis Russia.' The report went on: 'An attack on Malaya will not be made by Japan until she has made up her mind to risk war with the United States as well as ourselves and possibly the Dutch. We do not believe she would be prepared to take that risk until the Russian position in the north has been weakened.' A further conclusion reached was that 'if Russia collapsed we believe that Japan would attempt to seize the maritime provinces before making an intensified attack on China.'

At that time much of the information from which the JIC drew its conclusions about probable happenings in the Far East came from the British Embassy in Tokyo. *We were influenced by the people in Japan*, Bentinck said, *and we had an Ambassador, Craigie, who was a worthy character, but not the shrewdest and most far-sighted fellow*.

The Japanese attack on Pearl Harbor on 7 December and American lack of preparedness were to become the subject of a lengthy congressional inquiry, and volumes have been written on the attack itself and the events leading up to it. The clearest lesson which emerges from all this is that while the gathering of information, largely through the breaking of ciphers, was of a high order, the machinery for analysing and disseminating the information was gravely inadequate. One reason for this was that secrecy was all too often practised at the expense of efficiency. Another was the lack of liaison between the United States armed services.

The findings of the congressional inquiry, which were published in 1962, included the statement: 'The Pearl Harbor air attack was the only part of the Japanese war plan which took Washington unawares.' That may have been true, but unfortunately what was known in Washington was not always known to the commanders in the field. At the time of the attack on Pearl Harbor the Commander-in-Chief of the Pacific Fleet, Admiral Kimmel, was not on the distribution list for decrypts of the Japanese ciphers. Nor was his army counter-part, General Short. Although the creation of a new joint army-navy intelligence committee, not unlike the British JIC, was authorized on 11 October 1941, the committee did not actually meet until after the Pearl Harbor attack, and there was, in consequence, no inter-service organization for evaluating intelligence of Japanese intentions.

Much of the reluctance of even the best-informed people to believe that the Japanese would attack Pearl Harbor did of course stem from the intrinsic improbability of such a happen-ing. That the Axis powers should, in the course of less than six months, commit two acts of such catastrophic miscalculation as the invasion of the Soviet Union and the attack on Pearl Harbor, which between them ensured their ultimate loss of the war, was indeed barely credible.

One consequence of the entry of the United States into the war was an enhancement of the efficiency of both the American and the British intelligence services. Already in the summer of 1941 Churchill, against the advice of Stewart Menzies, had insisted on the sending of Ultra decrypts to Washington. About the same time four American cryptographic experts arrived in Bletchley with information about how the Japanese diplomatic ciphers could be read, a process which had the code-name 'Purple'. In certain respects Purple was even more enlightening than Ultra. Decrypts through Ultra were primarily though not exclusively, of tactical value. Purple decrypts included summaries of far-reaching conversations on political and strategic objectives which the Japanese Ambassador in Berlin had with Hitler and Ribbentrop. The pooling of information from the two sources was reflected in the appreciations of Japanese intentions made by the JIC in 1942.

On 18 April, for example, the committee reported that Japan intended to complete the occupation of Burma and the Philippines, achieve peace in China, occupy bases in the south-west Pacific to cut the sea route from the USA to Australia, and compel the Allies 'to disperse troops and naval forces by raids or threats of raids'. It went on: 'In the east Japan is likely to avoid a major fleet action. In the west Japan aims at occupying Burma and possibly pushing beyond the frontier into parts of Bengal and Assam. In the south we do not believe that Japan aims at the occupation of Australia and New Zealand, but believe that she would be content with their isolation.' Six months later, in a paper on communications between Germany and Japan, the JIC was able to present the Chiefs of Staff with details of every vessel known to have been engaged in blockade-running, flights of all aircraft between the two countries and the war materials required by both.

For the processing and distribution of intelligence the USA continued to adopt British models. *The Americans were good*, Bentinck said, *but they hadn't had the practice we had. They followed our set-up of the JIC, and there was a direct contact through a representative of the JIC (London) in our mission in Washington. We got on well with them, and we made every effort to get on well. The same thing with them. Anyone who didn't get on well was sent somewhere else. The collaboration was, I would almost say, impeccable.* He did however add: *Immediately after Pearl Harbor I had to preside over a joint meeting between the JIC and the American intelligence representatives in London. After the meeting I said to Alec Cadogan I thought the US Navy and Army would just as soon fight each other as the Japanese.*

There were other improvements too in the operation of the British intelligence services in the latter part of 1941 and 1942. General Claude Auchinleck, the Commander-in-Chief in the Middle East, was later to express the opinion that but for the intelligence received through the reading of enemy signals

Rommel's army would have reached Cairo. (Against this must be placed the fact that Rommel himself was considerably helped by the reading of the highly informative messages which the US Military Attaché in Cairo was transmitting.)

Increased aircraft production made it possible for most photographic requirements to be met by the spring of 1942. A limited number of aircraft were also made available for dropping agents into enemy-occupied territories. This was at first of particular benefit to the Royal Navy and the Royal Air Force in the war at sea. An excellent chain of coast-watchers was set up in Norwegian ports, and the movements of German warships in and out of French harbours were also regularly reported. In addition to the agents despatched or equipped by SIS were those of SOE who, although not primarily engaged in espionage, frequently sent reports of value. Indeed in one occupied country, Denmark, SIS eventually handed over the gathering of intelligence to SOE, which had much better links with the Danish resistance.

A new body was set up, with the cover-name of London Controlling Section, to co-ordinate projects for the deception of the enemy. Its head was a stockbroker, Lieutenant-Colonel John Bevan, who in September 1942 was made responsible to the Director of Plans. *I rated Johnny Bevan's section very highly,* Bentinck said. *Johnny Bevan was in the army in the first war and then a junior military secretary at Versailles. He was very quiet, very shrewd. Dennis Wheatley was one of the most active members of the section. He had a mind for that kind of thing.*

Problems of internal security were also appreciably lessened by the outbreak of war between Germany and the Soviet Union. Although Hitler and Mussolini had had their admirers in Britain before the war, the number of them who carried their admiration to the point of committing treason was infinitesimal. There was therefore no difficulty in containing any threat to security which the British Union of Fascists presented. The Communist Party, believing, as it did until June 1941, that Britain was engaged in a capitalist war which it had no reason to support, presented a more complex problem.

In principle communists were debarred from employment in highly secret organizations, though, as is now well known, the bar was not always imposed in practice. Whether communists did represent a serious threat to Britain's security against attacks by the Axis powers before June 1941 is questionable. What is certain is that once the Soviet Union had been attacked British communists became enthusiastic supporters of full-scale war. This in itself relieved MI 5 of one of its burdens and enabled it to concentrate all its resources on the more immediate threat.

At one time or another Bentinck encountered during the war all the most notorious undercover agents of the Soviet Union operating in Britain. *I met Philby once*, he said, *when he came to a JIC meeting. I recollect saying as he left the room: 'That's a queer fish. What's his background?' I received the answer, 'He's old St John Philby's son,' to which I said: 'I suppose that accounts for it,' and moved on to the next item. Guy Burgess I met twice, and on each occasion I had a clear impression that he had formed as great a dislike for me as I had for him. Donald Maclean was known by the typists in the Foreign Office as 'Smarty-pants' Maclean, as against 'Fitzwhiskers' Maclean. I knew him to be drunken and rackety, but it never occurred to me that he was a spy. Nor did this occur to people in the service who knew him very intimately, e.g. Tony Rumbold. It's important, though considered rather distasteful, to take an intelligent interest in the private lives of one's subordinates.* Nor at any time did Bentinck suspect Anthony Blunt, who occasionally attended JIC meetings as a representative of MI 5. *He struck me as being rather a dull dog.*

With all the improvements in sources of intelligence there remained one important theatre of operations from which information remained extremely hard to come by and on which JIC assessments had to be subject to reservations. This was the Soviet side of the fighting front. On 1 June 1942 a JIC report contained the statement: 'Our information about the dispositions, resources and war potential of our Russian ally is considerably less than our information about the enemy.'

A week before the German invasion took place the JIC had been instructed 'to consider the principle of sending advisers on a mission to the USSR if she were attacked by Germany'. In the event a mission was despatched. It contained representatives of the intelligence services, which had a chain of command comparable with that of the admirable organization in the United States headed by William Stephenson. In practice as an intelligence-gathering machine it was wholly ineffectual. It was given no information of importance and could learn little else. In order to assess the strength of Soviet forces, therefore, the British intelligence services had to analyse what was known of the German order of battle through Ultra and other sources and then make the appropriate estimates.

The Western Allies for their part were faced with a continual problem when deciding how much information to pass on to the Soviet Government. On the one hand, it was clearly important to reveal as much as possible of what was known of German strengths and intentions. On the other, it was learnt through Ultra that the Germans were reading a number of the Soviet codes and ciphers. This in itself was a compelling reason for not revealing the secret of Ultra to the Soviet Government. Fortunately, the Soviet agents in Britain, such as Philby, were not able to reveal it. What the effect on the Allied conduct of the war might have been if Philby and the other Soviet agents had been privy to the secrets of Ultra must remain a subject for speculation.

In practice one of the methods adopted for conveying information of strategic importance to the Soviet Union was to leak it through SIS to known Soviet agents in neutral countries, particularly Switzerland. This served incidentally to enhance the credibility, and also the post-war reputations, of the Soviet agents involved.

An important change in the management of the Chiefs of Staff's Committee took place in the spring of 1942 when Admiral Pound gave up the chairmanship. He did so ostensibly on the ground of increasing deafness, though he remained First Sea Lord and therefore a member of the committee. By the system of rotation Pound was succeeded by General Sir Alan Brooke, who remained chairman until the end of the war and was to be the committee's dominant personality.

Brooke completed the agenda of meetings in about half the time which Pound had taken. His authority over the army commanders in the field was impressive, and his was the voice which represented the views of the Chiefs of Staff to Churchill. *Brooke*, Bentinck said, *was a powerful personality. He used to gobble like an irate turkey. He was very difficult and could be pig-headed. He got an idea into his head, and it required a great deal of intelligence and facts to dislodge it. Even then it wasn't altogether dislodged.*

Among the beliefs to which Brooke firmly adhered was the existence of what he called a German 'mass of manoeuvre', i.e. large forces not yet committed to the Russian front. *All the members of the JIC*, Bentinck said, *were convinced that this large 'mass of manoeuvre' did not exist and wrote this in our reports.* This did not satisfy Brooke. *Both Pound and Brooke tended to operate on hunches and preconceived ideas. One of Pound's hunches led to the loss of a large convoy to Russia.* This was the famous convoy P Q 17, described by the naval historian, Patrick Beesly, as 'the only British convoy to be abandoned by its escort in the face of a predictable and devastating attack by the enemy' as a result of a decision 'taken against the advice of two of the most experienced and capable officers in the Operational Intelligence Centre'.

One of Brooke's strengths was, in Bentinck's judgement, in *standing up to Churchill*, but Portal, he considered, was still the ablest of the Chiefs of Staff.

Changes also took place in the composition of the JIC itself. Beaumont-Nesbitt had already been replaced by Major General Francis Davidson, *a very mediocre officer*, in Bentinck's opinion, *with a permanent desire to make our reports fit in with the views of the CIGS*. Then in 1942 the question arose of whether Godfrey's appointment as Director of Naval Intelligence should be renewed.

Both the DMI and Medhurst, Bentinck said, *wrote to their respective Chiefs of Staff asking that it shouldn't be, as he was so difficult to work with. Pound was furious at this, considering it a reflection on the senior service, and he instructed the Second Sea Lord, Admiral Moore, to hold an inquiry.*

I made every effort to keep out of this, but I was summoned to go and see Admiral Moore, who greeted me by saying he wanted to have a private talk about John Godfrey and not to bother about his old shipmate, a paymaster-captain, being in the room.

I spoke frankly to Moore. For Godfrey's ability Bentinck had a high respect. *But I did say he was difficult at the meetings with the other directors. I added that when I came to a JIC meeting and found that Brigadier Lamplough, R M, was representing Godfrey I breathed a sigh of relief.*

John Godfrey was appointed to command the Indian Navy. When he came back from India I had luncheon with him, and he told me that I'd said this about heaving a sigh of relief. I couldn't deny it. He knew it was the sort of language I would have used. After this episode I became a little wary when dealing with high-ranking naval officers.

Godfrey's replacement, E. G. N. Rushbrooke, was, in Bentinck's judgement, *a very nice fellow, but, as regards ability, not a patch on Godfrey.* The RAF was more fortunate in its representation at the highest level of intelligence, Medhurst being replaced by Frank Inglis, described by Bentinck as *also an extremely able officer.* Geoffrey Vickers, a solicitor in the firm of Slaughter and May, continued to represent the Ministry of Economic Warfare and to contribute, in particular, skills in conciliation and in drafting.

In the autumn of 1942 the Western Allies began to move consistently on to the offensive on land. This altered the character of much of the JIC's work. As the authors of the official history of intelligence put it, 'By June 1942 the needs of the planners had inaugurated that process by which the work of the JIC, in addition to assessing Germany's long-term intentions, were devoted to organising, to an ever-increasing extent down to the end of the war, the intelligence required for the planning of Allied operations.' This called for a closer relationship between the Joint Planning Staff and the JIC, which was achieved largely by making Bentinck a member of the Joint Planning Staff with the title of Foreign Office Adviser to the Director of Plans.

The J P S officers, Bentinck said, *were head and shoulders above the 'I' officers. They were the highest calibre of people I have ever worked with. The sailor there always became First Sea Lord. The airmen too went to the top.* The two he particularly selected for praise were in fact an airman and a seaman. *The outstanding ones were Bill Elliot and Charles Lambe.*

Churchill was less inclined to be eulogistic about the Joint Planning Staff. 'Those damned planners of yours,' he once told Brooke, 'plan nothing but difficulties'. He was also heard to refer to them as 'psalm-singing defeatists'. These were, in effect, indirect tributes to the intellectual rigour with which the JPS examined all proposals, a rigour which led to the abandonment of projects which Churchill had himself advanced, such as landings in Norway and an expedition to capture Sumatra.

For the beginning of the offensive in North Africa the Eighth Army was well served by decrypts. Four days after Montgomery assumed command a detailed summary of Rommel's intentions was provided for him. What had not been foreseen was that Montgomery would make a tour of his command, not only announcing that Rommel would be defeated, but explaining in some detail what the German plans were. The assurance with which Montgomery spoke to officers and men had an important effect on the outcome of the battle, but his revelations of Rommel's plans caused understandable concern in Whitehall. It was already known that the Germans had instituted an inquiry into the security of their ciphers as a result of their heavy shipping losses in the Mediterranean; yet once again the possibility that Enigma might have been broken was not faced. The reprimand which he received for his indiscretions did not diminish the stature of the victor of the battle of Alamein, but it may help to explain his later reluctance to acknowledge the part played by information received through Ultra in the formulation of strategy.

For the Anglo-American landings in North Africa in November 1942 an elaborate deception plan was prepared. In a report on this to the Chiefs of Staff the JIC stated: 'It is clear that an overseas operation by the Allies is expected. Most of the reports suggest that the operation will be against Morocco and Algeria and/or Dakar, although other areas, as far afield as Norway, have been mentioned. So far there is no indication of any move by German or Italian forces to combat the threat of an imminent invasion of French North Africa.'

In fact the confusion within the enemy high commands was even greater than the JIC report implied. German forces remained on the alert in north-west Europe, and none were moved to the western Mediterranean before November. Canaris produced evidence shortly before the landings that the Allies were planning to establish a second front on the

Cherbourg peninsula. Late in October Kesselring thought that a powerful convoy was coming to reinforce Gibraltar and then Malta.

A huge Anglo-American amphibious force, including 300,000 troops, was landed in North Africa, having been admirably provided with topographical intelligence. Convoys sailing from the Clyde in the last ten days of October consisted of 158 merchant ships and 52 escorts. They caught up on the way to the Mediterranean with six slower convoys, which had sailed earlier.

That such a vast operation could be carried out without serious interference, and that tactical surprise could be achieved at the landing beaches, was evidence not only of a successful deception plan, but also of the ineptitude with which the enemy intelligence services were performing.

CHAPTER 14
Return to the Continent of Europe
(1943–44)

By the end of 1943 nearly everyone who played an important role in the British intelligence services had found his place within them, and the structure of the services, modified as it had been to meet the demands of war, was in all important respects complete.

The last two changes in the composition of the Chiefs of Staff Committee took place in the course of the year. Early in 1943 Vice-Admiral Lord Louis Mountbatten, the Commander-in-Chief of Combined Operations, became a member of the committee. When Pound was finally forced to give up he was replaced in October by the new First Sea Lord, Admiral Sir Andrew Cunningham.

Cunningham came with a huge reputation as a fighting admiral and has been accused by some naval historians of having little interest in intelligence. Sir Ian Jacob considered him as unsuitable for his new post as Nelson would have been. Bentinck defended him against both these charges, although Cunningham himself wrote of his new appointment: 'I had an almost complete lack of staff training and have to confess to an inherent difficulty in expressing myself in verbal conversation except when really roused.' Mountbatten Bentinck described as *highly intelligent and a very good showman. He got good people and got the best out of them, rather like Monty did. He also got on well with Churchill.*

A new Director of Military Intelligence was also appointed in 1943. This was Major-General John Sinclair, known to his friends as Sinbad. *Better than Davidson*, Bentinck said, *but not a very sparkling officer.* Sinclair later became head of SIS after Sir Ian Jacob had refused an offer of the post. (It was perhaps a tribute to the quality of the members of Churchill's military secretariat that Jacob should be asked to become head, first of the secret service, and then of the BBC.) *Winston didn't organize*, Bentinck once observed. *He said he wanted this, that and the other, and he had very good officers to do the organizing. Pug Ismay above all, Ian Jacob and Joe Hollis.*

In the JIS from 1942 onwards officers holding wartime commissions played an increasingly important part. One of the many benefits which Britain derived from the fact that, for the first two or three years of the war, only a small proportion of her armed forces was regularly engaged in combat was that of time for training civilians for service responsibilities, and for finding the right people for specialized jobs. The intelligence services benefited particularly from infusions of civilian talent.

In the Government Code and Cipher School at Bletchley Park some of the country's leading mathematicians and chess-players were engaged in breaking Enigma. Alongside them were several Fellows of the Royal Society, historians of the calibre of J. H. Plumb and Asa Briggs, future politicians with the intellectual stature of Roy Jenkins and Edward Boyle, and writers such as Angus Wilson and the first master of the radio short story, L. H. Lambert, who adopted the pseudonym A. J. Alan. SIS took in men as gifted as Graham Greene, Malcolm Muggeridge and Hugh Trevor-Roper. The JIS too attracted men of evident talent.

Bentinck did not himself select the JIS officers. *They were wished on us*, he said, *but if somebody wasn't really suitable we agreed that something else would be found for him*. One of the first War Office representatives on the JIS who was not a professional soldier was Laurence Kirwan, a future President of the Royal Geographical Society.

Recalling his time in the JIS, Kirwan said: 'We had an enormous amount to read, perhaps too much. Sometimes we worked all night, as all appreciations had to be ready by 8 a.m. for the Chiefs of Staff.' Bentinck he described as 'marvellous, tremendously autocratic, Byzantine. He would have made a wonderful Greek archimandrite. He was very adroit at getting his way, good at steering things in the right direction and influencing people, very amusing. He was supposed to represent Foreign Office policy, but I sometimes wondered whether it was Bentinck policy.'

Another War Office representative was Noel Annan, the future Vice-Chancellor of London University, historian and Director of the Royal Opera House, Covent Garden. Annan described himself as 'an uncritical admirer' of Bentinck. 'He was a very impressive figure. He never burdened himself with unnecessary detail. He would never dream of drafting a document unless he had to. That was for other people to do. He looked at you in an apparently benign way, yet you could see he was making judgements about people and what they said all the time.'

Annan accepted Kenneth Strong's judgement that Bentinck was the outstanding intelligence officer of his time, his closest rival in this respect being perhaps Strong himself. 'I would never have had a clash of opinion with Bill,' he said. 'If there had been a difference, I'd have accepted that his judgement would be superior to mine.'

War Office representatives on the JIS frequently found themselves having to counter what they considered the excessive optimism of the RAF. Knowledge of German skills, they felt, had to be set against evidence of German reverses. This even involved, as Annan recalled, pointing out that 'the British armies and the new American armies were not the match of the German armies in professionalism and perhaps bravery. It was here that Bill was so extraordinarily diplomatic in the way he produced harmony between the three services. Everybody had complete trust in him. Nobody ever thought that he pulled a punch or that he was trying to plough a self-interested furrow. He had a temperament of extreme scepticism, yet total belief that the Allies were going to win.'

The Air Ministry representatives on the JIS who had been brought in from civilian life were both able and persuasive. They tended also to be more experienced than their service colleagues. Annan's opposite number, Francis Ogilvy, was some twenty years older than he was and a partner in the advertising firm of Ogilvy, Mather. Ogilvy's superior officer, Howard Millis, had served in the first world war, and later was, like Geoffrey Vickers, a solicitor with Slaughter and May and a banker with Baring Brothers.

The senior naval representative, the stockbroker Charles Drake, was described by Noel Annan as 'extremely able'. His assistant, Charles Fletcher-Cooke, later became a QC and Member of Parliament for Darwen in Lancashire.

'All of us,' Fletcher-Cooke recalled, 'plus some augmentation from other services, would gather once a week under Bill's chairmanship for a general discussion on the state of our knowledge of enemy formations and intentions. These weekly meetings were really fascinating, because Bill had to keep about thirty officers on the ball and in play and go round the table and have a general discussion. He would encourage you to speak your mind and give your opinion in front of officers far senior to you. Bill was simply marvellous. I admired him enormously. One saw at second hand how he handled the intelligence directors themselves.'

From early in 1943, as a result of British victories on land, the intelligence services had a valuable additional source of information. This was the presence in Britain in appreciable numbers of senior German officers, including generals, as prisoners of war. In captivity a number of them talked freely, apparently unaware that their conversations were being recorded. *When you're in the state in which they were*, Bentinck said, *morale is pretty low. If you've been a general who's been a failure and has had to surrender, you're ready to blame everybody except yourself.*

Charles Drake expressed the opinion that 'the bugging of POWs at high level in Trent Park was perhaps the most important source of political information'. Particularly revealing were the observations of General von Thoma, who had been captured in the western desert. Bentinck described the recordings of conversations, to which he listened closely, *as highly constructive and frequently entertaining*. He added: *This also applied to the telephone conversations of members of diplomatic missions in London.*

At a meeting of the Chiefs of Staff on 14 September 1943 Bentinck was on record as stating that 'though the morale of German troops remained high whilst they were fighting, it now broke very much more quickly when they were taken prisoner. This had become particularly noticeable during the last three months.'

The mastery of enemy ciphers became increasingly

sophisticated in 1943 and the early months of 1944. Peter Calvocoressi, historian of Ultra, who himself worked at Bletchley Park, made the interesting observation that 'if from the middle of the war you had been looking for the half-dozen persons who knew most about the Luftwaffe in all its operational and organizational aspects, you would have found them all in England'. In addition to Enigma the Government Code and Cipher School was able to read messages from the so-called Geheimschreiber with the code-name 'Fish', which was used for high-level communications to and from the German High Command.

In the autumn of 1943 the Germans did introduce important changes in the operation of Enigma, but this was done not out of a belief that the ciphers were being read, but in order to reduce the dangers which might result from the capture of individual machines or keys. The problems arising from these changes were duly solved at Bletchley Park, and as mastery increased the security of the Allies' own ciphers became more and more important.

In October 1943 the JIC called attention to the difference between the American practice of sending meteorological information *en clair* and the British practice of sending it in cipher, and the consequent risk that the enemy, by continually comparing the two, might be able to break the ciphers. The Chiefs of Staff agreed that this discrepancy should be brought to the attention of the Joint Staff Mission in Washington.

On 13 January 1944 the JIC reported that some communications systems used by the French and other allies were 'dangerously insecure' and recommended that Allied governments should be asked to communicate information of importance to the enemy under British or American ciphers. The upshot was an agreement that Allied ciphers should be investigated for purposes of security. *We knew*, Bentinck said, *that our Allies' ciphers were not ultra-secure. We therefore didn't give them information that would have been of vital use to the Germans. That led to a good deal of soreness, but it had to be.*

The work of the Inter-Services Topographical Department continued to expand. One reason for this was the public response to an idea which had been put forward by John Godfrey in 1941. This was that an appeal should be made to the public through BBC broadcasts for private photographs, such as holiday snaps of beach scenes, which might be of use to the planning staffs. No fewer than 80,000 photographs were received. Their value became apparent when landings on the continent of Europe began to be planned in detail.

For purposes of deception increasing use was made of the so-called black radio stations, that is to say stations purporting to be operated by German or other opposition groups. By 1943 twenty-three black stations were operating under British control from four transmitters. The guiding spirit in all this was the former *Daily Express* correspondent in Berlin, Sefton (Tom) Delmer. The main purpose of the stations was to undermine German civilian and military morale, but as vehicles for occasionally passing items of information which might serve to mislead the German High Command their value was evident.

In general, the co-ordination of British intelligence was by 1943 almost complete, so much so that Kenneth Strong was able to write later; 'Cavendish-Bentinck became the first intelligence officer in any country to have a reasonable measure of co-ordination over all intelligence activities.' There was, however, one area of untidiness which continued to cause Bentinck concern. This was the lack of unity, expressing itself here and there in hostility, between SIS or SOE or, as Bentinck put it, *this awful quarrelling between MI6 and Gubbins.*

That better co-ordination would have been desirable is clear. Major General Sir Colin Gubbins, who was the head of SOE during the second half of the war, stated in a lecture in 1970 that he had come to the conclusion that secret intelligence, political warfare and the kind of subversive activities for which SOE was responsible should be placed under the control of one minister and one executive head. This did not happen in the second world war, SOE remaining responsible to the Minister of Economic Warfare and SIS to the Foreign Secretary.

It would have been better, I think, Bentinck said, *if there'd been one single organization,* but he agreed that it would have been unfortunate had this been SIS as it was constituted when war broke out. *In SIS there were a lot of old boys, people who'd been there from World War I and had been hanging on between the wars. They fancied themselves as spy-masters. You'd have had to get in new blood. SOE had good people, very good people. There were Charles Hambro and Terence Maxwell. Gubbins was, I suppose, a fairly good organizer, though I didn't rate him very highly.*

The problem of co-ordination remained intractable, and Bentinck was not himself able to offer any wholly satisfactory solution. *I don't know just how you should organize it. CIA is much too big.*

In practice SOE representatives were in close contact with the JIC and at times attended meetings of the Chiefs of Staff. J. G. (Jack) Beevor, a senior SOE staff officer, recalled that relations with the JIC were 'less cordial' than those with the Joint Planning Staff, but described Bentinck himself as 'an outstandingly intelligent and shrewd diplomat'.

Bentinck found his own associations with SOE on the whole somewhat painful. This was chiefly in consequence of the greatest blunder, by far, which SOE committed. The blunder occurred in the Netherlands, where a radio operator named Hubertus Lauwers was captured by the Germans and correctly used the prearranged code-words indicating that he was transmitting under duress. The SOE officers involved failed to notice the use of the code-words, and the so-called *Englandspiel* followed, in which SOE activities in the Netherlands, including parachute drops, were controlled by the Germans for some two years. This was a small-scale operation in comparison with what was happening to German agents in Britain, but it caused wholly unnecessary losses among members of the Dutch resistance, RAF crews and aircraft, and organizers of escape routes for prisoners.

Bentinck, assisted by Capel-Dunn, produced the report which exposed the extent of SOE's failure. *There was no doubt*, he said, *that SOE had been too happy-go-lucky. SOE would gladly have murdered me. I arranged with Victor Rothschild that if I suddenly died he was to carry out an autopsy.*

As the campaign in North Africa progressed the JIC was called upon to forecast both how long Germany would try to maintain forces in Africa and how she would respond to threats to southern Italy. 'Hitler,' the committee stated on 3

December 1942, 'will do his best to retain a foothold in North Africa and to keep Italy in the war. If Italy collapses he will concentrate on the defence of the Balkans and leave Italy to her fate.' Three months later, while maintaining, correctly, its earlier assessment of Germany's strategy in Africa, the JIC, in the light of further information, revised its forecast of her intentions in Italy. 'Her strategy,' it stated, 'will be to hold the Tunisian bridgehead as long as possible, and when driven from there to hold the defensive outposts of Sicily, Sardinia and Crete, and ultimately the coasts of Southern France, Italy and Greece.'

The Allied intention of following victory in North Africa with an invasion of Sicily was not difficult to foresee, and to disguise it an elaborate deception plan was formulated. This included the most famous individual exploit in the field of deception in the second world war: the dressing of a suitable corpse in the uniform of a major in the Royal Marines; the planting of documentation, including personal letters written by Mountbatten and General Sir Archibald Nye, the Vice-Chief of General Staff, which indicated that an attack on Sardinia was planned; and allowing the corpse to drift ashore.

The deception worked as it was intended to. *Canaris*, Bentinck said, *smelt that it might be a plot. The others swallowed it hook, line and sinker.* Ultra decrypts showed that the documents planted on the corpse had been accepted as genuine. German reinforcements were sent to Sardinia, and the German High Command revised its appreciations of Allied intentions in the Mediterranean.

The creation of the fictitious major in the Royal Marines was only one part of the deception plan. Another was the promotion, through SOE officers in Greece, of increased sabotage of communications, of the kind which would precede Allied landings. This too had the intended effect. On 14 May the German High Command sent a signal to Kesselring, the German commander in Italy, informing him, on the basis of what was called absolutely reliable information, that Allied landings could be expected in both the western Mediterranean and the Peleponnese.

The landing in Sicily began on 10 July 1943. Just over a

fortnight later Mussolini was forced to resign. This had been foreseen by the JIC, which had stated on 11 April that Allied landings, first in Sicily and then on the mainland, might well lead to an Italian collapse, giving as one of its reasons the general unpopularity of the Germans in Italy. In making this forecast the JIC differed somewhat from opinions held in GHQ in Cairo, having the advantage of much information from Italian prisoners of war. In reporting on 27 July on the consequences of Mussolini's fall the JIC made the slightly startling forecast that 'it is possible that the German generals will note for future reference the ease with which a dictator has been removed'.

For some time after the invasion early in September of the Italian mainland the Chiefs of Staff continued to feel concern about the possibility of a German counter-offensive which would drive the Allies out of Italy. There were good reasons for this concern. A Purple decrypt, for example, had reported a conversation on 7 October in which Hitler and Ribbentrop informed the Japanese Ambassador that just such an offensive as the Chiefs of Staff feared was being planned.

The JIC remained hopeful. On 29 October it stated that it 'could not envisage any circumstances in which the enemy will be able to increase his air power in Italy to a scale in any way sufficient to support a major offensive'. Brooke was not satisfied. 'There has,' he said at a meeting of the Chiefs of Staff on 2 November, 'been a tendency over the last two years to underestimate the forces which the enemy could bring to bear in any particular theatre.' The JIC was therefore instructed to prepare a new paper, in which it was to ask itself the question whether 'there is any possibility that by using their interior lines the Germans could deal us a decisive blow in Italy, well knowing that our build-up there must be incomparably slower than theirs'.

The JIC reiterated opinions it had advanced earlier and yet another paper was called for. In this the committee had to examine the possibility that Germany would accept 'all risks in other theatres of war in order to deal the Allies a decisive defeat in Italy'. The paper was produced, and at the end of this commendably thorough examination of every possibility of defeat the Chiefs of Staff accepted the JIC's opinion that the Germans would be unable to achieve the necessary air superiority.

On 12 November 1943 the JIC was instructed to examine a report on Yugoslavia made by Brigadier Fitzroy Maclean, the former Foreign Service officer and Member of Parliament whom Churchill had personally selected as head of the British military mission to Tito's guerrilla forces. After doing so the committee recommended that help should be increased to Tito and withdrawn from Mihailovic's Cetniks. This ran counter to most Foreign Office thinking and to opinions held earlier in the intelligence directorate of the War Office. The JIC was influenced by the first-hand impressions formed by Maclean and his fellow officers and also by evidence received through Ultra. One Ultra report contained a German claim to have killed six thousand of Tito's Partisans and only fifteen Cetniks during a period when more than twice as many Cetniks as Partisans had been taken prisoner.

A few months later the JIC was asked to advise whether the Island of Vis could be considered a secure headquarters for a few weeks for Tito, who had been temporarily driven off the mainland. It reported that enemy operations 'for the capture of the island are highly unlikely'. Once again Brooke was dis-satisfied. The committee had, he considered, underrated the threat to Vis, and a signal was sent to General Maitland Wilson, the Commander-in-Chief in the Mediterranean area, stressing the importance of maintaining Vis's garrison at the necessary strength.

Elsewhere in the Balkans and Central Europe in late 1943 and 1944 evidence began to accumulate of a weakening of the will to fight among Germany's allies. Reporting on 20 January on the effects of recent Russian advances, the JIC wrote of 'increasing fear, tension and confusion in the Balkan countries. In Bulgaria the present crisis might result in the defection of that country from the Axis. Hungary is concentrating on the defence of her own frontier. In Roumania the present Govern-ment may shortly lose control.'

Nine days later the JIC produced a report entitled 'Effects of Allied Bombing of Balkans'. This stated: 'Sofia was raided twice in November and twice in December. The achievements have been out of proportion to the efforts expended. Wholesale evacuation of the city has resulted. The disruptive effect on the administration of the country has been great.' Almost a month later the Chiefs of Staff formally took note of a telegram received from President Roosevelt. This reported conversations which Averell Harriman had been having as a result of peace feelers put out by the Bulgarian Government.

After its report of 29 January the JIC was called upon regularly to submit a list of priorities for bombing targets in the Balkans, it no doubt being felt that decisions should be influenced by political as much as by military considerations. Rail targets in the area of Bucharest and Ploesti usually headed the JIC's list.

In December 1942 the JIC examined the possibility that Germany and the Soviet Union might agree to end the war. *We were always on the look-out*, Bentinck said, *for the possibility of a German-Russian peace, knowing that if it suited them the Russians would not hesitate to change sides*. This was a sensible precaution. Secret talks were held between German and Soviet representatives in Stockholm in both April and June 1943, but nothing came of them, chiefly because of Hitler's antipathy to any idea of making peace. By that time too the Russians had won the battle of Stalingrad and would not consider peace except on their own terms. 'We adhere to the view,' the JIC reported on 23 June 1943, 'that Germany and Russia are unlikely to find a basis for a separate peace. We do not think that in present conditions the Russians would begin even to negotiate.'

When analysing the fighting on the Russian front the JIC continued to make reservations. Its forecasts, it stated in January 1944, must be 'subject to a wide margin of error, because we have so little intelligence about Russia's strength and intentions and no information, official or unofficial, from Moscow other than communiqués.' The committee did however state in October 1943 that 'the Germans, in spite of their failure to prevent the Russians from establishing bridgeheads across the Dnieper, are not contemplating any further large-scale withdrawal until they are forced to do so by Russian pressure.'

By 20 January 1944 the position had become such that the

JIC was able to state: 'The Russians hold the initiative every-where and have marked superiority on land and in the air. Germany's strategy can be opportunist only.' But it commented shortly afterwards: 'There is practically no evidence as yet of any weakening in the fighting efficiency and discipline in battle of the German army.'

On Soviet policy the JIC was not at this stage called upon to comment. But Bentinck did have one encounter, which was to be of some significance in his post-war career. This was when Anthony Eden introduced him to the Soviet Foreign Minister, Molotov, as 'our chief intelligence officer'. Molotov gave Bentinck a look which indicated that this unsolicited piece of information had been duly noted and its significance registered. This was reflected in the subsequent attitude of the Soviet authorities.

Japanese strategy in 1943 could be expected, in the JIC's judgement, to be almost wholly defensive. 'We believe,' the committee reported in February, 'that Japan's intention to conduct a basically defensive policy will have been strengthened by the experience of the past months. This period has shown that Japanese detachments have been able to hold out for considerable periods against much larger and better equipped Allied forces, backed by air superiority. Moreover, the relative ease with which Japanese troops can be maintained suggests that the defence of her sphere against the Allies will not easily succumb to attempts to cut her communications.'

In December the JIC forecast: 'Japan's aim is to prevent, by every means, both political and military, an acceleration of the pace of the war, in the belief that a prolonged campaign will produce war weariness in Britain and America and so lead to a negotiated peace. She will not carry out voluntarily any strategic withdrawal. The garrisons in Burma, Malaya, Sumatra and Indo-China have been strengthened by about four divisions in the past three months. These reinforcements are probably prompted by fears of an impending Allied attack and do not presage offensive action by the Japanese, at any rate on a large scale.'

From the time of the decisive American naval victory at

Midway in June 1942 onwards, the conduct of the Allied war effort in the Pacific zone had been more and more under the control of the United States. The land fighting in which the British were involved was largely the concern of the Indian Army, which had long enjoyed a considerable degree of autonomy. For these reasons the number of the JIC's appreciations concerned with the Far East, in comparison with the number which dealt with the German war, was fairly small. There was however one report, made in August 1943, which indicated that in intelligence, as in other fields, the Anglo-American harmony, which had been so carefully fostered in the European sphere, was not always evident east of the Suez Canal.

'Troubles and difficulties,' the JIC wrote, 'have arisen largely as a result of unnecessary and often unwanted penetration of and interference in India by the personnel of various US bodies. This cannot be compared with our own attempts to secure collaboration with the Americans in the South-West Pacific. This matter now requires clearing up firmly.'

By far the most important tasks of the JIC in 1943 and the first half of 1944 were to assess the total fighting capacity of Germany and to estimate the proportion of it which would be deployed against the Allies when they attempted to land in northern France.

On 12 November 1943 the committee produced a detailed analysis, industry by industry, city by city, of the effects of bombing on the total German war effort. 'The extreme gravity with which the German High Command view the extension of the air offensive during the last three months is,' it stated, 'evidenced by changes effected between 1 July and 1 October. At the beginning of this period approximately fifty per cent of the total German fighter strength was employed on the Western front. Today it is not less than seventy per cent.'

Between five and six million people were estimated to have been 'rendered temporarily or permanently homeless'. Five U-boats were said to have been destroyed by the bombing of yards, and the bombing of factories in Schweinfurt had reduced steel production. 'In other industries,' the committee stated, 'damage has been too widely distributed to make a deep impression on any of them.' The reduction in industrial output in September 1943, compared with the early part of the year, was estimated at about ten to fifteen per cent.

More than six months later, on the eve of the Normandy landings, the JIC stated: 'There is no evidence to suggest that the Allied bombing may shortly foment any effective opposition to the regime, or that the stamina and discipline of the German people have deteriorated to such an extent that a collapse may be considered likely within the next two weeks.' Earlier in the year, in January, the committee had examined the reasons why discipline was being so successfully maintained.

'Two main factors at present,' it stated, 'combine to prevent the fall in German morale, which has already taken place, from developing into a breakdown of discipline sufficient to bring about an internal crisis. These factors are fear of the Gestapo and fear of the consequences of defeat. The formula of "unconditional surrender", as interpreted by Nazi propaganda in default of any explanation by the United Nations [the Allies], is having a big effect in making Germans afraid of the consequences of defeat to themselves individually and collectively. Few Germans retain any hope of a German victory.'

Portal suggested that this JIC report should be referred to the Joint Planning Staff, who should be asked: 'What military arguments, if any, prompted the original declaration of unconditional surrender? Do these arguments still hold good?' The other Chiefs of Staff agreed with Portal, but nothing effective came of his suggestion.

While the JIC was engaged largely in collating and analysing intelligence relating to the plans to land in Normandy new events occurred which suggested that Britain might once again find herself on the defensive.

In the autumn of 1939 R. V. Jones, the principal scientist on the staff of the Air Ministry, after studying SIS reports on the subject of Hitler's supposed secret weapon, had suggested that both a pilotless aircraft and a long-range gun might be under development. In December 1942 SIS had reported a conversation in which a professor in the Berlin Technische

Hochschule had spoken of a rocket containing five tons of explosive and having a range of 200 kilometres. General von Thoma talked in captivity of rocket development, but was sceptical about progress. Then in March 1943 SIS received a fairly detailed report from some Luxembourgers who had been engaged in construction work in Peenemünde, where long-range rockets were being assembled.

In the light of all this it was decided that a special committee should be set up in April 1943 to investigate such reports and recommend counter-measures. The established machinery of the JIC and the JPS was to be by-passed, and the chairman of the committee was to be the Joint Parliamentary Secretary to the Ministry of Supply, Duncan Sandys, who was also Churchill's son-in-law.

Reports of German production of long-range weapons of one kind or another came flooding in during the summer of 1943, and for a time the JIC wondered whether some of them might have been planted by the Germans. In July the committee commented that 'there are some signs that we are receiving too much information about a rocket or a long-range weapon, and there are therefore grounds for hoping that German experiments in this direction are proving unfruitful'. By the end of September it was calculated that 159 such reports had been received from SIS, 35 from prisoners of war and 37 from diplomatic posts abroad.

Before long the conclusion was reached that Germany had produced both pilotless aircraft and long-range rockets, weapons which the Germans themselves called V1 and V2, and that both would be used before long in attacks principally against London. After a time almost the only doubter was Lord Cherwell, who had long been Churchill's principal scientific adviser. The rocket, he stated, would be found to be a mare's nest, and when shown an aerial photograph of what was in fact a V2 being loaded on to a railway wagon at Peenemünde, he expressed the opinion that it was a barrage balloon.

The gathering of intelligence about the V1 and V2 was an operation in which Ultra played a relatively small part. The principal sources were aerial photography and reports from agents. Photographic reconnaissance units were instructed to cover all areas within 130 miles of London and Southampton from which V1s might be launched. The first of the launching pads, known from their appearance as 'ski-sites', was discovered in October 1943. By the end of November thirty-eight sites had been confirmed by photography. By the beginning of 1944 the figure was eighty-eight.

Much of the information about the V2 came from Polish agents. Some of their findings were confirmed when an experimental rocket crashed in Sweden and the British Air Attaché was able to send a fairly full report. Then in May 1944 a V2 landed in a bank of the River Bug in Poland and did not explode. The Polish underground army captured the rocket, held it and secretly prepared a landing ground, on which a Dakota aircraft piloted by a New Zealander came down. The rocket was loaded on to the aircraft and brought to England for detailed examination.

In the assessing of information about V1 and V2 there was inevitably a certain amount of duplication of work between the Sandys Committee and the JIC. The Chiefs of Staff therefore decided in November 1943 that the Air Ministry should take over some of the responsibilities of the Sandys Committee and the JIC should take over the rest. Sandys himself was invited to continue to attend meetings of the Chiefs of Staff where appropriate.

When the re-allocation of duties was decided the JIC was instructed 'to make its own arrangements about getting scientific advice'. The JIC's practice had always been to call in scientists for guidance and advice, but not to include them in the committee itself. This it continued. *There was a little fair-haired Welshman called Jones*, Bentinck recalled, *who came in for consultations. He was very good, very useful, with a very good brain.*

When on 13 June 1944 Air Marshal Bottomley informed the Committee of the Chiefs of Staff that the enemy had launched his first attack with pilotless aircraft the night before, there was little about the scale and nature of the forthcoming assault which the Chiefs of Staff did not know. The launching pads of the V1s had been bombed continuously and measures could be taken against the pilotless aircraft themselves. Bombing had also limited production of the V2s, although against the rockets themselves, once they were launched, there was at that time no defence.

As part of its preparations for the Allied landings in Normandy the JIC proposed a clear division of responsibilities for intelligence between the Supreme Headquarters of the Allied Expeditionary Force (SHAEF) on the one hand and itself and the service ministries on the other. 'The JIC and Service Ministries,' it stated, 'must remain the primary authorities for any appreciation of the enemy's war effort as a whole. Service Ministries are the centres to which information from all sources flows. Army Groups and Tactical Air Force Headquarters must be responsible for appreciation of the enemy situation on the Army group front. The Supreme Allied Commander and the Allied Air Commander-in-Chief will call on the JIC or Service Ministries to furnish any appreciations or strategic estimates which they require.'

Of the division of responsibility between London and Washington the committee wrote: 'Intelligence agencies in the United Kingdom must be the main collecting centres for all information relating to the Western front owing to the distance of Washington from London.'

The Chiefs of Staff approved these proposals. For bringing information received from Ultra to commanders in the field special liaison units were formed which had this task as their sole responsibility.

On 1 March 1944 the JIC wrote: 'Germany is aware that Allied forces are rapidly being built up in the United Kingdom, and there is some evidence that at present she expects that the main attack will be made against the coastline facing the English Channel or possibly against Brittany, probably in conjunction with diversionary landings on the west and south of France.'

By that time a complex deception plan was already in operation. Its primary purpose was to convince the German High Command that the main Allied assault would come in the Pas de Calais area and that the landings on the Cherbourg peninsula, when they took place, would be a diversionary or subsidiary attack. For this a phantom army was created in Scotland. Its credibility was sustained by a large volume of signals traffic which it appeared to be operating. The double agents too reached the climax of their services. A Spaniard named Juan Pujol Garcia, in whom Hitler had full confidence, gave it as his considered opinion that the main attack would be in the Pas de Calais area. By then Hitler had already awarded him the Iron Cross. *It was*, Bentinck said, *one of the two most important and fruitful pieces of deception in the war*. (The other was the use of the corpse dressed as a marine major.) *We made the Germans believe that there was going to be a second landing in the Pas de Calais under General Patton, which led them to keep five divisions in that area.*

On 19 April the JIC was called upon to assess the value of the help which French resistance forces could give to the Allied armies. 'There are now about 100,000 men provided with arms and ammunition,' the committee wrote. 'The total numerical strength of the resistance is much greater, but cannot be considered of military value without arms. The standard of efficiency varies from bad to excellent in individual groups.' The conclusion reached was: 'At the worst, resistance cannot fail to be of value, and at best may so derange the German lines of communication as to be a major factor in the battle. Thus, from a military standpoint, resistance will yield a result which can be described as a bonus. The size of the bonus cannot be reckoned and could not therefore be taken into account in operational planning.'

When the landings finally took place on 5 June, the JIC stated that 'the Allied armies will have to overcome desperate resistance by the maximum forces which the Germans can bring against them without denuding the coasts of France and so enabling the Allies to effect an unopposed landing elsewhere.'

A week later the committee wrote: 'All the evidence suggests that the Germans did not accurately assess in advance the timing, scale or location of the operation. The initial hesitancy in the German build-up against the Allied bridgehead was partly due to the German over-estimate of the forces available in this country. Although there are indications that the Germans are moving armoured formations from the Pas de Calais area and the south and south west of France, we believe that they still fear subsidiary operations against these areas.' It added: 'The Germans still think that diversionary operations threaten against southern Norway.'

As late as 26 June the JIC was able to state: 'It is clear from our intelligence and from the German dispositions in France as a whole that the enemy still expects a large-scale landing between the Pas de Calais and the Seine.' Once again deception had been successful, and once again the German intelligence services had failed their armies, which continued to fight so tenaciously.

CHAPTER 15
The End of the German War
(1944–45)

During the last year of the war against Germany the JIC, and
Bentinck in particular, became increasingly concerned with
political rather than military problems, with the consequences
of the war as well as with its conclusion.

Once the Allied armies had successfully broken out from the
bridgehead in Normandy the principal task in the military
field which the Chiefs of Staff gave to the JIC was to assess
how long German resistance was likely to last. Intelligence
required for the battlefronts was by then the concern of
General Eisenhower's headquarters, where Kenneth Strong,
whom Eisenhower had appointed as his chief intelligence
officer, had more than a thousand people working for
him.

In the summer of 1944 the JIC's forecasts of Germany's
power to resist were consistently optimistic. On 14 July it
wrote: 'It is difficult to see how Germany can, if Allied attacks
on the three major fronts are ceaselessly pressed home, pro-
long the struggle beyond December.' On 5 September it
stated: 'Whereas the Germans have at the moment an organised front between the Russians and the German frontier, in
the West they have nothing but disorganised remnants incapable of holding the Allied advance in strength into Germany
itself.' The committee addded: 'Whatever action Hitler may
now take it will be too late to affect the issue in the West, where
organised German resistance will gradually disintegrate under
our attacks, although it is impossible to predict the rate at
which this will take place.'

The last forecast was contested by Churchill. Three days
later he wrote to Ismay: 'It is at least as likely that Hitler will be
fighting on January 1 as that he will collapse before then.' In
the event Churchill was right and the JIC was wrong.
Whether by the adoption of a different strategy the war in the

west could have been over before the end of 1944 is a question which can be, and indeed frequently has been, argued.

The JIC's miscalculation was due to economic and military, rather than political, appreciations. In the Ministry of Economic Warfare it had long been believed that shortage of oil would be a decisive factor in bringing German resistance to an end. On 4 July 1944 the Ministry's representative on the JIC, Geoffrey Vickers, said at a meeting of the Chiefs of Staff: 'The enemy's oil situation is now such that he is being forced to eat into oil stocks and dumps.' His conclusion was that, provided bombing attacks kept oil production down to the prevailing level and Germany was forced to fight intensively on three fronts, 'current supplies will fall short by some thirty-five per cent of the minimum needed to avoid hampering military operations'. Similar forecasts continued to be made by the JIC in the months that followed, yet, threatening though the shortage of oil was, the German armed forces were never paralysed through lack of it.

The most effective German military resistance in the west was the remarkable counter-offensive which von Rundstedt launched in the Ardennes in December 1944. This too was the subject of a somewhat overoptimistic JIC report. On 11 November the committee wrote: 'The Germans may be planning a limited spoiling attack designed to upset Allied preparations and thus postpone the major allied offensive, possibly even until the spring of 1945. Such a spoiling attack would be characteristic of German military practice. We do not think that the evidence warrants the conclusion that the Germans are planning a spoiling offensive.' Eisenhower's headquarters was similarly deceived by the scale of the German operation. In making his preparations von Rundstedt imposed radio silence, thereby neutralizing the advantage of Ultra, and the offensive itself was launched under cover of thick fog. At one stage it achieved a penetration of fifty miles in depth.

In its assessment of political conditions inside Germany in the summer of 1944 the JIC retained its normal sureness of touch. In a report made some three weeks after von Stauffenberg's attempt to assassinate Hitler it wrote: 'The recent unsuccessful attempt to assume control in Germany by a group of senior officers has resulted in greatly increased control of the German armed forces passing to the Party. So long as the Allies insist on unconditional surrender we do not think that the Nazi Government will sue for an armistice in any quarter. It seems likely that Germany's collapse will be brought about primarily by military defeat in the field, leading to a collapse of organised resistance by the German armed forces.'

Once it became clear that German resistance in some form would continue until the spring of 1945, and possibly later, one of the JIC's concerns was the relative speed of advance of the Russians and of the Western Allies. Another was the persistence of reports that the Germans were planning a final prolonged resistance in the so-called alpine redoubt in southern Germany.

In a paper which it issued on 6 February 1945 on the probable effects of the latest Russian offensive the JIC, after making the usual reservations about lack of knowledge of Russian 'intentions, dispositions and, above all, administrative capabilities', wrote that it might be 'impossible for the Russians to seize and hold Berlin until after a pause to improve their communications and build up their stocks. This would be in spite of the great prize which Berlin offers to them.'

Eisenhower had the choice, Bentinck said, *of pushing on to Berlin, and taking it, or cutting south-east to Leipzig and Czechoslovakia. There was a meeting held one night.* Among those present were Eisenhower, his Chief of Staff, Bedell Smith, Omar Bradley (in Bentinck's opinion *the best general on our side apart from Alexander*) and Strong. *There it was decided to go to Leipzig and not to push on to Berlin. This was not reported to the PM. Morgan and Tedder didn't regard it as necessary to report to London what was happening at SHAEF. God knows why.*

Kenneth Strong came back the next day to London and had dinner with me at the Turf Club. He told me of this meeting and explained it all with pepper-pot and mustard-pot and so on. I promptly dictated a memorandum to Anthony Eden reporting this. Anthony took it for granted that it had been passed to the Chiefs of Staff and to the PM from SHAEF. The PM heard of it some hours later — too late. The PM was furious.

Reports of German plans for a final desperate resistance in a mountain stronghold in the south were given credence in certain American intelligence quarters and also in the press. As late as 24 April 1945 OSS produced an elaborate analysis of the possibilities. The day before the *Daily Express* had carried a headline: '100 German Divisions in the Redoubt'. Bradley himself later wrote: 'Not until after the campaign ended were we to learn that the redoubt existed largely in the imagination of a few fanatical Nazis.'

The JIC had remained sceptical. *As regards the Alpine redoubt story*, Bentinck said, *this was not believed by the JIC.* In various reports on the subject it went no further than to suggest that the possibility of some guerrilla activity should be taken into consideration in the drawing up of plans, but the conclusion reached in February 1945 was: 'We do not think that prolonged large-scale resistance against organised attacks would prove possible.'

The spectre was also raised of the possible use of chemical warfare by the Germans as a last desperate form of defence. From time to time during the war the JIC had been called upon to report whether there was any likelihood that the Germans would resort to this kind of warfare. The answer given by the JIC was consistent throughout. It was expressed for the last time on 23 April 1945. 'We have no evidence,' the committee wrote, 'of any intention on the part of the Germans to initiate chemical warfare. They are, however, in a position to do so.'

Churchill divided his wartime Government into three main parts. Operations against the enemy were controlled by the Chiefs of Staff, over whose deliberations he himself, when he chose, presided. The Cabinet under his general direction was concerned with the normal business of government or, as it was then called, the home front. Foreign affairs were decided by himself and Eden with advice from the Foreign Office. On the whole the arrangement, which could be flexible when needed, worked well, at least so far as operations and the home front were concerned.

The Committee of the Chiefs of Staff was therefore not a political body, nor were its members by training or inclination politicians. This sometimes became apparent when the business of the committee extended into the political field, as for example in relations with the Soviet Government.

Men of the generation and upbringing of the Chiefs of Staff had been imbued with a general antipathy towards what was known as 'bolshevism', but of the actual working of the Soviet system they had little knowledge. When Brooke visited Moscow in August 1942 and talked with the future commander of the Polish forces in the Middle East, General Anders, he was surprised to find Anders tapping a table with a cigarette case and speaking in a very low voice. Afterwards Brooke recorded in his diary: 'I must confess that till then I had not realised that my sitting-room was full of microphones.' Similarly in the atmosphere of bonhomie which was so sedulously created by the Soviet leaders at the time of the Yalta conference Portal, after a banquet, wrote in his diary of Stalin: 'I reaffirm my impression that Uncle J is the goods—sincere, simple and big.' Of one of the Directors of Military Intelligence, General Davidson, Bruce Lockhart, who had first-hand knowledge of revolutionary Russia, wrote: 'Interested in Russia and obviously bitten by the propaganda bug.'

In reporting to the Chiefs of Staff on political matters, as he had to, in 1944 and 1945, Bentinck was not therefore addressing the ideal body, and some of his reports could be expected to fall on stony ground. This helps to account for the fact that in dealing with one problem to which he gave a good deal of attention he failed to make any progress. The problem was that of the treatment of the large number of Soviet citizens who had been recruited or conscripted into the German services.

In March 1944 Bentinck wrote a paper in which he estimated the number of these people as 470,000. 'I do not see,' he wrote, 'why we cannot say to the Russians that this is our estimate; that 200,000 of these are in France and the Low Countries; that we intend to direct broadcasts to them in Russian and drop leaflets; and that we shall be delighted if the Russians will collaborate with us in this.'

Nothing much resulted from this, and two months later, on 10 May, Bentinck returned to the charge: 'These Russians,' he wrote, 'are mostly men who have been put into the German Army under compulsion or have nominally volunteered in order not to starve. They will probably fight well if they have no incentive offered to them to desert and if they have some German *Feldwebel* behind them, but I expect that if leaflets printed in Russian and offering good food and pardon for past sins in return for desertion were scattered over Russian units, most of these Russians would come over.'

The British Military Mission in Moscow was instructed to make an approach to the Soviet Government on the subject and received a reply that 'the number of such persons is insignificant and no political interest would be served in making a special appeal to them'. This satisfied certain sections of the Foreign Office. Christopher Warner wrote in a minute: 'The Soviet Government would deeply resent and suspect our harbouring large numbers of anti-Soviet Russians.'

The reply did not satisfy Bentinck. 'It is just over two months ago,' he wrote, 'that the suggestion was put forward that we should try to undermine the morale of the Russians in France. If the consideration of this matter continues at the same rate as hitherto this question will end by ceasing to be of practical interest.'

On 16 May 1944 Bentinck recorded in the minutes of a meeting of the JIC that he had arranged for the question of desertion by Russians to be raised by the Director of Military Intelligence 'in order that it should not be thought that I used the JIC for pushing ideas that receive no support from elsewhere'.

The Chiefs of Staff remained largely indifferent to the question, and the Foreign Office continued to express anxiety. A note appeared on a Foreign Office file to the effect that SHAEF had refused to allow propaganda to be directed to Russians. This, Bentinck had to point out, was untrue. He also wrote of the Soviet assertion that the numbers of potential deserters was negligible: 'This, as the Soviet Government are well aware, is a lie.'

On 19 May the Chiefs of Staff took action of a kind. This was to send a telegram to Washington stating: 'FO advise they will consider subject a political one which should therefore be put to Molotov.' Ten days later a letter drafted by P. J. (Bob) Dixon of the Foreign Office, assisted by Christopher Warner, to the Chiefs of Staff in Washington settled the question. It was of the kind which makes normal humans despair of officialdom.

'If the Chiefs of Staff,' the letter ran, 'attach great importance to the matter, the Secretary of State would be prepared to consider an approach to M. Molotov by Sir A. Clark Kerr and the US Ambassador in Moscow, asking the Soviet Government to reconsider their negative reply. The Secretary of State is, however, very doubtful whether the Soviet Government would change their minds and, unless the Chiefs of Staff are very keen that we should make the attempt, he would let the matter rest.'

The remainder of the story is well known. In the words of Nikolai Tolstoy in *Victims of Yalta*, 'well over two million Russians were handed over to Stalin in the years 1944–7. The fate accorded to almost all of them was terrible.'

One largely political question on which the JIC was required by the Chiefs of Staff to report in December 1944 arose from a proposal by the United States Chiefs of Staff for a wider exchange of information with the Soviet Government on weapons developed by the Germans. The JIC pointed out that a request by the Western Allies to send some officers to visit a German research centre captured by the Russians, which had been combined with an offer of full reciprocal facilities, had led nowhere. 'We believe,' the committee wrote, 'that in an exchange of the nature now proposed by the US Chiefs of Staff we are likely to give the Russians much more information than we receive.'

Immediately after the war in Germany came to an end the Chiefs of Staff instructed the JIC to consider, in consultation with the Foreign Office, 'our general relations with the Russians and to submit recommendations as to any change in our attitude which they consider desirable'.

It was three weeks before the report was produced. One reason for this unusual delay was that Bentinck was away from London when the report was called for. Another, no doubt, was the need for consultation. It is also clear that the report was carefully thought out and carefully drafted.

The committee began by stating: 'We exclude any discussion of questions of high policy. We assume that the policy of His Majesty's Government is to achieve the maximum collaboration with the Soviet Union compatible with our own vital interests.' After pointing out that 'the Russians have throughout the war shown the utmost suspicion in their dealings with us' and that 'the Russian method of negotiation is to drive in every way the hardest political bargain', the committee laid down a number of guide-lines for future negotiations. The chief of these were:

'Nothing should be given to the Russians gratuitously. No Russian request should normally be granted unless some request of ours to which we attach importance is granted in connexion with it.

'It should be our aim to let the Russians know exactly where they stand in their dealings with us. This means that we should take longer to make up our minds but should always hold to our decision unless completely new circumstances supervene.

'The issues on which we are prepared to be really tough should be very carefully selected.

'We should when possible avoid making requests which would put the Russians in the position of having to expose any shortcomings.

'In dealing with Russian officers and officials it is important to treat them with strict formality and punctilio, even more than friendliness.

'Officers who have to deal with the Russians should be very carefully selected.'

Had this sensible and workmanlike document been published at the time it was written, it would no doubt have been widely condemned as provocative and even outrageous. Bentinck, Lord Annan said, 'had a realism towards the Russians which was refreshing'. It was also in 1944 and early 1945 somewhat rare.

Our mistakes, Bentinck said, *were in not being tough enough with the Russians. I think the P M and Anthony Eden, above all that dreadful Beaverbrook, had a curious personal liking for Stalin. The trouble happened not at Yalta—it had gone a little far by then—but at Teheran.*

In advocating a policy of realism when dealing with the Soviet Government Bentinck insisted on scrupulous observance of undertakings which had been given to it. Early in March 1945 Eisenhower reported that an approach had been made in Switzerland, ostensibly on behalf of some senior German officers, to discuss the possibility of bringing the war to an end.

Commenting on this, the JIC wrote: 'We cannot say whether this approach is genuine or whether it has been made under the control of Himmler. An approach of a somewhat similar nature, allegedly from Kesselring, was made through Lugano last October, but was found to be controlled by Himmler. For this reason it was not reported to the Chiefs of Staff. Should it be decided to follow up the present approach, the Soviet Government would have to be consulted. The British, United States and Soviet Governments agreed at Moscow in 1943 to inform each other immediately of any peace-feelers.'

The German officers had also asked for certain personal assurances. On this the committee commented: 'It will be necessary to ascertain whether these officers are regarded by the Soviet Government as war criminals.'

The same scrupulousness, Bentinck considered, should be shown in dealings with senior German officers who were held prisoner, even though the Soviet Government did not feel under any such restraint in its own use of captured German generals, as its fostering of the so-called Seidlitz, or Free German, movement showed. On 23 January 1945 the JIC issued a report summarizing past happenings and pointing the contrast between the attitudes of the Soviet and British authorities.

'Since September 1943,' the committee stated, 'the senior German officers in this country have shown an ever increasing interest in the Free German movement in Russia. In April 1944 General von Thoma suggested that a Free German movement should be instituted in Great Britain. In May 1944 General Bassenge with the sanction of General von Thoma offered, without any conditions whatever, to try and contact General von Rundstedt if the consent and support of the British Government were given. In August 1944 General Bassenge, as a result of a request from the Political Warfare Department, SHAEF, agreed to attempt to persuade the German Commander of the Channel Islands to surrender. The parley party were, however, refused permission to land by the German commander, and no interview was possible. In September 1944 General Bassenge outlined a plan for a simultaneous approach by broadcast and leaflet and any clandestine means possible to all German commanders in the field and all commanders in the Wehrkreis, to assume executive control in their districts, liquidate the party and hand over to the Allied commanders. In November 1944 General Bassenge agreed to a proposal from the 12th US Army Group and OSS, made with the sanction of SHAEF, to canvass his colleagues with an invitation to join him in forming an unofficial advisory section at SHAEF, charged with the examination and development of plans to hasten the end of hostilities. This proposal is under further consideration by SHAEF.'

In conclusion the JIC went no further than to state: 'No immediate decision appears to be called for in respect of these developments, except that the attitude of German generals in our hands would provide a basis for an enquiry from the Russians as to the use they propose to make of the Seidlitz movement.'

Whether the British could or should have made better use of senior officers such as von Thoma and Bassenge is debatable. In fact, when their help was finally called for in the concluding stages of the war nothing much resulted. In April 1945 General Sir Andrew Thorne, C-in-C Scottish Command, had a meeting with von Thoma and others to discuss whether they would broadcast an appeal to German forces in the west to surrender. In the JIC's report of the meeting von Thoma was quoted as saying that 'the German officers would like to be cooperative but were unwilling to jeopardise the lives of their families'.

As the end of the war approached, Bentinck was able occasionally to absent himself from London. In April 1945 he visited Washington accompanied by Lieutenant-Colonel Harold (Bunny) Phillips. *I went to see the FBI*, he said, *and had a talk with Hoover's No. Two. He excused himself to go out and make a telephone call for two or three minutes. I noticed that the armchair I was in was immovable, and I knew the room was bugged. He thought we'd say all sorts of interesting things which would be duly recorded. All I did say was what a fine, intelligent fellow he was.*

Later Bentinck dined with General Donovan at his Georgetown home. After dinner the guests went down to an underground cinema to see a musical film. This was interrupted by an officer who brought an urgent message. Donovan read it and then announced that Hitler was dead. 'There was a strange silence,' Donovan's biographer, Anthony Cave Brown, recorded. Then 'Donovan shook hands with Cavendish-Bentinck.'

Bentinck also visited SHAEF headquarters in Germany. Kenneth Strong described later how he 'picked his way in his smart London suit with neatly rolled umbrella through the mud'. Strong added: 'When he had completed his tour he was more than ever convinced of the importance to the western world of the immense military strength and potential of the United States.'

Bentinck was accompanied by Kenneth Keith, later Lord Keith of Castleacre, who was Strong's military assistant. Together they visited General Patton's headquarters in Frankfurt. *Too late*, Bentinck said, *the Americans began to see what the Russian game was. Bedell Smith did say to Kenneth Strong he regretted breaking up SHAEF. After the war we had to re-form SHAEF in the form of NATO. Had we kept together we'd have been able to talk to the Russians.*

Shortly after the war ended in Europe *I went*, Bentinck said, *to the hotel at Mondorf in Luxembourg in which the topmost members of the German Government, Army, Navy and Air Force were interned. This place went by the code-name of 'Ashcan'. The purpose of my visit was to have preliminary interviews with the civilians.*

Steengracht, who had been Minister Counsellor at the German Embassy in London before the war, was brought to me with no boot-laces, tie or braces. I asked him why the Germans did not make more use of puppet governments in the territories they occupied. Steengracht replied that the Nazis would not trust anybody in these territories and were on the whole dreadfully mistrustful of each other. He thought this mistrust was one of the main reasons for the Germans' defeat.

Although the JIC had been in existence before the second world war it became an effective body only in war conditions. Its subsidiary, the JIS, was wholly a wartime creation. To Bentinck it was clear that the structure of the two, which had served the country so well, ought not to be dismantled in time of peace. He therefore set about making the necessary arrangements.

I initiated, he said, *the Joint Intelligence Bureau. I'd noticed that there were junior officers in the intelligence divisions in the Air Ministry, the War Office and the Admiralty all doing the same job, writing the same things, gathering the same information, most of it not secret in any way. I thought this should be rationalized. I put it up to the Chiefs of Staff, and they took it. The departments didn't like it at all.*

From the Joint Intelligence Bureau grew the Intelligence directorate of the Ministry of Defence. The institution of the JIB was also an early blow in the prolonged battle which still had to be fought before the three armed services came under the control of a single political head.

Bentinck was also called upon, together with two other members of the Foreign Office staff, to make recommendations for the future organization of the SIS. *We had a small committee consisting of Neville Bland, Ivone Kirkpatrick and myself. Ivone Kirkpatrick had a lot of other things to do and didn't turn up very much. The Secretary was Capel-Dunn.*

The report of this small sub-committee was presented to the Chiefs of Staff on 5 June 1945. A decision was later taken that it should not be made public before 1996. When it is released it will no doubt be a document of appreciable historical interest, summarizing, as it will, some of the clearest thinking on intelligence as it was conducted before the business of gathering information had the benefit of the satellite, and that of collating it the benefit of the computer.

Bentinck was able to reveal a few of the recommendations. *We instructed Stewart Menzies*, he said, *to hoard all the money he could before the war ended because we knew that after the war the Treasury wouldn't give a penny if it didn't have to. I've been told that this was done.*

The sub-committee also considered the quality and use of

agents. *It's very difficult*, Bentinck said, *to cover up people. Personally I think the fellow who's really worth while is your high-level one. The people who get you bits and pieces out of waste-paper baskets—it doesn't really give you a good picture. The high-level fellow will talk freely and get inside information. That was what we said we should go for and, of course, money for intercepting communications.* As an example of the 'high-level fellows' wanted, Bentinck cited the film producer Alexander Korda, *who became Sir Alexander Korda for having been helpful. He was looked after by Claude Dansey, and after the war Claude Dansey was looked after by him.* The sub-committee considered too the working of the Official Secrets Act. *We came to the conclusion that the best thing to do was to leave it alone.*

In making his recommendations for the future Bentinck was uniquely well qualified to assess the relative value of the different sources of information which had served to guide decision-making during the war. The importance of Ultra had, he believed, been exaggerated in certain quarters. Although it had been the principal British source of intelligence, he had been conscious of Ultra's limitations. *We did not always know in advance what the Germans were going to do. Ultra was of great use tactically but not of such vital importance when it came to longer-term appreciations of German intentions. For the political side Ultra was very valuable, but not absolutely indispensable. If you'd relied on Ultra only you might not have got the picture quite right.* This assessment of Ultra did not differ greatly from that of Peter Calvocoressi, who wrote: 'If I were to single out its most typical contribution, I would pick its constant and thorough delineation of the German order of battle.'

On the use of agents Bentinck disagreed with the judgement of Strong, who wrote: 'The importance of the secret agent is vastly overrated in wartime, when everything is moving so fast.' *The SIS*, Bentinck said, *developed with time. We had people who were remarkable.* Of the contributions by Allied services he said: *The Poles were the best people by far.*

In pronouncing these and other judgements, Bentinck had the unique qualification of having been the chief British intelligence officer in a war in which, after an unpromising start, the British had shown themselves overwhelmingly superior to all their enemies in every aspect of intelligence and in all other forms of clandestine warfare. One aspect in which superiority was most marked, and with which Bentinck was throughout the war most closely concerned, was the presentation of facts and analyses to those who had to make decisions at the highest levels.

Among the most extraordinary facts of the second world war was the number of disastrous decisions which Hitler and the German High Command made. *The Germans*, Bentinck said, *could have won the war five times over. We were lucky that they didn't try to invade. They would have succeeded. They would have had losses, but only a fraction of what they had in Russia. If they'd gone on steadily bombing we wouldn't have been so happy. If they'd got the Japanese after Pearl Harbor to push into the Indian Ocean and cut our communications with Egypt. It would have been easily done, for our old R-class battleships weren't able to stand up to the Japanese fleet. If they'd given a couple more panzer divisions to Rommel, Alamein mightn't have taken place. The greatest mistake was going into Russia. Once they'd gone into Russia I knew the Germans weren't going to win the war.*

That these and other blunders were committed cannot be attributed primarily to faulty strategic thinking or even to Hitler's intuition. Hitler did make errors of judgement on a colossal scale, but he was not without military competence, and there was plenty of expertise in the higher ranks of the German armed forces. A major contributory factor to all the mistakes made was faulty intelligence.

The main causes of the inadequacy of the German intelligence services as a whole were to be found in the nature of the national-socialist system: in the mutual distrust of which Steengracht spoke to Bentinck; in the rivalry, particularly between army and party, which led to duplication in all branches of intelligence, even cryptography; above all in the fear of provoking the anger of a superior by bringing unwelcome news or expressing an unpopular opinion.

Without this distrust, duplication and fear MI 5 could not have kept so many double agents in play so long and so successfully. Nor could the fact that Enigma ciphers were being read regularly have remained a secret until the end. There were a number of breaches of security by those who had access to information from Ultra, a few of which have been mentioned here. Yet all were overlooked or explained away.

Even more extraordinary was the fact that deciphering of Enigma was continued on French territory long after the French defeat of 1940. The staff of the cryptology section of the French Deuxième Bureau in the early months of the war had numbered about seventy. Several of them fell into German hands when France was overrun, as did archives and other material. Nevertheless the head of the section, Gustave Bertrand, made his way to Vichy France, where he continued his work on Enigma with a staff of thirty-two, of whom fifteen were Poles. Seven were Spaniards, most of them communists.

When the Germans occupied Vichy France the two senior Poles tried to escape over the Pyrenees, but were betrayed and captured. From them the Germans seem to have learnt nothing. Bertrand himself continued to travel regularly between Vichy and Paris. Eventually he fell into the hands of the Abwehr, to whom he was known as a member of the Deuxième Bureau. Yet, according to his own account, his offer to work for the Germans was accepted; he then escaped from them, and was picked up, together with his wife, by the RAF and landed in England. However all these events are explained, it remains a fact that, whereas a number of Germans had good reason to believe that the British were reading Enigma ciphers, Hitler and the High Command continued to base policies on the assumption that the secrets of Enigma were inviolate.

For reasons perhaps not dissimilar to those which operated in Germany the Japanese also ignored a number of warnings that their ciphers were being read. One of these was a front-page report in the *Chicago Tribune*.

In Britain, by contrast, duplication within the intelligence services was largely eliminated after the first year of war. Rivalry existed, but seldom as anything worse than an irritant. Fear of senior officers was also limited and was certainly not felt at the highest level. Bentinck stood up to Brooke and told him the truth as he saw it. Brooke in his turn stood up to Churchill and did the same. Neither Bentinck nor Brooke feared the loss of his life in consequence, or even his job.

The United States intelligence services, as they developed, enjoyed a similar relative freedom of operation. To what extent the huge apparatus for intelligence and security in the Soviet Union suffered in wartime from the kind of defect which characterized Nazi Germany must remain, in the Western world, largely a subject for conjecture. Certainly it would have required a brave man to make a habit of bringing unwelcome news to Stalin. It seems everywhere to be characteristic of the kind of megalomaniac who becomes an all-powerful dictator that, on the one hand, he is highly suspicious and, on the other he needs a constant diet of the kind of flattery which consists of telling him what he wants to hear.

Bentinck was not required to remain in office until the end of the war with Japan. He was replaced as Chairman of the JIC by Harold Caccia, a future British Ambassador in Washington and future Permanent Under-Secretary at the Foreign Office. Lord Caccia, as he became, later described the Committee of the Chiefs of Staff as a formidable body which demanded concise, accurate intelligence and had no time to spare for anything else. He was also aware that another civilian would not have been tolerated as Chairman of the JIC unless Bentinck had filled the role with outstanding success.

For Bentinck two appointments were considered, both of major importance in the Europe of the first years of peace. One was to the post of political head of the military government of Germany. The other was to the Embassy in Poland, the country whose invasion had been the immediate cause of the war, whose territorial boundaries and future form of government had been discussed at seven out of the eight plenary sessions at the Yalta conference, and over whose management of her affairs in the immediate post-war years Britain had been accorded by the Yalta agreement certain limited rights of supervision.

For personal reasons Bentinck was reluctant to take either appointment. He had met Mrs Kathleen Tillotson, who came from Montreal, had seen much of her during the war, and wished to marry her. His wife would not grant him a divorce, and he therefore decided to bring divorce proceedings himself. In either Germany or Poland he would be in the public eye and in a representational post, and the publicity likely to accrue to a contested divorce could be damaging. All this he pointed out to the Foreign Office.

Eden was aware of Bentinck's problem. Bruce Lockhart recorded in his diary on 4 July 1945: 'Drove down to Binderton to spend the day and night with Anthony. We got on to the new Ambassador in Poland. He was in a quandary. He wanted to appoint Bill Cavendish-Bentinck, but Bill could not get away because of his divorce case.' According to Bruce Lockhart, Eden went on to say that Churchill's choice for the post was Duff Cooper, but that he himself did not want to appoint anybody from outside the Foreign Service.

Bentinck's qualifications for the post were evident. Apart from his wartime record he had served in Poland after the first world war. He was aware of Polish achievements in clandestine as well as overt warfare against the Germans. He had performed with grace as disagreeable an assignment as any which fell to a British diplomat during the war. This was to tell the Polish Ambassador, Count Edward Raczyński, that because of crippling losses in the flights to and from southern Italy the R A F would no longer be able to drop supplies to the people of Warsaw to help them in their rising against the German occupier.

Consideration of Bentinck's qualifications was decisive. Eden came to the conclusion that the advantages of having Bentinck in Poland must outweigh any possible unpleasantness arising out of his divorce action. Bentinck was therefore offered the post of Ambassador and accepted.

CHAPTER 16

Return to Poland
(1945–47)

I first met Bentinck in the summer of 1945. I had been appointed to serve as his Press Attaché in Warsaw, and he received me in a small room in the Foreign Office. A tall, impressive, good-looking, bespectacled man in his late forties, with perfect manners, he gave me the impression of being probably somewhat cold and even austere. The meeting was not a long one.

Press attachés were at that time appointed by the Ministry of Information. (The title 'press attaché' was shortly afterwards abolished in favour of 'information secretary' in recognition of the fact that the press was no longer the principal medium of information and persuasion.) The method of our recruitment was slightly haphazard. Among fairly recent appointments had been that of John Betjeman to Dublin.

During my rather cursory briefing at the Ministry I made some inquiries about living conditions in Poland. Not much seemed to be known, and I was advised to take a week's British rations with me. These did not occupy much space in my suitcase.

I flew to Warsaw on a perfect September day. As the aircraft came down over the city I could not discern a single roof on such buildings as remained. After sixty-three days of intensive street warfare in the summer of 1944, at the end of which the Poles were reduced to fighting with scythes and their bare hands, the Germans had emptied the city apart from that section to the east of the Vistula which was already occupied by the Russians. They had then set about systematically destroying it. This they had done with notable efficiency.

As I was driven from the makeshift airfield through the acres of rubble the depression this induced was lifted by the sight of women selling large bunches of flowers and evidently doing a good trade.

The British Embassy staff, I discovered, occupied most of

the fourth floor of the Hotel Polonia, a former railway hotel, which had served as a German military headquarters and had therefore not been demolished. The hotel also housed the embassies or legations of a number of other Western countries, including the United States, as well as workers for international relief organizations, journalists and others who, for various reasons, had made their way behind what Churchill was shortly to call the Iron Curtain. Our bedrooms were also our offices.

Later on my first day I was taken down to the hotel restaurant and presented with a menu which astounded me. Among other dishes I had a large and excellent steak cooked in butter such as no law-abiding subject had seen in Britain for years. How this was possible I soon discovered. Warsaw is the centre of a large food-producing area; the peasants continued to bring their food to the markets; and, because of the devastation of war, transport for removing it eastwards was not available.

I soon learnt that the Foreign Office had chosen a staff of outstanding quality for its representation in Poland. The two senior Foreign Service members, after the Ambassador, were the Counsellor, Robin Hankey, and the Head of Chancery, John Russell. Hankey was the son of Maurice, later Lord Hankey, the great administrator, who could be regarded as the creator of the JIC. Russell also had a distinguished father, Sir Thomas Russell Pasha, the famous Chief of the Cairo Police and Director of the Narcotics Bureau.

Hankey had opened up the Embassy and had first been noticed in public when relieving an old woman of the burden of a huge sack of either coal or potatoes. (Later accounts of the incident varied.) The qualities of kindness and spontaneity which this revealed were blended with shrewdness of judgement and, at times, a forthright expression of what that judgement demanded.

Russell, who was still only thirty, was a tall, commanding figure, already bald, with lively eyes and an incisive manner. He was to die suddenly in 1984. *The Times* then wrote of him: 'He was one of the last British ambassadors to conduct his missions successively in the grand aristocratic manner as a personal representative of the sovereign rather than an official of the government of the day.' It added: 'There was never any doubt of the enjoyment or humour which he brought to his work.'

There were other gifted members of the staff whom I came to know before long, but surpassing them all in ability and commanding them effortlessly was Bentinck himself. Among the qualities in him I soon perceived were humanity, humour and quickness of mind. My initial judgement at the Foreign Office had been wrong.

Bentinck held a daily meeting of all his senior staff at 9 a.m. I had to begin by giving a summary of the contents of the Polish morning newspapers. After that various subjects of general interest were discussed, Bentinck encouraging everyone, irrespective of rank, to speak his mind, just as he had done when controlling the Joint Intelligence Staff. The atmosphere was friendly and informal, yet I do not think anyone ventured to appear as much as a minute late for a meeting more than once. Bentinck's dog, an Aberdeen terrier named Angus, was always present, and when he wanted to fly a kite or report information from a source he did not choose to reveal, Bentinck would begin by saying: 'Angus tells me . . .' One soon learnt to pay particular attention to anything Angus said.

For preparing the summary of the press I had the assistance of a distinguished-looking, grey-haired lady of about fifty named Maniuta Marynowska, whom Hankey had known when he had served in the Warsaw Embassy before the war. She was later to become a pawn in a ruthlessly conducted political contest. For the rest, I adopted the simple expedient of engaging some of the prettiest girls in Warsaw and placing a large order for drink, under the export quota, with Saccone and Speed in London. As a result my office-cum-bedroom soon became the recognized meeting ground of the foreign correspondents of the Western world, of whom the unofficial doyen was Larry Allen, of the Associated Press. These arrangements, I was glad to observe, seemed to meet with Bentinck's approval, particularly the employment of the pretty girls. Before long it caused some concern in the Press Department of the Polish Ministry of Foreign Affairs, which was driven to establish similar and rival attractions.

The Government to which Bentinck was accredited was known as the Polish Provisional Government. Its formation had been the result of prolonged bargaining between the Soviet Union on the one hand and the United States and Great Britain on the other, in which the Soviet Union was overwhelmingly successful. As a preliminary to obtaining full recognition the Provisional Government undertook to hold 'free and unfettered elections'. This tautology was to be open to more than one interpretation, as was the commitment to allow 'all democratic and anti-Nazi parties' to take part in the election.

The Soviet Government had assembled during the war a group of Polish communists, most of whom had lived outside Poland for many years. They became known as the Lublin Committee. The legitimate Polish Government was established in London, and for the fusion of the two in a future administration Stalin suggested that four-fifths of the ministers should come from Lublin and one fifth from London. He achieved roughly what he wanted.

Apart from the elderly Professor Władysław Grabski, who had been Prime Minister shortly after the first world war, only one Polish politician of distinction coming from the West was accepted within the Provisional Government. This was Stanislaw Mikołajczyk, who had become Prime Minister when General Sikorski had been killed in an air crash. *A very honest, genuine peasant leader*, in Bentinck's judgement, Mikołajczyk was also a man of courage and strength of character. He had returned to Poland after considerable pressure had been exercised on him by both the British and United States governments. According to his own account, Churchill had told him that the Lublin Poles had no authority among the Polish people and that they needed him, to which Mikołajczyk replied: 'All they need is the Red Army and the NKVD.'

The holding of genuinely free elections, as the term is generally understood in the Western world, could never have been more than a hope. That the Soviet Government, which had at no time allowed its own people to vote freely, should accord this privilege to a nation with such a long and understandable record of hostility towards Russia, and whose territory lay across the Red Army's lines of communication with its occupying forces in Germany, was beyond reasonable expectation. Nevertheless one of the principal instructions given to Bentinck was to do his utmost, in conjunction with his United States colleague, to ensure that elections of the kind agreed upon at Yalta were held.

The American Ambassador, Arthur Bliss Lane, had been on friendly terms with Bentinck since they had both been posted to Warsaw in 1919. 'A friendship of many years,' Lane wrote in his book on Poland, *I Saw Freedom Betrayed*, 'and the fact that we saw eye to eye on the attempts of the Polish Government to avoid its international obligations, resulted in our always speaking with the utmost frankness to each other.'

Lane (*Blissful Arthur* as Bentinck called him) was a genial, likeable and capable diplomat. My impression, and that of a number of my colleagues, was that he was wise enough to accept not a little guidance from Bentinck. *I was accused*, Bentinck said later, *by Sidney Gruson of the* New York Times *of having too much influence on Blissful Arthur.*

The excellent working relationship between the two ambassadors was to be slightly impaired after a time. *On one occasion, Bentinck said, I went down to Cracow and got a message from Blissful Arthur asking if I would come up to Warsaw, as he was worried. I found him in rather a state of nerves and couldn't make out why he wanted me to come. We were always absolutely frank and told each other what instructions we had had, which worked very well.*

He was very loyal. Some years afterwards, when he came through London, he told me what had worried him. He had had some instructions from Byrnes, who was Secretary of State, and at the end of the instructions were the words: 'You should not, repeat not, discuss this with your British colleague.' Byrnes of course was an Irish American.

The effective Polish Government was a small oligarchy. The man who, in some respects, was its most powerful member had the unimpressive title of Under-Secretary of State for the Council of Ministers. This was Jakob Berman, who had been arrested in Poland in 1937 and sentenced to three years' imprisonment as a high-ranking Soviet agent. Berman had one telephone on his desk connecting him with Molotov and another connecting him with Zhdanov, the head of the Polit-buro. The President of the Republic, Bolesław Bierut, was also a powerful figure and also an agent of the N K V D. He had startled Churchill during the war by demanding, in the name of the Polish people, that the largely Polish city of Lwów should be incorporated within the Soviet Union. Economic affairs were largely controlled by a communist named Hilary Minc, whose wife was, in Bentinck's judgement, an even more dedicated Marxist than he was. (The ineffectual Prime Minister, Osóbka-Morawski, admitted to Arthur Bliss Lane that he knew nothing about his Government's economic policy.) Another man with wide-ranging powers and modest title was the Deputy Speaker, Roman Zambrowski, who had formerly gone under the name of Nussbaum and who now, in his additional capacity of Special Commissioner for the Pros-ecution of Embezzlement, Fraud and Economic Sabotage, could dispose of his enemies much as he chose.

One member of the oligarchy differed from the others in that he had spent the war years in Poland. This was Władysław Gomulka, the Secretary-General of the Polish Communist Party. *Gomulka*, Bentinck said, *was the only one who was mentally genuinely a Pole*. A man of violent temper, Gomulka was to fall from power shortly after the break between Tito and the Cominform because of 'nationalistic-communistic tendencies'. He was later to enjoy fourteen years of authority following the Poznań riots of 1956.

According to Mikołajczyk, who was extremely well in-formed, the most powerful man in Poland was a Soviet general named Malinov, who never appeared on public occa-sions and who was unknown, even by name, to more than a handful of Poles. He considerably outranked the Soviet Ambassador in Warsaw, Lebedev, who was also super-vised by his First Secretary, an officer in the N K V D named Yakovlev. *Lebedev*, Bentinck said, *was a nice fellow. I tried to be friendly with him. I said to him – and he didn't deny it – 'There'll be plenty of people trying to make mischief between us.'*

For a man of Bentinck's experience and capacity it was not difficult to judge the character or foresee the intentions of the effective majority in the Polish Provisional Government. Moreover he and his staff had the benefit of plenty of information from Polish sources. It takes time to install the full apparatus of a police state, particularly in a country where the security policy and the great bulk of the population are mutually antagonistic from the outset. As a result, for the first year or more of the Embassy's presence, although press and radio were rigidly censored, there was considerable freedom of private speech. Of this the Poles took advantage to the point of foolhardiness.

On 10 October 1945, some two and a half months after his arrival in Warsaw, Bentinck wrote in a despatch: 'With the exception of four Ministers out of twenty-one, the Government of Poland is composed of Communists and their supporters; the Communist Party have a complete grip on the administrative machine, in which all but a few of the key posts are occupied by their nominees. The press is regimented. The Russian and Communist controlled "Security" police produce an atmosphere of terror. Except as regards commerce and industry the situation has not deteriorated during the last two months. The Polish Peasant Party led by Mm. Witos and Mikołajczyk is now well organised, and it is generally acknowledged that if a genuine election were to be held now this party would certainly secure over sixty per cent of the votes cast.'

Bentinck went on: 'It is clear to me that the Polish Communist clique who have the Government of this country in their hands have no intention of abandoning power if the elections should go against them. They are convinced that they will bring about a form of Government and of life that will be best for Poland, and hotly deny that they are aping the Russians.'

Witos, who had been Prime Minister when Piłsudski had defeated the Soviet forces at the approaches to Warsaw in 1920, died very shortly after this despatch was written. This served to increase Mikołajczyk's authority in what was becoming the effective party of opposition and his popularity among the nation as a whole.

For his day-to-day dealings with the Polish Government Bentinck found himself mostly in contact with the Vice-Minister of Foreign Affairs, Zygmunt Modzelewski, with whom he established a certain *rapport*, and whose intelligence and ability he respected. After a meeting with an influential member of the Polish wartime Government, Professor Kot, who paid a short visit to Poland in September 1945, Bentinck wrote to the Foreign Office: 'Kot tells me that Modżelewski, who is a Communist, was originally called Fischhaut and that he was for some time employed by the Soviet commercial organisation (Sovtorg) in Paris. One of the attractive features of the present administration here is that nothing is known about the past of many of its members, where they came from or what names they formerly bore. They are colloquially known as the "ski-ers" as they have mostly taken names ending in -ski.' Bentinck went on: 'Modżelewski is the real Minister for Foreign Affairs. The titular occupant of that post, Rzymowski, is an unattractive old stooge with the reputation of an unsavoury turncoat. When I saw them together this morning Modżelewski and myself did all the talking and rather ignored Rzymowski. A strange state of affairs, but it is better to deal with Communists than with their stooges.'

These despatches, written a few months after Bentinck's arrival, although they show that he had no illusions about the nature of the Government to which he was accredited, have an underlying quality of cheerfulness. This in itself reflected a buoyancy in the people of Warsaw of which in 1945 it was impossible not to be aware. It manifested itself in a number of ways, most clearly in the determination with which, having returned to their devastated city, they set about creating a new life there.

Rather over a year later, on 27 December 1946, Bentinck was to write: 'The principal feeling in Poland is fear, although pride may cause individual Poles to conceal this when in the company of foreigners. Fear of the Soviet Union, fear of the resurrection of a powerful and vengeful Germany, and above all fear of the Security Police.'

He went on to state that the Soviet Government's nominees, 'who will unfortunately remain in power here after the elections, will continue and probably intensify this method of rule with a view to drawing Poland even more into the Soviet orbit. The two main obstacles which they will have to overcome are the character of the Polish people and the influence of the Roman Catholic Church. Despite two years' rule by a government, which could not remain in power for forty-eight hours without a police similar to the Nazi Gestapo or the Soviet M V D and now almost as expert as the latter, the spirit and vitality of the Poles are not yet broken, though their spirit is certainly cowed.'

Emphasizing again the influence of the Church, Bentinck added: 'Services are packed, sermons are heard with close attention, political injunctions from the pulpit are obeyed.'

Bentinck travelled extensively in Poland, usually accompanied by a young Third Secretary named Lewis Massey, who was bilingual and who acted as his interpreter. On one of his visits to Cracow I saw him being bodily seized, somewhat to his consternation, by a group of students and then carried shoulder-high through cheering crowds. Not many British ambassadors in modern times, or indeed at any time, can have been accorded similar treatment.

In Warsaw itself, largely because of the lack of accommodation, almost any British subject who arrived was drawn immediately towards the Hotel Polonia and therefore to the British Embassy. One of the most striking of these was Rabbi Solomon Schonfeld, who after the war made a determined and widespread search for Jewish orphans.

Schonfeld's day-to-day dealings were largely with Alan Banks, a shrewd and able Vice-Consul, who during the war had served in SIS in West Africa. Banks later wrote his memoirs. Of Schonfeld he stated: 'When he had got a party of about forty orphans together it was his custom to take a room in the Polonia Hotel and bring them to me in groups of four to receive entry visas into the United Kingdom. As a result of this contact, I was able to report to the Ambassador information which had a bearing on the demand to increase the number of admissions to Palestine. An Anglo-American committee was formed to collect evidence of the Jewish plight in Europe and to estimate the numbers wishing to leave. The committee came to Warsaw and, with the Ambassador, those of us who were informed of the situation were invited to say our piece before its members. Subsequently they decided that 100,000 immigrants per annum should be admitted.'

Of Bentinck Banks wrote that he had 'the greatest admiration and affection' for him. Once Bentinck had moved into the small villa which he acquired, Banks recalled: 'He made a point of asking three or four members of the staff, from the most junior to the senior, to lunch at his house every day he was free to do so. He was able to evoke loyalty without apparent effort and was greatly loved and admired.'

The villa was made available to John Russell, who had returned briefly to England to be married, for his honeymoon. Bentinck subsequently became godfather to the Russells' daughter Georgiana. Russell recalled one incident with particular pleasure. At a time when there was no accepted rate of exchange between the zloty and the pound sterling the Foreign Office solved the problem this presented by ceasing to pay any allowances. Bentinck informed the Foreign Office that its methods were reminiscent of those prevailing in the Sublime Porte in the days of the Sultan Abdul Hamid.

Michael Winch, a member of the staff with scholarly inclinations, who reported most knowledgeably on Polish political affairs, told me how grateful he was to Bentinck for teaching him the importance of speed in reporting. Robin Hankey, looking back over nearly forty years, said unequivocally: 'Bill was a great Ambassador.'

For my part I found him the perfect chief. If I had a problem or needed a decision I did not trouble to explain the details or the background, as he always knew them. Yet he let me run my office as I chose without any interference, expecting the highest standards and receiving as a result the best we were able to give.

He supported me in all my efforts, open or surreptitious, to circumvent the censorship and to counter the persistent hostility to Britain to be found in the Government-controlled media. He was aware that some of the charges made against British policy were beginning to have an effect on Polish public opinion. This caused him concern, and he reported to the Foreign Office accordingly.

In a long despatch written towards the end of 1946 he listed the main causes of complaint against Britain which could be considered to have some substance. One of these was the reluctance of the British Government to accept as final the delineation of Poland's western frontier with Germany. This reluctance was contrasted in the Polish press with the Soviet Government's unequivocal acceptance of the frontier.

While the Polish Government continued to be styled 'provisional', the British Government did not feel obliged to release gold and naval vessels which had been the property of the Polish Government in exile. As these were bound to be returned eventually, Bentinck suggested that the sooner this was done the better. He also called attention to certain anomalies in the payment of bonuses to former members of the Polish armed forces in the West who had decided to return to Poland. The final cause of complaint was one which a more cautious man than Bentinck might have omitted. This was the hostile attitude shown by certain British trade unions towards the employment of men demobilized from the Polish armed forces. As a dedicated trade unionist the Foreign Secretary, Ernest Bevin, cannot have found this agreeable reading.

Of the various efforts made by the Polish Provisional Government to improve its reputation in Britain, and thus its international standing generally, the most successful were those which involved the support of British members of Parliament. Success was not invariable. In October 1945, for instance, four members of the British Co-operative Society, led by the newly ennobled Labour peer, Lord Palmer, were invited as guests of the Polish Government. The aircraft bringing them was forced to land on an airfield near Poznań, where the Russian commander refused to allow it to continue. Only after strenuous personal intervention by Bentinck were the four guests able to reach Warsaw. They drew, I noticed, their own conclusions from this incident.

Much better stage-managed was the reception of an official parliamentary delegation which came to Poland early in 1946. This included members of the Labour and Conservative parties as well as Phil Piratin, one of the two communists returned at the 1945 election. In practice the delegates formed themselves into two sections. The guiding spirit of one was a politically minded doctor of medicine named Stephen Taylor, later Lord Taylor. The other consisted of two Conservative MPs, one of whom was a young man who had served alongside Polish forces in the war—Tufton Beamish, later Lord Chelwood.

Of the manner in which they conducted their investigations and the guidance they received from Bentinck, Taylor and Chelwood later gave varying accounts. Chelwood said he had found Bentinck 'a man of very penetrating mind. However serious the comment, there was always that twinkle in his eye.' The delegation's briefing, in which Hankey and Russell had joined, had been excellent, and Bentinck had advised him, when he reached Cracow, to plead a headache, escape from the official guides, and pay some private visits. This he did and as a result was able to spend two hours with the Cardinal Archbishop Sapieha, considerably to the annoyance of his guides.

Taylor, by contrast, found Bentinck, 'very charming, very amusing, and a great ladies' man', but 'a very poor intelligence officer'. He added: 'His advice was of no value. He sent us off to see people who were supposed to be middle-of-the-road socialists, but were pretty broken down and useless—no match for the communists.'

One of the proposals which the Polish Government was then considering for the better management of the future elections was to present all candidates, including members of Mikołajczyk's Polish Peasant Party, to the electorate in a single unified *bloc*. Division of the spoils would have been made once the election was over.

In the majority report, which Dr Taylor drafted for the parliamentary delegation, it was stated: 'With regard to the forthcoming elections, there is much to be said for having a complete *bloc* of all Parties.' Other statements contained in the report were: 'There have recently been less reasons for complaint about the Security Police'; and 'we had no evidence of Russian interference in Polish internal affairs'.

A minority report was also produced. This was drafted by Beamish: 'We think it is a mistake,' the minority report stated, 'to in any way gloss over the fact that tens of thousands of Poles are imprisoned without trial for alleged political offences. There was no subject on which we heard more bitter complaints than this.' The report added: 'We were struck by the fact that, in the comparatively small area we saw, Russian troops were scattered in small parties in practically every village of any size.'

It was perhaps a telling reflection on British political theory and practice that on such a matter-of-fact question as whether the people of Poland were or were not being allowed the kind of government they wanted, opinion should be divided so clearly along party lines.

I did not meet any members of the parliamentary delegation while it was in Poland because, shortly before their arrival, I was knocked down while on the pavement by a Red Army lorry. As the back wheel of the lorry and two wheels of a trailer ran over the middle of my body in the area of the pelvis, I was necessarily out of action for some weeks.

There were, however, visits from several other members of Parliament who, after a few days in the country, formed a picture of contemporary Poland which bore little relation to anything which I had been able to discern.

Of these, the best informed and the smoothest was Konni Zilliacus, who was of Finnish origin and whom the historian of MI5, Nigel West, listed, almost certainly correctly, as one of the agents of the KGB. The most engaging, in some respects, was a member for a constituency in the Potteries named John Mack. He spouted left-wing slogans rather in the manner of machine-gun fire, but he had the good sense to relish the benefits of expenses-paid, vodka-laced trips to various capitals in Eastern and Central Europe. The most aggressive, certainly to me, was a small member for a Cardiff constituency named George Thomas, who expressed to me with some fervour his enthusiasm for what was then happening in Poland. He later became Speaker of the House of Commons.

I took it as a compliment that both Thomas and Zilliacus asked questions about me in Parliament with hostile intent. I did not then appreciate the power which some of the more determined MPs who concerned themselves with Polish affairs could wield in certain circumstances, or how this could affect Bentinck.

The Polish Provisional Government decided at some time late in 1945 or early in 1946 that it did not yet have the machinery for holding elections which would both produce the results it wanted and be in any way convincing. Mikołajczyk refused to accept the proposal of a single *bloc*, and the growing popularity of his party was evident.

A decision was therefore taken to hold a referendum in June 1946, which could serve as a rehearsal for the future elections. Three questions were to be put to the electorate, which had to approve, or not, the abolition of the senate; the principles underlying the nationalization of industry and agrarian reform; and a Polish–German frontier on the line of the Oder and the western Neisse.

Mikołajczyk's party decided to oppose the Government only on the first question, that of the abolition of the senate. Its decision to do so was the signal for an intensification of the persecution to which members of the party were already subjected. The executive committee of the Polish Peasant Party in the Wrocław region was arrested in its entirety. In the Puławy area 333 farms were burnt in a day as a warning to peasants. Murders by the Security Police were common. The facts were reported by Bentinck, and on 23 January Ernest Bevin stated in the House of Commons: 'I am seriously concerned at the number of political murders that have been committed in various parts of Poland in recent weeks in circumstances that in many cases appear to point to the complicity of the Polish Security Police.'

The preparations for the referendum were also extensively covered by British and American newspaper correspondents. Among the British contingent were Tom Delmer, the wartime expert on black propaganda, now back with the *Daily Express*; Willie Forrest of the *News Chronicle*; Christopher Buckley of the *Daily Telegraph*; and Ossian Goulding of the *Daily Mail*. These were all men of ability and experience, who believed opinions should be formed to fit facts. Bentinck made himself readily accessible to them.

The fraudulent conduct of the referendum was barely concealed. Delmer described it as 'inartistic'. Here and there officials of Mikołajczyk's party were able to check the results. Where they did so they found that more than eighty-three per cent had voted against the abolition of the senate. The official results gave the total figure as thirty-two per cent.

These and other facts were reported in the British press and made known by Bentinck to the British Government. As a result he was instructed to deliver a note to the Polish Government, which called attention to the widespread belief in Poland that 'grave irregularities' occurred during the referendum. The note went on to remind the Polish Government of its obligations concerning elections under the terms of the Yalta agreement.

As a pointer to how the elections should be conducted the referendum may have served a useful purpose. As a public relations exercise it was a failure. For this the Polish Government attributed much of the blame to Bentinck, and it came to the conclusion that he must be removed.

The first move with this end in view was made at a comparatively low level, when a representative of the Protocol Department of the Ministry of Foreign Affairs suggested on a visit to London that Bentinck might be replaced. This was not a formal *démarche*, and it was not stated that Bentinck was *persona non grata*. No action was taken by the British Foreign Office.

The next move was an arrest, which was prominently announced through all the controlled media. The victim was Count Grocholski, whose family Bentinck had known since 1919. Bentinck learnt of the arrest before it was made public. As a gesture of friendship, and in order to show that their relationship was in no way clandestine, he deliberately went to Grocholski's house. It was, arguably, an injudicious step, but it probably had little, if any, effect one way or another on Grocholski's fate or his own.

Grocholski was charged with being an agent of illegal underground forces and also of collaboration with the Germans, although he had in fact been a serving officer in the Polish Home Army. As Bentinck wrote in a despatch, the real objects of Grocholski's trial were:

'i) to be a large red herring as regards the election;
'ii) to frighten Poles from contact with foreign diplomatists;
'iii) to deter us in the future from attempting to make any contact if we should so desire with the underground movement.'

Shortly afterwards he sent a telegram to Robin Hankey, who by then had left Warsaw to become head of the Northern Department in the Foreign Office, which read: 'I presume you realise that Grocholski case is part of a campaign to get rid of me.'

To the Polish Government's supporters in London the Grocholski trial afforded a welcome opportunity to attack Bentinck personally. 'The Labour movement,' the *Daily Worker* wrote, 'should insist on a thorough purge of Britain's diplomatic representation in order to put a complete and final stop to the peculiar activities revealed by the Warsaw trial. The new Britain does not require the old Cavendish-Bentincks.' Willie Gallacher, communist Member of Parliament, asked the Foreign Secretary 'if he will consider withdrawing the present Ambassador in Warsaw and replacing him by someone who will make social contacts more in keeping with the policy of the Labour Government'.

To this Hector McNeil replied on behalf of Bevin: 'I do not consider as valid the reasons for which the hon. gentleman would like to see a change of ambassadors in Warsaw.' It was a feeble answer, but by then the Government was in a quandary. When a foreign government makes it clear that it would like to see an ambassador removed it is not usually desirable to keep him in his post much longer, even when the reason why he is found unwelcome is, as it was in Bentinck's case, that he knows too much of what is going on. It had therefore already been decided to appoint Bentinck Ambassador to Brazil, but before this was made public the Polish Government made another move in its campaign against him. This was to arrest my press reader, Mrs Marynowska.

At that time there was a journalist working in Warsaw named Joel Cang, who was a Polish citizen but who reported regularly for *The Times*, the *Manchester Guardian* and the *Jewish Chronicle*. He was extremely well informed and highly intelligent. Among his regular contacts was Jakob Berman, arguably the most powerful man in the Polish Government. *It was from Berman*, Bentinck said, *that I got a message through Cang that they had nothing against me personally—they liked me personally— but they had to get rid of me*. Another item of information which Cang brought from Berman was that, if the letter announcing Bentinck's transfer had been received at the Ministry of Foreign Affairs a day earlier, it would not have been found necessary to arrest Mrs Marynowska.

Lewis Massey attended her trial as an observer. There, he told me, it was made clear, as we ourselves had known, that she had no access to any secret information, and she was charged in effect with nothing more than retailing general gossip to Bentinck.

Nevertheless she was sentenced to twelve years in prison. She did not serve the full term, but died almost immediately after her release.

Gocholski was sentenced to death on 14 January 1947. Five days later the Polish elections were held: 337 seats were deemed to have been won by the Government *bloc*, 24 by Mikołajczyk's overwhelmingly popular Polish Peasant Party and 21 by other minor parties. On 23 January Arthur Bliss Lane resigned from his post. In his letter of resignation he wrote: 'For all practical purposes my mission to Poland is ended. I believe I could do more by educating American public opinion as a private individual than I can by remaining in Poland.'

Mikołajczyk remained, but the Polish Government decided that it would not be for long. Fortunately he received news of his impending arrest and decided to escape. At least it can be said that he did so on board a British ship, thinly disguised as a British naval officer and through the contrivance of an old S O E hand and wartime associate of his named Ronald Hazell.

With the rigging of the elections and the departure of Mikołajczyk further darkness descended on Poland. But the darkness was to be neither total nor permanent. *Before I made my sorrowful departure from Warsaw in February 1947*, Bentinck recalled, *I had an interview with Modzelewski, the acting Minister of Foreign Affairs, who said to me that within ten years the people of Poland would fully understand the benefits of communism and there would be no opposition. I replied that this would take four or five generations, if ever. He inquired why. I answered: the Roman Catholic faith and Church.*

The departure of Bentinck was a cause for satisfaction to the Polish Government and to its allies in Britain, and more was to come. Bentinck brought his action for divorce in March 1947, and his wife showed that she was in no mood for compromise. The eminent KC, Sir Patrick Hastings, said he would not continue to act for her on the ground that she seemed primarily interested in destroying her husband's career, but this did not deter her.

In the 1940s divorce proceedings still tended to revolve almost exclusively around questions of adultery. On this subject Bentinck was advised to be wholly frank with the court. He accepted this advice, disagreeable though it was, and thereby ensured colourful and, in effect, highly damaging headlines and paragraphs in the evening and national newspapers.

As Mr Justice Hodson, when summing up, put it, Bentinck 'gave frank evidence', including admissions of what in judicial language were described as 'extra-marital adventures of an isolated character'. In summing up the judge said: 'No one could fail to sympathise with this husband in the way he had been treated.' Nevertheless he granted his wife's plea for a judicial separation, an arrangement which can serve to inflict punishment and encourage adultery, but is unlikely to achieve much else.

Eight months later a decision of the Court of Appeal gave Bentinck his divorce on the ground of his wife's infidelity, and in July 1948 he and Kathleen Tillotson were married. By then Bentinck was no longer a member of the Foreign Service.

Bentinck was dismissed by the personal decision of Ernest Bevin, the Foreign Secretary, because of his involvement in divorce proceedings. Exactly how the decision was arrived at is still not wholly clear. Lord Bullock, Bevin's biographer, told me he could find no more than casual references to Bentinck's dismissal in the papers he had studied. Lord Mayhew, who was a junior minister in the Foreign Office at the time, had no recollection of the event. Sir Frank Roberts, a personal friend of Bentinck, who became Bevin's Private Secretary shortly after Bentinck's dismissal, said that although Bevin would sometimes reminisce to him until the small hours of the morning, he made no reference to Bentinck. When I asked Lord Taylor if he could throw any light on the question he said: 'Didn't he get into trouble with a girl?'

The only clear pointer which Bentinck himself received came from Bevin's Private Secretary, Bob Dixon, to whom Bevin said of Bentinck: 'I could have saved him if his name had been Smith.' As it is difficult to sustain the proposition that adultery is less reprehensible in a man named Smith than in a man named Cavendish-Bentinck, the conclusion which must be drawn from this is that the real victor was class hatred, to which the British Foreign Secretary found it expedient to bow.

Not only was Bentinck dismissed from the Foreign Service. He was also deprived of all his pension rights. The *Evening Standard* described this, reasonably enough, as 'a monstrous injustice'. Tom Delmer was similarly indignant in the *Daily Express*. Unfortunately for Bentinck both the *Daily Express* and the *Evening Standard* were then owned by Lord Beaverbrook. The relationship between Bevin and Beaverbrook was one of mutual hatred, and both were powerful haters.

Bentinck had never been a rich man. Virtually all his resources were disposed of by his divorce proceedings and their consequences. At the age of forty-nine he found himself without money, without pension, without work, and having to start a new career.

CHAPTER 17

Metamorphosis of a Diplomat
(1947–54)

On 17 May 1947 Bentinck wrote a letter to Bevin's Private Secretary, Bob Dixon, which began: 'Many thanks for your nice letter of sympathy on my recent misfortunes. Whilst I am sad at leaving a service in which I have so many good friends, I find the task of seeking other employment exciting and rejuvenating.' He added that he hoped for employment which would continue long enough to spare him 'the years of enforced and irritating idleness between sixty and whenever I become too senile for work'.

He mentioned that he had had a pleasant final meeting with Bevin and described himself as one of Bevin's 'strong admirers'. He went on: 'The one matter on which I have strong feelings is that I should receive my pension, as I do not consider that an unfortunate divorce suit should be placed in a lower category than idleness or incompetence, and I understand that those who have to resign for these reasons are granted pensions.'

He never received a pension, but he did find employment which, in the event, would cause him to be actively at work for more than a quarter of a century after he reached the age of sixty. He retained his friendships with his former colleagues, and his readiness to accept the past and concern himself with the present and future struck many who knew him.

Bentinck was not without offers of employment or suggestions for what he might do. *Gomer Kemsley*, he said, *offered me the job of foreign editor of the* Sunday Times *and generally of the Kemsley Press. I looked into this and came to the conclusion that if Gomer dropped dead or sold his papers—which he later did— I should be out on my ear, because I hadn't got a union card, I hadn't been in the press world at all, and I was a protégé of a press baron.*

Efforts were made to see whether I could be placed as one of the Gauleiters of some province in Germany, but that fortunately didn't materialize. I wouldn't have been keen on it. I could see it wasn't going to last. I like things to last.

Claude Dansey suggested that Bentinck might be taken on Sir Alexander Korda's payroll but (*I couldn't see anything up my street*). He was given the opportunity of going into partnership in an enterprise called the Continental Assets Realisations Trust with Leonard Ingrams, *the father of the man who runs* Private Eye *so successfully*. Then he was invited to lunch with Felix Guépin, *an up-and-coming and very able executive at Shell*. The purpose of this was to discover whether he would be interested in helping a number of leading British companies to recover their property in occupied Germany and resume business operations there. For these purposes a body had been formed called the Committee of Industrial Interests in Germany, which was financed by the companies participating.

A meeting of this committee was held at Unilever House on 16 June 1947, when it was decided to appoint Bentinck as a full-time officer of the committee. The appointment was to be for a year in the first instance. He was given the title of Vice-Chairman, the Chairman being Sir Charles Tennyson, a direct descendant of the great poet. Tennyson was Secretary of the Dunlop Rubber Company, but his interests were literary rather than commercial. Within two years Bentinck was to become Chairman, with Tennyson given the courtesy title of President. Two years after that Tennyson wrote to Bentinck: 'The receipt of your committee's extremely satisfactory accounts reminded me that I am still—is it?— President. Really I have now receded so far into limbo that my continuance in that office seems rather absurd.'

Bentinck's salary was £3,000 a year. This enabled him, within the limits imposed by the age of austerity, to live fairly comfortably. He and his wife set up house in Trevor Place, off Knightsbridge. Bentinck's son and daughter were both living in London, and he was able gradually to soften the effects of the destructive and divisive bitterness of the divorce action and the events preceding it. The daughter, Mary Jane, was described to me as being at that time 'a Junoesque beauty'. Their mother had appealed to the House of Lords against the Court of Appeal's judgement, but in July 1948 it was announced that she had withdrawn this appeal because satisfactory financial arrangements had been made. That was the end of the litigation.

Unilever, Bentinck said, *provided me with an office. To begin with I just had a secretary, Sheila Owen, a model of efficiency and tolerance. She had a thorough knowledge of German, also French and Dutch, and was my prop and mainstay for twenty-two years.*

Much of Bentinck's work in the early years consisted of dealing with the Allied Military Governments of Britain, France and the United States. He did not visit the Soviet Zone. *They wouldn't let me travel about.* Nor did he see any likelihood of being able to protect British commercial interests there. *One of the reasons why I didn't join Leonard Ingrams*, he said, *was that we had different opinions. He thought you were going to get something out of the Russian zone and I said: 'No, you can write that off.'* In October 1947 Bentinck did propose to the Foreign Office, on behalf of the committee, that 'in view of the unsatisfactory treatment of British property in the Soviet zone His Majesty's Government should inform the Soviet Government that, unless they improved things, His Majesty's Government would be compelled to compensate British companies out of plant or other materials which would otherwise be sent from the British zone to the USSR as reparations'. Nothing came of the suggestion.

From an early stage Bentinck was sceptical of the benefits and merits of occupation by the Western powers. After a visit to Switzerland in August 1947 he reported to his committee: 'The Swiss are unable to understand why the British do not take any advantages they can from their victory and why they adopt the attitude that they are trustees for the German people. They are convinced that the Germans could look after themselves and that if the three western zones were to be handed over to a German government, with certain Allied forces being maintained solely for security, the recovery of Germany to the west of the Soviet zone would within five years outstrip that of France, Italy or the United Kingdom—so long as His Majesty's present Government remain in office.'

The people in military government who were the good ones, Bentinck said, *were the people who put the drains right, who got the electricity and the trains working and directed repairs to the roads.* Trade union and currency reform were also, in his opinion, well arranged. *Bevin sent out some very good people from the Ministry of Labour with instructions to organize the German trade unions prompted by all our mistakes. Shell had to deal with about thirty-eight unions here. In Germany they only had one. The whole of finance had to be reorganized. That was done very efficiently. It was directed by the Americans and ourselves, and the Germans took part in it. It was ruthless, but it set the finances on their feet. At one time five cigarettes had been equal to one ton of first-class steel scrap.*

Nevertheless, *occupation*, he said, *is soul-rotting. The temptations are so great. The best people left after completing their tasks, or to return to business. Others wanted to stay on and believed the occupation would last twenty years.* By the end of 1949 Bentinck went so far as to report to his committee that 'the working of the High Commission in Germany has struck me as being in a poor way'.

The failures of the three Western occupying powers to co-ordinate their policies also seemed to him unfortunate. 'I think,' he wrote in one of his earlier reports, 'that we may well have sacrificed the tangible benefits of really close Anglo-American co-operation in our pursuit of quadripartite control.' Although he had a high opinion of the American Military Governor, General Lucius Clay, he deplored, particularly so far as the companies he represented were concerned, what he called 'the American zeal for decartelisation and deconcentration'.

Bentinck had many advantages in carrying out the tasks entrusted to him by the committee which others might have lacked. As Sheila Owen put it, 'He could get results which other people couldn't and unlock doors that the Unilever people couldn't. I don't think a lesser mortal would have managed to get to Germany early on. It was terribly difficult.' In Germany he had numerous friends in leading positions by whom he was invited to stay or to dine, and he knew where to go for information. Sir Peter Wilkinson, who became British Ambassador in Vienna and who saw something of his work in Germany in the 1950s, stated: 'Of all the diplomats I have come across he was perhaps the most professional. When he came to Germany he always made a beeline for the Labour Attaché as the surest source of information.'

To equip himself for his new fields of activity he read widely. His regular reading, Miss Owen noted, included, in addition to the leading British newspapers, the *Economist*, the German *Handelsblatt*, the *Neue Zürcher Zeitung* and various economic digests and summaries produced by Unilever or Shell.

Thus fortified he was able to present the problems of British industry, at first to the Allied Military Governments, and later to the German authorities, with expertise in addition to diplomatic skill. After a meeting with Christopher Steel, the Political Adviser to the Military Governor, General Robertson, he reported: 'I detected a tendency on his part to consider that the protection of British interests in Germany must take second place when political considerations are involved.'

This attitude was widespread and understandable, but it was Bentinck's task to oppose it so far as he reasonably could. In February 1948, after a visit of some two weeks, which took him to Berlin, Hamburg, Frankfurt, Cologne, Düsseldorf and the Ruhr, he wrote to his committee: 'A communication should be addressed to the Foreign Office asking whether His Majesty's Government wish to maintain and further British industrial interests in Germany and, on the assumption that the answer is in the affirmative, requesting that they should ensure that these British interests are exempted from exceptional taxes, levies and imposts for meeting charges arising out of the war, or meeting the costs of the occupying forces or of reparations.'

It was the first salvo in a campaign which was to engage much of Bentinck's energy over the next four years.

Among the tasks specifically assigned to Bentinck by his committee was 'the collection of information regarding business conditions in Germany'. This he carried out with characteristic thoroughness, and in one year he made thirty-two trips abroad.

In the summer of 1947, he said, *German industry was a shambles. Essen was all rubble.* Yet before the end of the year he informed his committee: 'The Germans are coming up now. We cannot have it both ways. Either the Germans will be competitors, and we shall not have to keep them alive, or else we shall have to continue to pay for them.'

Of the German capacity for hard work, which was transforming the industrial scene, he had plenty of evidence. Of one company he said: *The work force used to wait outside the gates until they opened in the morning at six o'clock. Then they dashed in in order to do enough piecework to earn an extra wage.*

In February 1949, after a visit to Germany, Bentinck reported: 'This month I reached the conclusion that economic recovery is now on as firm a basis as that of any country in Western Europe.' A year later he stated: 'Whereas formerly I felt quite well dressed in Germany, my latest visit made me feel I should buy at least two new suits.'

Much of the improvement he attributed to the efforts of the new German administration, with some of whose leading figures, particularly Dr Ludwig Erhard, he was in close contact. Of Erhard himself he said: *He was really rather a simple soul.* But he was an early champion of Erhard's economic policy. 'Dr Erhard's policy of liberalisation,' he reported to his committee in February 1950, 'has met with the strongest disapproval of the British Government, and the US High Commission are beginning to think that he may have gone too fast and too far. Dr Erhard, with whom I spent some four hours at dinner, seemed to be in no way lacking in self-confidence.'

Bentinck went on: 'The first stage of Dr Erhard's plan, which was to satisfy the home market, raise morale and establish confidence, has been completed.' Prices had fallen, union leaders had shown themselves to be 'practical persons and not doctrinaires', and the conclusion Bentinck reached was that 'Germany will be a strong competitor in a year's time, if not sooner'.

These reports were of value in alerting British industrialists to the kind of competition they would soon have to face. But the most immediate benefit to the companies represented on the committee of Bentinck's friendly relations with leading German politicians, bankers and industrialists was to be seen in his efforts to obtain exemption from a particular fiscal measure. This was known as the *Lastensausgleich* or Equalization of Burdens.

The *Lastensausgleich* was a tax which was due to come into effect on 1 April 1952 and to replace other methods of raising revenue to pay for making good the damage inflicted by war. It was to be levied on all companies operating in Germany. To Bentinck it seemed inequitable that British companies, whose plant and other assets had been treated as enemy property during the war, should now have to pay for the consequences of a war which Germany had started, and he was determined to fight on the companies' behalf.

The negotiations were long and complex. They also called, in Bentinck's judgement, for a united front among the wartime Western Allies. French and Benelux support was readily forthcoming, but in dealing with American representatives Bentinck found himself handicapped by what he described as 'the all-consuming urge to appease the Germans in any matter which will not have a harmful effect as far as the Administration is concerned in this presidential election year'.

In the end total exemption from the *Lastensausgleich* was obtained for companies which were one hundred per cent British-owned. Those which were eighty-five per cent or more British-owned were made exempt for six years. For Shell, Unilever and Anglo-Iranian Oil in particular this was a considerable benefit. Certainly the money saved greatly exceeded the companies's outlay on Bentinck's salary and office and travelling expenses.

The skills with which Bentinck reported on German political and economic affairs, freed British industrial concerns from the shackles of military government, and obtained a number of concessions from the German authorities, derived from his diplomatic training and experience. So too did the dexterity with which he handled the committee that employed him. At one stage the committee included representatives of forty companies, but its affairs were conducted without serious disputes. *I dealt with things by circulars*, Bentinck said, *which I sent out to all the members, and remained in personal touch with Shell and Unilever and the big boys, and just ran it.*

Before long, however, he had to develop other skills, the skills by which businessmen may be distinguished from diplomats. In December 1949 he was invited to become a technical adviser to the International Chamber of Commerce. In informing Hugh Saunders, the Secretary of Unilever, of this Bentinck wrote: 'I find difficulty in checking a latent suspicion that the International Chamber of Commerce must be very hard up if they are inviting an amateur like myself.' Nevertheless the invitations grew, and with them the amateurism steadily receded.

The Committee of Industrial Interests had accepted that Bentinck should be free to take on other work on the understanding that he gave priority to his responsibilities to the committee. As Bentinck pointed out, the committee might not last indefinitely and he had to think of the future. For him the future was still clouded by the fact that he had no pension to look forward to.

The dismantling of the great I. G. Farben combine was a political objective to which the Western occupying powers, the USA in particular, attached considerable importance. To protect their interests the foreign shareholders in I. G. Farben held a meeting in Brussels in 1948 and decided to form a committee. Bentinck was invited to be its chairman. Not long afterwards Dr Adenauer's Government formed its own committee to deal with the liquidation of I. G. Farben, and on this Bentinck represented all the foreign shareholders. One of the major successor companies of I. G. Farben was Bayer, and in 1951 Bentinck was invited to join its board. The Shell group raised an objection to this on the ground that it would be incompatible with his chairmanship of the Committee of Industrial Interests. Although he believed the objection to be mistaken, Bentinck did not dispute it, and he proposed to the Bayer Company that Leonard Ingrams should be appointed in his place. Two years later Ingrams died suddenly. Shell now waived its objections, and Bentinck became a director of Bayer, thereby starting an association which was to last for over thirty years.

Another company in Germany of which he was made a director was called Keramag. *There was an officer in World War I,* Bentinck said, *called Jim Slater, who had been a professional footballer with Bolton Wanderers. He borrowed some money and bought a sanitary ware plant when the mark was very low. After the second war the plant was with Military Control. I got it out of their grip and they asked me to join their board. I looked after Slater's widow's shares. After about twenty years we sold it to a French company.* Part of the proceeds served to keep Mrs Slater in comfort and part to establish the Slater Foundation.

Shell made Bentinck a director of its supervisory board in Austria, and Unilever appointed him its adviser on foreign affairs. One of the tasks he performed for Unilever involved him in a number of visits to Israel over a period of two years in the early 1950s. The purpose of these was to look into the affairs of an enterprise with which Unilever was associated, but which it did not wish to acknowledge openly for fear of being put on an Arab black list.

It was a soap and margarine company, Bentinck said, *and I was asked to take on the chairmanship. After a while it became clear to me that our Israeli partners, the brothers Liechtenstein, would probably make some money out of it and the brothers Lever would probably not. So I managed to get, not very easily, permission to close the company.*

Although commercially unrewarding, Bentinck found his visits to Israel instructive and stimulating. *It was very interesting,* he said, *seeing a race and a religion becoming a nation.* To his committee he reported in December 1952: 'Israel has come to stay as a State. The administration will in time improve, and the self-sacrifice of those Jews who have returned to Israel, despite the fact that they could do better for themselves elsewhere, will not be lost. Both as regards agriculture and industry, Israel is bound to develop, mainly owing to the spirit of the people, particularly the younger generation.'

He added: 'Foreign residents have commented on the fact that whilst persons of Jewish race in Europe and the United States have a keen sense of humour, the Israelis tend to be dour and to see everything as it affects their own country. However, the Pilgrim Fathers, the Dutch Voortrekkers in South Africa, and the early Mormons were not famed for their joviality.' After his visits to Israel, Sheila Owen recorded, Bentinck 'came back saying "Shalom" to us at every conceivable opportunity'.

Early in 1954 Bentinck came to the conclusion that the main task for which he had been appointed by the Committee of Industrial Interest some six and half years earlier had been completed and that he should now devote his energies to the various industrial enterprises which wanted his services. He therefore formally tendered his resignation to the committee. At the same time he suggested that the committee should 'remain in being as a forum for the exchange of ideas and to deal with Government departments'.

A special meeting was called on 16 February to discuss these proposals. At this a representative of Babcock and Wilcox said he considered the committee should continue, but he would not like it to do so without Bentinck as Chairman. Elmore Metal's representative then said that Bentinck's reports were particularly valuable to the smaller companies, as they gave information which could not be got from other sources.

These two set the tone for what followed. After some discussion Hugh Saunders formally proposed that Bentinck should remain as Chairman and that he should 'be enabled to devote more of his time to outside interests which did not conflict with those of the committee'. This was agreed. Bentinck renounced his salary, but he continued to have the services of Miss Owen and her assistants and the use of an office. *I could do other things*, he said, *take on other jobs*.

Bentinck was then fifty-six, the age at which in the Foreign Service he could have expected retirement in about four years' time. Instead he was now being launched on a new career, no longer as a political and diplomatic adviser to industrial concerns, but as an industrialist in his own right.

A few years earlier a tentative proposal had been made to him which, if he had followed it, would have brought him back to his former occupations. This was that he might be appointed head of SIS. *It was suggested to me*, Bentinck said, *by Harold Caccia. I said I was not at all keen on it. It's a soul-rotting business*. 'Soul-rotting' was the expression he had also used to describe the post-war occupation of Germany.

For Bentinck by the early 1950s secret intelligence belonged to his past. His future was in industry.

CHAPTER 18

Wider Still and Wider
(1954–   )

From the mid-1950s onwards Bentinck's business career was one of almost uninterrupted success. He continued as an adviser to Unilever until, after reaching the age of seventy, he was obliged by company regulations to retire. Among the assignments which Unilever gave him was to visit Indonesia in December 1957 and report on the company's future prospects there.

A Dutch director of Unilever, who had been in Indonesia two months earlier, had returned full of gloom. 'Indonesia,' he stated, 'is on the verge of chaos. If present conditions do not alter, Unilever's existence in Indonesia is in danger.' Bentinck, while agreeing that the prospects for the Dutch in Indonesia were of the bleakest, was much more sanguine about the prospects for Unilever.

I persuaded Unilever, he said, *not to leave Indonesia in high dudgeon. I said: 'There are ninety million of these people and two million Chinese. They will all require in the coming years hair oil, margarine, soap, all things that we produce. They'd just have to put Englishmen in charge at first and get some Indonesians.* This in fact was what was done. *I picked out two Indonesians, and after a time they became heads of the business there.*

Bentinck reached the age of seventy in June 1967. Unilever asked him, exceptionally, to continue working until March 1968, and when he finally left he appointed, in effect, his successor as adviser on foreign affairs. This was Sir Frank Roberts, who had recently retired from the Foreign Service.

Bentinck's retirement from Unilever was the signal for the Committee of Industrial Interests in Germany to bring its existence to an end. Its final meeting was held on 11 March 1968 when, after suitable speech-making, the members presented Bentinck with a portable typewriter. Latterly Bentinck had arranged for certain companies with which he was closely associated, in particular Bayer and RTZ, to contribute to the expenses of the committee's office, and he continued to the end to report fully on German economic and political developments. In his final report, which was circulated four days before the committee was wound up, he wrote: 'Economically and financially the Federal Republic is as sound as Germany was prior to 1914.' He added: 'Towards the United Kingdom the German attitude is one of condescending pity.'

Of his appointment to the supervisory board of Bayer in Germany Bentinck later said: *We met four or five times a year. I was getting these handsome fees for doing very little, and I said to myself: 'Bill Bentinck, this can't last.' I said to Bayer: 'I ought to do something for you.' They said: 'We're starting a pharmaceutical company in England. Would you like to be chairman of it?'*

That was in 1958. The company, which was based in Haywards Heath, was known as FBA Ltd. For some years its position was precarious and losses were incurred, largely because of lack of suitable products. Of Bentinck's contribution as Chairman at that time, John Webb, who later became Managing Director of Bayer (UK), said: 'He was a great steadying hand and, if you like, a father figure, who stepped in at the board meetings and calmed everyone down. He nevertheless said: "Are you interested in the market? If you are we've got to persevere." That's why we're so successful now, with at least two excellent products. It was the faith he had in the future and the steadying influence that counted.'

There were at one time five subsidiaries of Bayer operating in Britain as separate companies. In addition to FBA, there was a company producing chemicals known as J. M. Steel Ltd. Another company produced fibres, another dyestuffs and another agrochemicals. Bentinck came to the conclusion that the five companies could with advantage be amalgamated while retaining a measure of autonomy.

I suggested this, Bentinck said, *to the Chairman of J. M. Steel, who viewed the suggestion with distaste. I could see that it would have to remain in cold storage for a while. Some time later I was invited to become Chairman of J. M. Steel, and I put forward the suggestion again as tactfully as possible.* John Webb, who was then Managing Director of J. M. Steel, shared Bentinck's opinion, and they were jointly mainly responsible for bringing about the amalgamation with minimal disruption.

The natural resentment felt by men who, having been managing directors of independent companies, found themselves heads of divisions and answerable to another managing director, was also overcome with some success. Bentinck, Webb, said, 'played a very important role there. There was so much respect for him as a person.'

After the amalgamation Bayer (UK) became a more and more successful concern. In the second half of the 1970s sales increased threefold, with an average growth of twenty per cent per year. By the mid-1980s total sales amounted to over £400 million. Within the Bayer organization in Germany the management in Britain was regarded as a model for other overseas territories, and it was allowed an exceptional degree of autonomy, largely because of the personal respect felt for Bentinck himself.

When I asked Bentinck which of the commercial enterprises in which he was engaged gave him the greatest satisfaction he replied: *Bayer. I built up something worthwhile.* To John Webb working with Bentinck was, as he put it, 'a great privilege and a great education'. The Bayer organization found it expedient to retain Bentinck as Chairman of Bayer (UK) when he was well into his eighties.

In the late 1950s the board of Rio Tinto, which had been supplying uranium to the United States Energy Commision, realized that its contract to do so was unlikely to be renewed and that new customers must be found. *Hugh Saunders*, Bentinck said, *who used to be Company Secretary of Unilever, and Frank Byers were both on the board of Rio Tinto, and they asked me if I could find a purchaser on the continent. The only people likely to be interested were the Germans.*

Bentinck, who was invited to join the Board of Rio Tinto in 1959, was friendly with Dr Felix Prentzel, the chairman of a Frankfurt company called Degussa, which had been carrying out research into methods of enriching uranium. It was also considering setting up a new company to manufacture fuel elements. The upshot was the formation of a company known as NUKEM (Nuklear-Chemie und-Metallurgie). This was formed in 1960, Rio Tinto being a forty-per-cent founder-shareholder. Bentinck later became Deputy Chairman of NUKEM.

NUKEM played an important part in the development of the German nuclear energy industry, whose products, as international agreements required them to be, were used wholly for peaceful purposes. It was also a consistently profitable company.

Through Bentinck's knowledge of the market and of the personalities involved Rio Tinto also gained an early stake in the nuclear energy industry in Belgium, where Bentinck represented Rio Tinto on the board of a company named MMN.

These European ventures were so successful that Rio Tinto which, after its amalgamation with Consolidated Zinc, became known as RTZ, asked Bentinck to investigate the possibilities of the Japanese market, even though he had no first-hand knowledge of Japan. *I have no meeting of minds with the Japanese*, Bentinck said, but, after seeing representatives of various companies and conducting discussions through interpreters, he recommended Mitsubishi as suitable Japanese agents for RTZ. The association of the two companies continued over a quarter of a century to the evident advantage of both.

Bentinck was a non-executive director of RTZ. When he was obliged to retire from the board at the age of seventy he was kept on as a consultant. No non-executive director of the company had ever before been retained in this way.

RTZ was partly responsible for the creation of another body whose affairs occupied much of Bentinck's attention. *Roy Wright*, he said, *who was a rather far-sighted director of RTZ, thought it desirable to have an international institute*. This was the Uranium Institute, to which Bentinck became a consultant. *The Uranium Institute is a body which follows the market in uranium, makes reports for its members, and tries to boost the use of nuclear power. I advise it on what is likely to happen.*

The Uranium Institute was founded in 1975. That it became a body of international consequence was to a large extent due to Bentinck who, together with the Institute's Secretary,

Terence Price, an able and resourceful scientist, understood from the outset the need to involve certain key individuals and organizations in Europe in the Institute's affairs. The most important of the individuals was Heinrich Mandel, a professor and board member of the great Essen electrical concern R W E. Price described Mandel as 'the nuclear pope of Europe'. Bentinck persuaded Mandel that R W E should join the Uranium Institute, and within a few years more than fifty other organizations from nearly twenty countries did so too.

Bentinck was also made President of the British Nuclear Forum, the trade association of the nuclear energy manufacturers. Later he was invited to become Life President and to attend all its meetings.

In the advice he proffered to the Uranium Institute Bentinck continually stressed the need for sustained, even aggressive propaganda in favour of the peaceful use of nuclear energy. He also called attention to the quarters from which much of the opposition to it was directed. In an address delivered to a symposium in London in 1978 he said: 'In Germany the shock troops of the attacking forces against the police protecting reactor sites were formed by the Communist Party and other, though less important, extreme left-wing organizations. In London the recent demonstrations against nuclear power and, especially, the outcome of the Windscale inquiry comprised such bodies as the Socialist Revolutionary Party and the Communist Party. A further powerful body opposed to nuclear power in the United Kingdom is the National Union of Mineworkers.' He added: 'I think it is a pity that the opposition was ignored until it had succeeded in seriously delaying the advance of nuclear energy.'

Six years later in another speech, delivered at the age of eighty-six, he said: 'We shall not succeed in defeating the opposition by merely replying to their attacks. We must go over to the offensive. We must devote our energies to selling nuclear power. Whatever nonsense may be talked by Greenpeace, Friends of the Earth etc., let us, where so possible, reply by ridicule and lose no opportunity to denigrate the so-called experts whose witness they call to their aid.'

Between 1954, when he began to work only part time for the Committee of Industrial Interests in Germany, and 1967, when he was obliged to retire from the boards of the public companies on which he sat, Bentinck's commercial interests were extensive. In addition to his work for Bayer, Unilever and the nuclear energy industry, he was a director of companies as diverse as Elmore Metal and Hill Samuel (Hamburg), Metrogate Property Holdings and the Skefko Ball Bearing Company. He was also chosen as one of the three British directors of an international organization called the Association for the Protection of Property Abroad, which was created largely by Sir Hartley, later Lord, Shawcross. Its other European representatives included Bentinck's old friend René Massigli and Hermann Abs, the banker who was financial adviser to Dr Adenauer and to whom the German Federal Republic owed so much for its financial and economic recovery.

The success which Bentinck achieved as a businessman bore out the judgement formed by Lord Annan that he could have reached the top in any profession he chose. His capacity derived, I believe, largely from a form of discipline which manifested itself in a number of characteristics. One of these was patience. Through patience he made good the potential setbacks he suffered in his Foreign Service career in the 1930s. Patience enabled him to transform the Joint Intelligence Committee from a body which some of its own members considered at first to be largely superfluous into a uniquely well-fashioned instrument for outwitting the enemy in wartime. With patience too he adapted himself to the requirements, aims and mental approach of the commercial world. *If you've been an official,* he said, *and go off into what might be called the private sector you have to have a complete change of mentality. As an official you don't think of the profit motive. After I came under the wing of Unilever it began to loom in front of my eyes like the star of Bethlehem.*

Bentinck's self-discipline was revealed in the conscientiousness he evinced in every task he took on: the attention to detail, the fulfilment of the smallest undertaking, the prompt and careful dealing with correspondence, the punctuality, the attendance at meetings. All this he brought not only to his commercial enterprises, but also to his voluntary work. Much of this voluntary work was concerned, as that of his father had been, with hospital administration. *I was asked to join the board of St George's Hospital. I said, yes, I'd be very happy to do so. I was also on the house committee of the Royal Dental Hospital. After a couple of years I became chairman. I used to go in most days.*

From discipline too stemmed, in part, Bentinck's unfailing courtesy, which made him not only acceptable but welcome on the many boards and committees on which he sat, and which allowed him to bring to them qualities of calm, reason and humour, sometimes when these qualities were most needed. Such was his courtesy that it served at times to mask strong feelings behind an appearance of equanimity.

It was also a kind of mental discipline which enabled Bentinck to effect his own peculiar fusion of a sanguine temperament and a sceptical mind. From this proceeded his exceptional judgement and inspiring leadership, which, when combined, had a quality of greatness.

From the 1950s through to the 1980s Bentinck enjoyed a happiness and contentment in his private life such as he had not known in his first marriage. When he learnt that I had remarried rather late in life he wrote to me to express the hope that this venture would be as 'successful' as his own second marriage had been.

He had a fairly active social life. *I have a wife who likes going out, and we go out to see people.* His friends were, as they always had been, predominantly those with whom he was or had been professionally associated. *I still see Roger Sherfield, Lord Gladwyn and Harold Caccia. Nobody senior to me in the Foreign Office is still alive except David Scott.*

He suffered a distressing loss when his only son died in 1966, but he remained emotionally close to his daughter and to his grandchildren by her, although physically separated by her marriage to a Harvard professor. His regular summer holiday latterly involved a visit to Canada, where his wife had inherited some property. Characteristically Bentinck soon became knowledgeable on the subject of timber.

From Trevor Place Bentinck and his wife moved to a house in Carlyle Square, one of those havens of greenery and calm which adjoin the King's Road, Chelsea. There Bentinck could regularly be seen exercising his dog, a vociferous but not unfriendly poodle.

In spite of age his mental faculties seemed quite unimpaired. Physically he suffered from a noticeable stoop and slight deafness, but his health was excellent and his vigour remarkable. He even continued to drive a motor car in a manner which caused one of his colleagues to say that he had never come across a driver who was so impervious to the abuse of other road-users.

In 1979 Bentinck's elder brother Ferdy died aged ninety-one, and he himself became the ninth and last Duke of Portland. At the same time he inherited three other titles, those of Marquis of Titchfield, Viscount Woodstock and Baron Cirencester.

My brother and I both became Duke of Portland, but by then the assets had been parted from the title, and we received nothing. The sixth Duke, with the consent of the Court, barred the entail in 1915.

In consequence a discretionary trust had been created, and by a deed of release dated 1 December 1971 the seventh Duke excluded future dukes, specifically mentioning Frederick and Victor Cavendish-Bentinck, and their wives, widows, daughters or issue of daughters, from being beneficiaries of the trust. The seventh Duke's only children were two daughters. The inheritors of the assets were one of the daughters, who remained unmarried, and the offspring of the other, who married an Italian, much to the disapproval of her parents.

As a latecomer to the House of Lords the new Duke of Portland soon became familiar with its ways and fascinated by its business. Lord Sherfield, who was the Chairman of a select committee concerned with energy, invited him to join the committee and afterwards said: 'He has been an extraordinarily good member and has enjoyed it very much.' Lord Chelwood, who had first encountered him in Warsaw, now described him as 'a liberally minded man, in the middle in politics; a very broad-minded man who makes his mind up on the facts with scrupulous care'. Terence Price told of his habit, after enjoying tea and biscuits at the Uranium Institute, of taking his leave 'by saying with a twinkle in his eye: "I'm off to legislate."'

Although restrained in his admiration for some of the

members of the Government, the new Duke of Portland took the Conservative whip, in accordance with family tradition after the eighteenth century, and attended on most days on which the House of Lords was sitting. In one of its debates he was able to speak with unique authority. This was a consequence of the Falkland Islands war in 1982.

During and immediately after this war concern was felt both inside and outside the Government at the failure of the British intelligence authorities to forecast the intentions and actions of the Argentine Government. A Committee of Privy Councillors was therefore appointed under the chairmanship of Lord Franks to consider this and related matters.

In its report the Franks Committee expressed the opinions that the joint intelligence machinery was 'too passive in operation to respond quickly and critically to a rapidly changing situation which demanded urgent attention', and that 'the assessment machinery should be reviewed'. The committee also examined the composition of the Joint Intelligence Committee and stated: 'Consideration should be given to the position of the chairman of the Committee; to the desirability that he or she should be full-time, with a more critical and independent role.'

The House of Lords held a debate on the Franks Report on 25 January 1983. In it the Duke of Portland, after summarizing briefly the history of the JIC, said: 'I understand that the Foreign Office chairmanship of the JIC had proved satisfactory until the unfortunate Falklands affair, and I wonder whether the appointment proposed by the noble Lord, Lord Franks, will prove equally satisfactory throughout the next forty years.' He went on to express the hope that 'the person appointed to be chairman will be someone with wide and practical experience in appraising foreign individuals and reports'.

The Duke concluded his speech by saying: 'I would finally urge that any expansion in the machinery of the JIC should be very closely controlled. After twenty-eight years in the Civil Service and thirty-five years in the private sector I have reached the conclusion that the efficiency of governments or organizations, also that of the head offices of large companies, is in inverse ratio to their size.'

Nearly three months later the Duke of Portland had another reminder of his past, when the Chancellor of the German Federal Republic visited Britain. *There was a dinner for Kohl in Downing Street. I was placed beside my hostess, with Kohl on her right and me on her left. I had to do the interpreting. When I came into this dinner party I said: 'The last time I was here for a dinner for a German Chancellor was at the time of the signature of the Treaty of Locarno. The Chancellor was Luther, the Foreign Minister Stresemann. The Foreign Secretary was Austen Chamberlain, and the Prime Minister was Baldwin.' I nearly said 'the tenant here was Baldwin', but I thought that would be too flippant.*

It was in the early summer of 1981 that I conceived the idea of writing a biography of the Duke of Portland. Between then and completing this book I spoke to many people who had encountered him at different periods in his life. Some had known him in the world of diplomacy where, although the expressions used are normally polite, rivalries and intrigue are not infrequent. Some had known him in a world of espionage and secret warfare, in which, it is often thought, normal standards of conduct are suspended. Some had known him in a commercial world which included mergers and takeovers with all the stresses, disappointments and, sometimes, suffering which these entailed.

Of all the people to whom I spoke, none had a harsh or unkind word to say about him as a man. That he made this possible was, arguably, as great an achievement as any other in his long and distinguished life.

BIBLIOGRAPHY

I have had six main sources. They were:

a) The conversations I had with the Duke of Portland and with men and women who have known him,

b) The ninety-two volumes of the minutes of the meetings of the British Chiefs of Staff during World War II and ninety-six volumes of related memoranda;

c) Foreign Office files from 1915, when Mr Cavendish-Bentinck took up his first appointment, until 1947, when he left the Foreign Service;

d) The minutes of the meetings of the British Committee of Industrial Interests in Germany;

e) *Documents on British Foreign Policy*, ed. W. N. Medlicott, Douglas Dakin and M. E. Lambert (HMSO);

f) The three published volumes of *British Intelligence in the Second World War* by F. H. Hinsley, E. E. Thomas, C. F. G. Ransom and R. C. Knight.

Other works I have found useful included:

Balfour, Michael, *Four-Power Control in Germany 1945–46* (O.U.P., 1956)

Baumont, Maurice, *La troisième république* (Rencontre, Lausanne, 1968)

Beamish, Tufton, *Must Night Fall?* (Hollis & Carter, 1950)

Beesly, Patrick, *Very Special Intelligence* (Hamish Hamilton, 1977)

Beesly, Patrick, *Very Special Admiral. The Life of Admiral J. H. Godfrey* (Hamish Hamilton, 1978)

Beevor, J. G., *SOE*. Recollections and Reflexions (Bodley Head, 1981)

Bertrand, Gustave, *Enigma ou la plus grande énigma de la guerre 1939–1945* (Plon, Paris, 1973)

Brown, Anthony Cave, *Wild Bill Donovan. The Last Hero* (Times Books, New York, 1983)

Bullock, Alan, *Ernest Bevin Foreign Secretary 1943–1951* (Heinemann, 1983)

Calvocoressi, Peter, *Top Secret Ultra* (Cassell, 1980)

Carlton, David, *Anthony Eden* (Allen Lane, 1981)

Carton De Wiart, Lieut.-General Sir Adrian, *Happy Odyssey* (Cape, 1950)

Carver, Field Marshal Sir Michael, *The War Lords* (Weidenfeld & Nicolson, 1976)

Castelet, André, and Decaux, Alain, *Histoire de la France et des français au jour le jour* (Perrin, France, 1977)

Chamberlain, Sir Austen, *Down the Years* (Cassell, 1935)

Chavardès, Maurice, *Le 6 février 1934. La république en danger* (Calman-Lévy, Paris, 1966)

Churchill, Winston, *The Second World War*, Vols 1–6 (Cassell, 1948–1954)

Cline, Ray S., *Secrets, Spies and Saboteurs. Blue-print of the CIA* (Acropolis, Washington, 1976)

Colville, Sir John, *Strange Inheritance* (Michael Russell, 1983)

Cruickshank, Charles, *Deception in World War II* (Oxford University Press, 1979)

D'Abernon, Viscount, *The Eighteenth Decisive Battle of the World. Warsaw 1920* (Hodder & Stoughton, 1931)

D'Abernon, Viscount, *Diary. An Ambassador of Peace*, Vol. 3: *The Years of Recovery* (Hodder & Stoughton, 1930)

Falkland Islands Review. Report of a Committee of Privy Councillors (HMSO, 1983)

Foster, Edward S., *A Short History of Modern Greece* (Methuen, 1958)

Fraser, David, *Alanbrooke* (Collins, 1982)

Galdarnes, Luis, *A History of Chile* (University of N. Carolina Press, 1941)

Garliński, Józef, *Intercept* (Dent, 1979)

Garliński, Józef, *The Swiss Corridor* (Dent, 1981)

Gilbert, Martin, *Sir Horace Rumbold. Portrait of a Diplomat, 1869–1941* (Heinemann, 1973)

Gilbert, Martin, *Winston S. Churchill*, Vol 6: *The Finest Hour 1939–1941* (Heinemann, 1983)

Gladwyn, Lord, *Memoirs* (Weidenfeld & Nicolson, 1972)

Halecki, O., *A History of Poland* (Dent, 1942)

Höhne, Heinz, *Canaris* (Secker & Warburg, 1979)

Hyde, H. Montgomery, *The Quiet Canadian. The Secret Service Story of Sir William Stephenson* (Hamish Hamilton, 1962)

Irving, David, *Hitler's War* (Hodder & Stoughton, 1977)

Jacobson, John, *Locarno Diplomacy. Germany and the West 1925–1928* (Princeton University Press, 1972)

Jones, R. V., *Most Secret War* (Hamish Hamilton, 1978)

Lane, Arthur Bliss, *I Saw Freedom Betrayed* (Regency Publications, 1949)

Lewin, Ronald, *Ultra Goes to War. The Secret Story* (Hutchinson, 1978)

Lewin, Ronald, *The Other Ultra* (Hutchinson, 1982)

Lockhart, Sir Robert, *Diaries 1939–1965* (Macmillan, 1980)

McLachlan, Donald, *Room 39* (Weidenfeld & Nicolson, 1968)

Masterman, J. C., *The Double Cross System* (Yale University Press, 1972)

Mikołajczyk, Stanisław, *The Pattern of Soviet Domination* (Sampson Low, 1948)

Montagu, Ewen, *Beyond Top Secret U* (Peter Davies, 1977)

Moravec, Frantisek, *Master of Spies* (Bodley Head, 1975)

Mosca, Rodolfo, and Agliati, Mario, *L'Europa a Locarno* (Dado, Locarno, 1975)

Newsome, David, *A History of Wellington College 1859–1959* (Murray, 1959)

Nicolson, Harold, *Curzon, The Last Phase 1919–1925* (Constable, 1934)

Nicolson, Harold, *Diplomacy* (Oxford University Press, 1939)

Nicolson, Harold, *Some People* (Folio Society, 1951)

Nicolson, Harold, *Diaries and Letters 1930–1939* (Collins, 1966)

Nicolson, Harold, *Diaries and Letters 1945–1962* (Collins, 1968)

Pack, S. W. C., *Cunningham the Commander* (Batsford, 1974)

Pallis, A. A., *Greece's Anatolian Adventure —And After* (Methuen, 1937)

Pearson, John, *The Life of Ian Fleming* (Companion Book Club, 1966)

Petrie, Sir Charles, *The Life and Letters of the Right Hon. Sir Austen Chamberlain* (Cassell 1939, 1940)

Phillips, Charles, *Paderewski. The Story of a Modern Immortal* (Macmillan, New York, 1934)

Popov, Dusko, *Spy Counterspy* (Weidenfeld & Nicolson, 1974)

Powys-Lybbe, Ursula, *The Eye of Intelligence* (Kimber, 1983)

Prittie, Terence, *Germany Divided* (Hutchinson, 1961)

Richards, David, *Portal of Hungerford* (Heinemann, 1978)

Ronaldshay, Earl of, *The Life of Lord Curzon* (Ernest Benn, 1928)

Rose, W. J., *The Rise of Polish Democracy* (Bell, 1944)

Roskill, Stephen, *Hankey, Man of Secrets.* Vol 3. *1931–1963* (Collins, 1974)

Shirer, William L., *The Collapse of the Third Republic* (Simon & Schuster, New York, 1969)

Simenon, Georges, *Maigret's Memoirs* (Hamish Hamilton, 1963)

Stevenson, William, *A Man Called Intrepid. The Secret War 1939–1945* (Macmillan, 1976)

Strong, Major-General Sir Kenneth, *Intelligence at the Top* (Cassell, 1968)

Strong, Major-General Sir Kenneth, *Men of Intelligence* (Cassell, 1970)

Tolstoy, Nikolai, *Victims of Yalta* (Hodder & Stoughton, 1977)

Tolstoy, Nikolai, *Stalin's Secret War* (Jonathan Cape, 1981)

Turberville, A. S., *A History of Welbeck Abbey and its Owners* (Faber, 1939)

Walters, F. P., *A History of the League of Nations* (Oxford University Press, 1952)

West, Nigel, *MI5. British Security Operations 1909–1945* (Bodley Head, 1981)

Wingate, Sir Ronald, *Lord Ismay. A Biography* (Hutchinson, 1970)

Woodhouse, C. M., *The Story of Modern Greece* (Faber & Faber, 1968)

INDEX